CHUCK WHITLOCK'S
SCAM SCHOOL

MACMILLAN · USA

MACMILLAN
A Simon & Schuster Macmillan Company
1633 Broadway
New York, NY 10019-6785

Macmillan Publishing books may be purchased for business or sales promotional use. For information please write: Special Markets Department, Macmillan Publishing USA, 1633 Broadway, New York, NY 10019.
MACMILLAN is a registered trademark of Macmillan, Inc.

Library of Congress Cataloging-in-Publication Data

A catalogue record is available from the Library of Congress.

ISBN: 0-02-862139-5

Manufactured in the United States of America
10 9 8 7 6 5 4 3 2 1

Book design by Christine Weathersby

To my Mom
Helen B. Whitlock
September 2, 1914-January 30, 1997

CONTENTS

ACKNOWLEDGMENTS

●

My great appreciation goes to Peter Miller at PMA for all his efforts to make this book a reality (and for making me laugh) and for negotiating my television contracts. My thanks to Gail Wayper, Eric Wilinski, Ed Goldberg, Jody Seay, and Lee Rooklin for their respective contributions and feedback.

Many thanks to all of the law enforcement agency personnel who've helped me with my investigations, including Detective Sergeant Mark Coffey, Detective Chris Peterson, Detective Chuck Warren, and Chief of Police Brent Collier.

Thanks also to the many watchdog organizations and associations, the prosecutors, prison authorities, victims, and the other investigative reporters without whose cooperation this book would not have been possible.

My deep appreciation for all their support of my work goes to Oprah Winfrey, David Boul, Vincent Bugliosi, Maury Povich, Jonathan Zager, Geraldo Rivera, Mike Rausch, Terry Murphy, Sally Jessy Raphael, Dave Jewitt, Susan Zirinsky, Cheri Brownlee, Ron Vandor, and Mark Benthimer. Thanks a million for all the help provided by my friends at KGW-TV Northwest Newschannel 8, *Hard Copy, Inside Edition,* NBC, CBS, ABC, CNN, CNBC, and *Steals and Deals.*

Many thanks to Mary Ann Lynch, my editor, Natalie Chapman, my publisher, and Michelle Tupper, assistant editor, who have been very supportive of this project.

A special thanks to Candace Smoral, whose love is a constant source of comfort and encouragement.

INTRODUCTION
• •

Scams have been around since the beginning of civilization. Some early caveman probably sold dinosaur dung as homemade apple pie. The caveman who figured out how to start a fire may have convinced his fellow cave dwellers that he was a god and told them that if they didn't contribute ten percent of their food, he'd give them a hot foot as they slept. If you're a biblical historian, you may remember that Delilah scammed Samson into revealing the source of his enormous strength and power by pretending to love him. Samson paid dearly for trusting this ancient love con artist: his hair was cut off, he lost his power, his eyes were burned out, and he was terribly humiliated by his captors.

While the actual scams may have changed a little over the centuries, the basic human elements remain constant. As long as people need products, services, and relationships, there will be rainmakers willing to dance for a price. Sometimes the price is no more than a few quarters at a rigged carnival game. The barker will tell you that all you have to do is shoot the red star out with a BB gun at ten feet. What he doesn't tell you is that the BBs are half the size of normal BBs, the paper twice as thick as regular target paper, and the air pressure in the gun half as great as a normal air rifle.

At the other end of the spectrum are countless victims who have lost their savings, property, self-esteem, and, in some cases, their lives at the hands of swindlers.

Unfortunately, scams are a cruel aspect of the fabric of our society. As technology becomes more sophisticated, so do the scams perpetrated on innocent victims. It's one thing to lose a dollar because you never found the peanut under the shell, but it's another to be bilked out of your life savings or even your identity by a college-educated criminal conversant in computer crime.

As the stakes get higher, it is up to the consumer—the potential victim, you and me—to get smarter. For the past several years I have researched, studied, interviewed, and investigated scam artists in my roles as investigative reporter and producer for the Portland NBC affiliate, *Hard Copy,* and *Inside Edition,* and I have appeared as an expert on cons on *Oprah, Geraldo, Maury Povich, Sally,* CBS's *Eye to Eye* and *This Morning,* CNN, and CNBC. I've written *Scam School* to give you tools to fight against con artists and the scams they perpetrate.

The first mistake most people make is to believe that they can't be conned. If you don't think you're capable of being scammed right now, wake up and smell the coffee. You don't have to be old, greedy, needy, lonely, or stupid to be taken to the cleaners.

After interviewing many con artists—some prior to conviction, some after—I observed a number of interesting—and frightening—characteristics common to the majority of them. The most striking is that they grew up breaking society's laws with no fear of punishment and little or no feeling for those hurt by their actions. Although some scams may seem humorous, it is important not to underestimate the scammer, not to forget that these are people who prey upon people's trust, who lie to make a living.

It is this sociopathic criminal that *Scam School* is about. This unique human creature is a predator and a parasite. Once he gains access to your greatest vulnerability, your weakest moment, your greatest fear, he will systematically take everything you own and laugh at your stupidity as you get weaker and weaker while he gets stronger and stronger. When you have nothing left to give, he will move on to the next host and never look back or lose a night's sleep. He is a human vulture with a compromised sense of morality.

In many ways, these manipulators, who come to you in doctors' smocks, ministers' collars, police officers' uniforms, or dressed any other way needed to win your instant trust, are much more dangerous than the mugger in the street with a gun. Muggers are oftentimes repentant and may even leave the noncash items in a nearby Dumpster to be found. A genuine con artist would never be so kind.

In *Scam School,* you'll meet honest, hardworking people just like you whose lives have been turned upside down by the schemes and swindles of white-collar criminals. I use these stories to acquaint you with the warning signs of a scam so that you can avoid being similarly ensnared in a con artist's deadly web. You will learn as you read. This is your school, with each chapter putting you deep inside true-life incidents.

Scam School is filled with information about scams being perpetrated right now across the United States and around the world. It includes real-life crime dramas that seem, at times, as if they've been taken straight out of a Hollywood thriller. You'll feel like you are right there with the police. You'll feel this way because I was there.

You'll be with the Immigration and Naturalization Service agent, the police, and me in Medford, Oregon, as we close in on a self-proclaimed faith healer who sold "human fat" candles for up to $900 a pop. You'll join me as I confront an impostor running a huge real estate scam. And we'll follow a victim in Oregon as she deftly pursues a swindler who bilked small business owners out of millions of dollars. From phony ATM guards to valets who steal your car and rob your home, you'll penetrate the criminal's confidence scheme and learn how not to get conned.

In some circles, people admire con artists because they often pull off remarkable stings that would rival any James Bond novel. I do not admire or respect these human parasites. I have seen firsthand the devastation and human suffering caused by their schemes. If there currently exists an Antichrist, he comes in the form of the antisocial, sociopathic con artist. Unfortunately, the con artist looks like you, your mother, daughter, doctor, and priest. He is whoever and whatever you need him to be, and he is everywhere.

In the pages of this book I attack this criminal in the most effective way possible: by teaching you how he operates. By throwing a spotlight on his behavioral patterns, you will be more likely to recognize him instantly. And, if enough people recognize him, we can collectively put him out of business. This is a do-it-yourself course in how to protect yourself from thieves who know how to make you an accomplice in the crime that is meant to steal you blind.

The stories you're about to read are true stories I've researched or investigated personally. While writing *Scam School* I frequently referred back to video copies of my investigative reports and reflected on the hundreds of grueling hours verifying sources, researching other information, and making certain the facts were accurate. But while the stories you're about to read are fundamentally real, I've taken liberties with *Scam School* which I would never have taken reporting a story for TV. I've changed victims' names, dates, and specific locations and added elements of fiction, where necessary, to disguise the identity of those involved. In some cases, this was done to protect the anonymity of victims who are embarrassed or fearful of retribution since they stepped forward to report the crime or testify against their perpetrators. In other cases, the criminal has not been tried in a court of law yet, or a known con artist is still wanted, and I don't want to jeopardize the fraud detective's case. In those instances where the victim committed suicide, there was no reason to cause the family additional grief or notoriety.

Finally, the step-by-step elements of the con may in some cases have had to be reconstructed based upon a paper stream and eye-witness accounts. For the few cases I didn't personally investigate, I have created conversations to make the crime more realistic. To avoid frivolous lawsuits, I've changed the names of most of the con artists as well. Con artists seldom take responsibility for their crimes. They may blame their parents, school systems, employers, addictions, spouses, and even their victims for their actions. Some might choose to blame me because I helped expose them to the light of day.

None of the changes materially affects the stories or the lessons to be learned. Make no mistake: Every con you read about here happened, and variations of it continue to happen every day around the world.

I wish I could promise that this book will protect you from all harm, that it will shield you from every known huckster, swindler, and flimflam man. I'd like to promise that, but in all honesty I can't. If I did, I would be no different from the bad guys I want to protect you from. Suffice it to say that you will know a whole lot more about protecting yourself from con artists when you finish reading this book than when you first picked it up.

A final note: The first and most important lesson I hope you take with you from *Scam School* is this: If it sounds too good to be true, it probably is! Forewarned is forearmed.

June 1997

GOING UNDERCOVER TO EXPOSE CRIME

Is it unethical? Sure it is, but you know, in business,
you have to be willing to scratch somebody's back.

—*Salesperson caught offering a $6,000 per month*
cash kickback in "Medicare Sting"

....

THE VALET PARKING SCAM

....

Enjoy your pizza!" I held open the door of the late model Acura and watched as the man escorted his wife into the pizza restaurant, waiting for him to turn around and say, "Hey, give me my car back! There's no such thing as valet parking at a pizza joint!"

But he didn't, and I slipped behind the wheel and drove off. My hands were shaking slightly, cold and sweaty. What was I doing? This was crazy. I was not a scam artist or con man. I was a businessman and an author. But here I was, posing as a valet and driving a very expensive vehicle, which, had I been a real con man, I would have been in the process of stealing.

Even though I had written about this very valet parking scam in *Easy Money,* my first book about scams, cons, and white-collar crime, I never expected I would end up perpetrating it—or any other scam—for television.

When I reached the corner, I looked across the street. There I saw a van with tinted windows. Inside it, I knew, was one of Oprah Winfrey's producers, Judy Banks, and a camera crew, recording my "scam" on video. Turning the corner, I pulled into a lot near the restaurant.

Parked there were the half-dozen other cars I had already taken from their owners. I surveyed my take: all luxury cars. Were I a con man running the valet parking scam for real, I would have been well on my way to a big score. It would have been unbelievably easy to load the cars on a truck, then drive to Mexico and sell them there. Or to have accomplices drive the cars south into Chicago, to any one of a dozen "chop" shops, where they would be stripped before my victims had finished eating their pizzas.

I looked over at the passenger-side visor of the Acura I had just been given to park. There, clipped to the visor, was a garage door opener. And chances were that the registration and proof of insurance were somewhere in the car, both of which would tell me where the owner's house was located. Plus, the owners had given me their house keys along with the car key; again, if I had been a real con man, while the couple were enjoying their pizza, I could have been back at their house, cleaning it out of valuables—without suffering any worry of being discovered by the owners and probably without arousing any suspicion in the neighborhood.

But the couple was lucky; I wasn't a real con man. I was in the process of creating an episode for on-camera scams for an *Oprah* show that would be titled "Scam School." Welcome to the classroom. Welcome now to Scam School as we go undercover together deep inside the world of white-collar crime and cons. Their car and their belongings were safe ... this time.

As I walked back to the restaurant, I checked to be sure that my valet parking vest and name badge were on straight. The people I passed on the sidewalk looked right through me, as if the vest somehow made me invisible. It was amazing; it made me think back to my days in Los Angeles, when I had used valet parking almost daily—like my victims, not once suspecting the person to whom I had entrusted my car and keys might not have been who he said he was.

My first experience with a con man had taken place not far from this pizzeria. It was 1954; at the time, the only televisions I'd seen were the new ones down at Goldblatt's department store on Chicago's Milwaukee Avenue. Whenever we could, my brother Jim and I would push through Goldblatt's revolving doors and stare at the images on the flickering screens: Howdy Doody; roly-poly Jackie Gleason; the Lone Ranger; Roy Rogers.

I was eleven, and I wanted a TV. So when a large, gregarious man in a suit knocked on our door one day and told my mother that she'd won a television, I was ecstatic. It would be easy to get our TV, the man assured my mother. All we'd have to do was pay the $32 delivery charge.

Thirty-two dollars was what my mother made in a week. She ran a punch press for Chicago's Appleton Electric, and she was a single mom supporting six kids. But, hey, this was a television! The man went into his briefcase and showed us a picture of the set. It was bigger and fancier than the ones at Goldblatt's. My brothers and sisters and I started talking excitedly about the shows we'd watch once we got it. The man stood by quietly as we sold our mother on the idea. Then, sensing the time was right, he pulled a lengthy contract out of his briefcase. "Sign it, Mom, sign it!" we all implored her.

My mother signed the paper, then went and got the cookie jar where we kept money for emergencies. This was our bank, the place where my mother put any extra money she had after paying the bills, where we put any money we'd made mowing lawns, delivering newspapers, and baby-sitting. My mother spilled out the money and started counting: dollar bills, quarters, dimes, nickels, pennies. Finally, there it was: $32. She gave the money to the man, and he gave her a receipt and went on his way.

Over the next few days, my brothers and sisters and I told our schoolmates and the neighbors all about our new television. It would be coming in the mail any day; the man had said we'd get it in two to three weeks. But two weeks came and went, and then three, and still there was no TV. Months passed, and still there was no TV. My mother tried to find the man in the suit, but the receipt he'd given her was no help—the company listed on it didn't exist.

At first I couldn't believe that the man was dishonest. He had been so nice, so happy for us; he had seemed to smile the whole time he was at our house. But then I understood: My mother had been stung by a con man. I've never completely forgotten that man, his smile, his suit, and the way he oozed charm.

Now, decades later, I was playing the role of the con man myself. For the first time, I felt I was finally doing something about the man who took my mother's $32. I was about to show the vast TV viewing public just how much misplaced trust can cost.

Back at the restaurant, Judy and her cameraman got out of the van. As our victims came out of the restaurant, we did what are known in TV as reveals, telling them just how they had been scammed. Without exception, the victims were amazed at how vulnerable they had been to the valet parking scam. How could they have so easily trusted a stranger with their two most valuable possessions, their automobiles and homes?

With the help of Judy Banks and her camera crew, in the next several days I conducted several other scams that would be televised on *The Oprah Winfrey Show*. There was the empty box COD scam, in which I convinced a series of marks to hand over cold, hard cash in return for COD packages that I claimed were meant for neighbors who weren't at home—packages that actually contained a brick, worth maybe ten cents.

There was the phony bank examiner scam, in which I convinced bank patrons to hand over hundreds of dollars each in withdrawals, claiming to be an FDIC inspector investigating claims that bank tellers were embezzling money from depositors. I couldn't believe how smoothly all these scams worked; it was so easy to trick people out of their money and belongings. I had already authored *Easy Money* at that point, so I understood more about cons than most people. But by placing myself for the first time on the other side of the con artist-victim equation, I was now learning more than I'd ever imagined possible about just how the con game works.

• • •

ON THE AIR WITH THE VICTIMS I CONNED

When I showed up at the studio for my first *Oprah* taping, I was even more nervous than when I had been doing any of my cons on camera. I was certain that my marks would have nothing but criticism for the way I'd deceived them. I entered the green room, and there they were: victims from the valet parking, empty box COD, and phony bank examiner scams. But their attitude toward me wasn't what I'd expected. There was a tense moment or two, but then a woman whom I had fooled with a phony package delivery approached me.

"I can't tell you how much you opened my eyes. I don't think I'll ever be taken so easily again." She shook my hand. "Thanks again."

That broke the ice; immediately, the other victims also started to approach me. Most asked me where they could get a copy of *Easy Money*.

The show was a tremendous success and elicited substantial viewer response. Millions of television viewers witnessed how effectively the cons had been perpetrated and marveled as the victims recounted how I had convinced them to hand over their cars or money. Their on-camera admissions of how easily had been taken in were powerful testimony to how even people who believe themselves to be savvy can be taken in by a smooth talker with an honest face and charming demeanor.

I also talked about other common cons and gave audience members guidelines on how to protect themselves against white-collar crime. Even though I had participated in pulling off the scams, I was still amazed at how effectively I had been able to perpetrate the cons on intelligent people—and I could tell that the studio audience was amazed as well. Even I felt vulnerable having experienced firsthand the ease with which innocent, trusting victims could be scammed.

The time it took to tape the show flew by. Afterward, Oprah came over and thanked me. Her producer, David Boul, told me that it had been one of the most effective shows they'd ever done. We had really struck a chord with the public. The show was such a success that soon I was asked to appear on other national TV news and talk programs, such as *The Maury Povich Show,* CBS's *Eye to Eye,* CNN's *Your Money,* and *Geraldo,* as well as radio talk shows and local television talk shows.

Then I was offered a new opportunity. After an appearance on KGW-TV, the local NBC affiliate in Portland, Oregon, I was approached by the station's news director about joining their news team to report on scams being perpetrated in Oregon and Washington. KGW was in fierce competition for news ratings with the other local network affiliates, and the news director at KGW wanted to hire me in the hopes that my investigative reports would boost ratings.

THE ALCOHOL NEUTRALIZER PILL

For my first exposé for KGW, I visited the Seattle Convention Center. I was legally wired for sound and had a cameraman with me. I had heard from very reliable sources that a number of products of questionable efficacy were being displayed at the current exposition. While looking around, the most blatantly suspicious product we found was something called the Alcohol Neutralizer, a pill alleged to have unique alcohol absorption properties.

"This miracle pill is going to save thousands of lives every year! It could save your life ... or the life of someone you love!" The huckster was a clean-cut ex-policeman from Chicago. Wearing a crisp white shirt and dark striped tie, he stood next to a table full of free literature set in front of a couple of prototype vending machines. As he spoke, his pitch attracted a small crowd. We stood near the back to watch.

He was a good speaker, confident and full of authority:

The Neutralizer pill reduces the blood alcohol level in anyone's system by 50 percent. No one needs to worry about getting stopped while driving home after having a few drinks anymore. The machines behind me will dispense the life-saving pills. For a small initial investment of only $5,000 per machine *and 60 cents per pill, which you can sell for $1.50 apiece, you'll be in business. You'll start to make money the very first night your machine is installed in your local bar, guaranteed!*

His pitch was very convincing. He claimed that judges, police-men, and other law enforcement officials were investing in this franchise based on the expectation of high profits and the chance to do a great public service by significantly reducing highway fatalities. As I listened, I found myself thinking it all sounded so wonderful. Immediately, my number one rule about scams sprang to mind: If it sounds too good to be true, it usually is.

At the end of the show we moved in to talk with the pitchman one-on-one. He was glad to cooperate with us in order to gain free publicity for his product. He explained once more that the Alcohol Neutralizer pill would help sober up people within an hour by absorbing up to 50 percent of the alcohol they'd con-sumed. A large sign behind him reported "confirmed studies done at Harvard." He pointed to an easel with a large blowup of a magazine article by a Harvard professor that reported "scientific proof" that the pill's active ingredient worked to reduce one's blood alcohol level.

During the drive back to Portland, I couldn't help but hope claims I'd heard about the Neutralizer pill were true. What a mira-cle a product like that would be! But one question kept running through my head: If this product was for real, why hadn't anyone publicized or reported on it before now?

Soon we were back at the station. We had the company's claim on tape, but our work had just begun. First, I called the professor at Harvard, who told me that although he had researched one of the pill's ingredients, he had never made the claims attributed to him in the magazine article.

Next, I contacted the manufacturer of the pill, who offered to send "exhaustive" research proving that all the claims made about the pill at the Seattle business exposition were true. The research I received was sketchy at best: one doctor, on the com-pany's payroll, had conducted some very minor studies without using acceptable research protocol.

With KGW-TV's blessing, we decided to experiment for ourselves. One day, at five P.M., we selected a random sample of six willing people from the newsroom and headed for a local bar. After an hour of serious drinking, our subjects were driven to the police station, where Breathalyzer tests were administered to them. All six, in fact, were shown to be intoxicated, with blood alcohol levels of between 0.12 and 0.18—drunk enough to be arrested for driving under the influence.

Next, we gave half our subjects the Neutralizer pill, while giving nothing, not even a cup of coffee, to the other three. According to the pitchman's claims, the three people who took the pill should have been much more sober than the others at the end of an hour. But an hour later, to no one's surprise, we found that there was no significant difference in the decline in blood alcohol levels between those who had taken the pill and those who hadn't.

A few weeks later, we decided to confront the distributors of the Neutralizer pill while they were in Portland at a business exposition. Up until then, I still considered myself a researcher, not an investigative reporter. During my research for *Easy Money,* I had traveled around the country talking with a number of con artists who were incarcerated or were out of jail working legitimate jobs, but I had never confronted anyone in the middle of perpetrating a con, and I didn't know how they would react. Even with the added protection of an off-duty policeman escorting me, my stomach was queasy. But there was no way I was going to pass up this story now.

When the distributors were late showing up at their hotel, I was sure they had sniffed us out. But then there they were, walking toward us across the lobby: a husband-and-wife team, accompanied by the ex-cop pitchman we'd met in Seattle. As soon as they started talking, I knew that they still did not suspect a thing.

Together we went up to the couple's suite. They had just started spreading out their sales results when I said, "Before we get started, there's something I'd like you to see."

As the tape of our investigation rolled, I watched my quarry very carefully. I could see their minds at work as they sat motionless, their eyes never leaving the screen. It was patently clear to us all that we were watching proof of the fact that their miracle pill was a dud and their claims about its efficacy fraudulent.

Finally, the woman turned to me and said indignantly, "Chuck, so what if the pill just makes people responsibly aware, or maybe cognizant of, 'Gee, I've had a few'? Is that so bad?"

When I reminded her that people wouldn't be getting what they paid for, she replied, "Chuck, it's just a buck-fifty a pill. It's not like it's a five- or ten-dollar pill. They spend more than three dollars for a beer!"

She responded so self-righteously that my first impulse was to lash out at her. What about all those people who shelled out $5,000 for the vending machines to dispense a worthless pill? Or those drinkers who relied on the pill to reduce their blood alcohol level before getting in their cars—and the innocent victims of all the accidents that might result?

But I stopped myself, realizing that the woman hadn't tried to refute any of our evidence. She knew that her and her husband's claims for the Neutralizer were nothing but a crock of nonsense. But con artists easily rationalize their nefarious ways. Typically, this woman just refused to acknowledge the harm she was causing.

A two-part investigative report resulted from our work. The response was tremendous. While on the air, I asked viewers to give me a call on a new 800 number if they had any information concerning a scam. Shortly after the broadcast, the lines lit up.

The calls came from everywhere and referred to almost every type of scam imaginable: street scams, phony investment offers, telemarketing scams, auto mechanic rip-offs, travel scams, retail rip-offs, scams against the elderly. (We also quickly discovered that a number of people who'd reported scams to us were attempting to scam *us* by making false allegations. In most cases, these callers had a vendetta and were looking for a way to ruin someone's reputation.)

During the following months, I never ran out of despicable con artists to investigate. There was the elderly man with cancer who desperately wanted to buy a private residence so that his blind wife would have a place to live after he died; a heartless con man sold them a nonexistent mobile home and then took off with their life savings.

There was the eighty-seven-year-old woman suffering from Alzheimer's disease who was convinced by her caregiver that he was her son; she willingly signed over power of attorney to the caregiver, who then sold her home, emptied her bank accounts, closed her CDs, and left town with every penny she had.

Soon the network news department of NBC found out about our reports and began to offer them over their satellite system so that their other affiliates could use them. Around the same time, CNBC's *Steals and Deals* started airing some of our reports as well.

THE WHITE-COLLAR CRIME ADVISORY COUNCIL

Still, I was frustrated by the idea that we had only scratched the surface of helping people fight white-collar crime. So together with various members of the law enforcement community—including the police, the FBI, state and local county prosecutors, fraud detectives, sheriffs, insurance fraud investigators, and Medicare fraud investigators—I started a white-collar crime advisory council. Our meetings gave me insight into the kinds of cases the law enforcement community was investigating, so my news team could cooperate with them whenever possible. At the same time, the meetings gave a variety of law enforcement agencies an opportunity to exchange information in an informal setting.

The advisory council offered us quite a change from the usual contention and distrust between law enforcement and the media. But the very nature of white-collar crime demands a different approach in order to help stem the tide of this growing crime wave. And there was one thing we all agreed on: An educated public is one of the most powerful weapons we have against white-collar crime.

My efforts to raise awareness about con artists and white-collar crimes continued when I contracted with a local radio station, KEX-AM, for a one-hour Saturday morning radio talk show. *The*

Scam Show with Chuck Whitlock was a huge success; the phone lines lit up with callers with questions or reporting ongoing scams. Members of the advisory board, victims of cons, and former con artists all came on the program to share information with the public. We were arming the public with the most powerful weapon they could have to fend off swindlers: information.

EXPOSING MEDICARE FRAUD

The more I turned the spotlight on white-collar crime, the more the camera seemed to turn on me. While producing investigative reports for KGW-TV, NBC's satellite feed, and then for Paramount Studio's *Hard Copy,* I continued to appear on programs such as *Maury Povich, Oprah,* and *Geraldo.*

Then I produced a landmark segment for King World's *Inside Edition.* Posing as a businessman in a suburb of Houston, Texas, I went to work investigating Medicare fraud. In order to play my role to the hilt, I interviewed a number of experts in the field and located a contact in Houston who furnished me with names of local companies that were under investigation by law enforcement.

I found a cooperative, honest administrator of a nursing home who agreed to allow me to use his facility. After placing several hidden cameras in his office, I invited vendors of medical equipment, supplies, and services to teach me the ropes and tell me how to make money on Medicare as an owner of new nursing homes.

The responses were shocking. More than half of the companies' representatives and owners immediately offered me kickbacks—everything from cash and "complimentary funding checks" to computers and big-screen TVs—to do business with them.

James Zeke, a salesman for Physical Care, a company that provides physical therapy and home health care to Medicare patients, told me that his company would pay generously for patient referrals. If he received thirty patient referrals from my nursing home, his company would pay me $100 per patient every two weeks. That was $6,000 per month in kickbacks just from this one company!

When I asked Mr. Zeke how this money would be paid, he replied, "Oh, I could give you cash. I mean, I don't have to write you a check. I could just bring cash."

The most blatant offer came in the form of a "complimentary funding check" for patient referrals from Ian Gross, director of operations for Speedy Ambulance Service. According to Mr. Gross, his ambulance service bills Medicare approximately $360,000 per year to transport just one dialysis patient. And many of these patients have no problem getting around. We witnessed one patient taking an ambulance ride from a dialysis center to the patient's nursing home for which Medicare was billed over $600 one-way. We took the same route in a cab for just $8.

Helen, a saleswoman for Current Laboratory, came into my office seeking a laboratory testing contract with a fistful of $25 gift certificates for free dinners, haircuts, dry cleaning, etc. When we confronted her later about her tactics, she swore that there was nothing wrong with what she had done. Her company's president, however, wrote us a letter condemning her behavior.

Some companies were willing to provide medical treatments and physical therapy to patients who didn't need them. The president of one physical therapy company explained to me how his company would reward us for patient referrals. If our nursing home billed patients for physical therapy at a higher rate, he would bill our nursing home at a lower rate. The difference—in the form of a kickback to my nursing home—would be their thanks for sending my patients their way. Just to show me that their hearts were in the right place, they would also give me $5,000 to let them fill our patients' prescriptions.

On hidden camera we caught one physical therapy representative assuring an elderly woman that more treatment with her particular company would help the woman's legs and knees when, in fact, the woman had already been told by several rehabilitation experts that more treatment of this type would do her no good.

One wound kit manufacturer's representative gave us the following advice about how we should treat our nursing home customers: "Don't walk them and don't turn them." Bedridden patients who don't move around develop bedsores, known as decubitus ulcers. These ulcers can be painful for the patient, but they can be extraordinarily profitable for a nursing home, since the nursing home charges the customer or Medicare every time a wound kit is changed. One company was charging $40 for a wound kit that cost less than $5. The more ulcers, the more wound kits are needed, and the more money can be made by unethical nursing home administrators willing to neglect their patients.

Keep in mind that we looked at only a few companies in just one city in the United States. Every day in cities throughout our country, patients are being billed for services they do not receive and Medicare is being overcharged for goods and services way beyond the realms of reasonable costs. According to former Senator William Cohen of Maine, who headed the Senate Committee on Aging at the time of our investigation, the Medicare system loses anywhere from $18 to $25 billion annually to the greed and fraud of companies like those we encountered in Houston. After witnessing firsthand the shady dealings of the companies we investigated in Texas, it's not hard to understand how the system we've all come to rely upon is going broke.

Cracking down on companies participating in fraudulent practices such as those we filmed will be a huge step toward righting the listing Medicare system. Tighter controls and more supervision over billing practices have to be put in force to keep tabs on companies that are quick to take advantage of a system that is far too easy to defraud.

If you are a Medicare patient, pay attention to what is prescribed to you. Be an informed consumer and ask questions. If you feel you have been cheated, lied to, or otherwise mistreated by unscrupulous people, blow the whistle. Family members should constantly monitor health matters for elderly family members. It's your health, the health of your loved ones, and your dollars that are paying for the Medicare system, so it is your responsibility.

• • •

The impact of this *Inside Edition* story on Medicare fraud was tremendous. Facts from the story were quoted on the Senate floor; revelations from the tape helped convince members of Congress to recommend that the Department of Health and Human Services hire more fraud investigators.

It was the first time an investigative report I'd been part of was submitted for national award consideration. When *Inside Edition*'s "Medicare Sting" won a 1996 National Headliner Award for Outstanding Investigative Reporting, as well as a Sigma Delta Chi Award for Television Investigative Reporting from the Society of Professional Journalists, I was thrilled.

I was completely hooked. Not only was I doing something worthwhile—I was having a great time doing it!

•2•

PROFILE OF THE PREDATOR

There can be no question that they are an unusually sick group in terms of mental health and an unusually antisocial group in terms of lack of regard for others and the lack of control over their own impulses.

—*Richard Blum,* Deceivers and Deceived

IDENTIFYING THE CON ARTIST

At the sound of the knock at the door, Veronica O'Brien slowly got to her feet. She glanced up at the mantle clock: Mr. Jensen was right on time. She made her way to the door, her hands growing cold and clammy. She always got nervous on first meetings, and the older she got, the more vulnerable she felt. But she needed to deal with people like Mr. Jensen in order to remain independent. The last thing she wanted was to have to move away from her beautiful house into some kind of old age home.

"Good afternoon, Mrs. O'Brien." Mr. Jensen looked to be at least fifteen years younger than Veronica, who was eighty-five.

They shook hands. "Good afternoon, Mr. Jensen," Veronica said, noticing that he held a cheap bouquet of flowers in his other hand.

"These are for you," he said, smiling.

"How sweet," Veronica said, warming up to him. "You are quite the gentleman, Mr. Jensen."

"Please, call me Oliver."

Veronica invited Oliver inside. There, in the living room, they talked about the room she had for rent. Veronica owned a big, old house near downtown Sacramento, renting out bedrooms to older men who were retired and needed a low-cost place to live.

As they talked, she was surprised at how observant and appreciative he was of all the knickknacks and prized possessions she had displayed around the room. In no time at all, she found she was completely relaxed with him; she even went so far as to ask him to call her Veronica.

Soon she served tea and cookies. As Mr. Jensen took his first sip, she got down to business. "The room's $500 a month. That includes breakfast and dinner, seven days a week. And I'll need first and last months' rent in advance before you move in."

"That's an awful lot of money all at once. I don't get my Social Security money for a couple of weeks," Mr. Jensen said sheepishly. Then he added, "I guess I can dip into my investment. I hate to do it, because it's making so much money for me. But I guess I'll have to."

Veronica liked Oliver. "You know, you look okay. I'll tell you what. You can go ahead and move in now and just pay me in a couple of weeks, when your Social Security check comes in. I'll even help you change your address so your check'll come here."

"That's awful nice of you, Veronica, but I do have the money," Oliver said. Then his eyes lit up. "As a matter of fact, I'm going to tell you about my investment. It's a new long-distance telephone card plan. Maybe you've got a dollar or two you'd like to grow."

Veronica smiled at him. She already had a small nest egg, but it was always good to have a plan to increase what you had. "That sounds nice. Let's get you moved in and situated; then you can tell me all about it."

So it was agreed: Oliver would move in by the weekend. Before Oliver left, Veronica helped him fill out his new-tenant paperwork, which included a credit information questionnaire. She also helped him fill out a change of address form for the post office. And before he left, Oliver pulled a brochure for the telephone card investment out of his coat and left it for Veronica to read.

On Saturday, Oliver showed up to move into his new home. The front door was open, so he walked right in. Two men in suits were waiting in Veronica's living room. One was looking through the investment brochure. Next to him, Veronica sat in a high-back chair. She looked pale and clutched a handkerchief to her mouth.

The man who was looking at the brochure put it down when he saw Mr. Jensen. Standing, he took out a police badge and introduced himself. "I'm Sergeant Warner. Are you Oliver Jensen?"

Oliver's first instinct was to turn and run. Instead, though, he froze, clutching his suitcases. "Yes," he responded.

"Mr. Jensen, it seems you're going to have to find yourself another place to live."

A puzzled look creased Oliver's face. "Has someone else taken the room?"

"No, sir. We're here to place Mrs. O'Brien under arrest for four counts of murder and felony fraud."

"Murder? Fraud?" Oliver sank into a nearby chair.

"Yes, sir. Mrs. O'Brien has been poisoning older retired gentlemen like yourself, then cashing the Social Security checks she receives in their names. We've already dug up two bodies in her backyard."

Oliver looked at Veronica. She stared up at him, expressionless.

How long did it take you to identify the swindler in this story? Like most people, were you surprised when it turned out to be the older, seemingly more vulnerable Veronica O'Brien? You shouldn't have been. There is no such thing as a typical swindler, no tried-and-true way to identify a con artist.

Con artists—like their victims—come from every race, religion, and socioeconomic background; they can be male or female, young or old. A con artist can be anybody—even the grandmotherly type who lives down the block.

• • •

DISTINGUISHING CHARACTERISTICS OF THE CON ARTIST

So how can we protect ourselves from swindlers? The first step is to try to understand what makes them tick. In *How Con Games Work,* author M. Allen Henderson remarks that the con artist considers the confidence game "the crème de la crème of crime." Henderson states:

• He looks down on thieves and muggers who have to resort to force in order to make a buck. He feels superior because he lives by his wits, making other people willingly give him what he wants.

• This sense of superiority in outsmarting others often results in compulsive scamming. The natural con man will resort to scams even when it would be more profitable to pursue more conventional avenues of endeavor.[1]

Why would someone with above-average intelligence, good communication skills, and a likable personality choose a life of deception and fraud when he or she could probably make a better-than-average living legally? Are there distinguishing characteristics that would enable a person to readily identify these predators?

Over the past few years, I have interviewed hundreds of con artists in an attempt to learn if there are any common denominators among them. They all seemed to be very sincere, very candid—until I started to ask some hard questions. At that point they all became hostile and angry—and in a couple of instances, near violent. Male or female, they pleaded their innocence to me, claiming that their convictions were all misunderstandings.

So while there are no obvious identifying features common to con artists—no common socioeconomic background, childhood experiences, education, or criminal history—there is one thing they share: They are always able to rationalize away accusations against them and to justify their actions, at least in their own minds.

Most con artists also have delusions of self-importance. They feel they deserve the riches they con out of their victims. From the young men who con young women out of their savings with promises of marriage to the old men who concentrate on widows and divorcées, they feel that they are only taking what is rightfully theirs. After taking a retired couple's life savings, one con artist told me that if they were not smart enough to hang on to what was theirs, they deserved to lose it.

Another thing common to almost all of the hardened con artists I talked with was their willingness to take everything they could get from each and every mark. They didn't think twice about promising their victims the world and giving them nothing in return.

Finally, while there are no hard-and-fast rules about con artists' backgrounds, I found that many happen to come from dysfunctional families or single-parent families with many siblings. As a result, they grew up feeling deprived of parental affection. Somehow, as these budding con artists grew into adulthood, they developed a cavalier attitude toward others and no longer feared the consequences of their actions. They had no respect for society's norms and laws, and little or no fear of punishment. The anger they repressed while growing up manifested itself in a selfish, manipulative personality. Indeed, the self-image of many con artists is so inflated as to border on narcissism.

Richard Blum is a distinguished criminologist who has studied and tested con artists extensively. In his book *Deceivers and Deceived,* he remarks that his tests revealed most con artists to be:

> *impulsive, amoral, uncontrolled and detached from normal relationships and thinking processes. They are also depressed and compulsive.... There can be no question that they are an unusually sick group in terms of mental health and an unusually antisocial group in terms of lack of regard for others and the lack of control over their own impulses.*[2]

When taken together, the behaviors most often exhibited by the con artist can be described as constituting Antisocial Personality Disorder. According to the fourth edition of the *Diagnostic and Statistical Manual of Mental Disorders*, published by the American Psychiatric Association:

> *The essential feature of Antisocial Personality Disorder is a pervasive pattern of disregard for, and violation of, the rights of others that begins in childhood or early adolescence and continues into adulthood.*
>
> *This pattern has also been referred to as psychopathy, sociopathy, or dyssocial personality disorder. . . .*
>
> *Individuals with Antisocial Personality Disorder frequently lack empathy and tend to be callous, cynical, and contemptuous of the feelings, rights, and sufferings of others.*[3]

THE CHAMELEON

While there may be some psychological characteristics shared by many con artists and some data that help explain how they become the amoral people they are, that doesn't change the fact that most people cannot detect the con artist in their midst. Take Jim Bakker, for instance. When he had his ministry, he seemed just as sincere and well-meaning as his colleague Billy Graham. Yet he ended up fleecing his flock. How is it that con artists can fool their marks like this?

One reason is that the good con artist is a chameleon, ready to be whomever he or she needs to be to fleece his unsuspecting prey. A swindler's greatest tool of the trade is his ability to camouflage his real identity and true intent.

Successful con artists know how to relate to their marks on an individual level. They are very intuitive about a mark's weaknesses and insecurities. The con man will look you right in the eye and lie to you, telling you he's a doctor, if that's what you need to hear—or a lawyer, or a police officer, or a businessperson. And if you are desperate or distraught enough, you'll believe the con artist in a heartbeat.

On a certain level all good con artists are impostors. Even a con artist who isn't lying about his name or profession is lying about something; at the very least, he's posing as someone legitimate when in fact he's not. But some con artists take posing as someone they're not several steps further. These are the professional impostors. Most of them operate by assuming brand-new identities. For some of them, posing as someone they're not is even more important than using their new identity to make money. Perhaps they get a rush out of acting their new roles so well that others are fooled; perhaps they are fulfilling secret desires they've had to be doctors, lawyers, princesses, or the like.

History is full of accounts of impostors. Remember Anna Anderson, who claimed to be Grand Duchess Anastasia, the sole survivor of the 1918 execution of the Russian Imperial family? Or Ferdinand Waldo Demara, "The Great Impostor," who made a career out of his impersonations? (His career as an impostor all but ended after a book was written and movie made about him.) And you might remember David Hampton, who claimed to be the son of Sidney Poitier, and conned his way into the homes of some prominent New Yorkers.[4]

CHUCK WHITLOCK: ALIAS BRENT COLLIER, CHIEF OF POLICE

Today, it's as easy as ever to assume a new identity. To prove this for *Hard Copy,* not long ago I assumed the identity of Brent Collier, the Chief of Police of Milwaukie, Oregon. Although Brent didn't think I would be successful, he gave me permission to give it a shot.

It wasn't a hard thing to do. First, I rifled through Brent's trash in his quiet residential neighborhood early one morning, where I retrieved one of his bank account statements and a utility bill. Next, I visited the Department of Motor Vehicles, where I used a story about having lost my wallet while fishing to finagle a new driver's license, with Brent Collier's name and license number next to my picture. Remarkably, I wasn't asked for any documents to verify my identification.

With just one phone call, I had valid checks with Brent's name, address, and bank account number in hand. For the next step in my plan, I needed to dress to impress, so I changed into a conservative black suit and newly shined shoes.

With my new driver's license and checks, I went apartment shopping. I told the landlord that I was Brent Collier, and paid her the $25 she requested to run a TRW credit report, often a standard step when applying for a rental unit. When I asked her if I could take the credit report with me, she didn't hesitate to give it to me; after all, it was mine.

I used the information on the TRW to complete my scam, phoning the credit card companies listed there and telling them to send replacement cards to my new address. At that point, who wouldn't have believed that I was Brent Collier? It was easy to pretend to be someone else. What was amazing was how readily everyone believed me.

WHAT'S THE DIFFERENCE BETWEEN A GOOD CON ARTIST AND A GREAT ONE?

Some people believe that all con artists have blatant, hard-sell, overtly sleazy personalities. That they have scarred faces, beady eyes, and flashy clothes. This is a misconception. There are no visual cues to tip a good con artist's hand. Each time I've been asked to pull cons for the camera, I have been surprised by the feedback from my victims after I've revealed who I really am. "But you looked so nice," they say. Or, "You didn't look like a con artist." That's just the point: no good con artist looks like a con artist.

Good con artists never seem to get caught. But the outstanding con artists are so good that their scams are rarely even reported.

Some swindlers pull off such perfect con jobs that their victims don't even realize they've been scammed.

So what's the difference between a good con artist and a truly outstanding one? Consider the following scam.

PARKING LOT PURCHASES

Joe and Betty wanted a big-screen TV. They shopped around, first in the department stores, then in the electronics stores. But the best price they could find was still much more than they could afford. Then, one day after emerging disappointed from a discount electronics store, they noticed a man standing next to a van.

"I couldn't help but notice that you wanted one of those big-screen TVs," the man said.

"Yeah," Joe said. "But they're too expensive. We're going to have to save our money."

"Why don't you finance it?" the man asked.

Betty answered, "We've had credit problems. . . . "

"Maybe I can help you. I, uh, I got my hands on six of these real good big-screen TVs. Just like the ones in the store. I need to get cash for them, so I can sell you one for $300."

"That's outrageous. They're selling for $900 or more in there." Joe said. He turned to Betty. "Let's go. This guy's trying to rip us off."

Quickly, the man said, "Look, you want a TV, and I need the money. Go ahead; take a look."

Joe and Betty figured they had nothing to lose. Inside the man's truck were a half-dozen identical, sealed cardboard boxes. All had a major TV manufacturer's name and logo printed on them. The man pulled one out of the truck and sliced open the box, revealing a brand-new TV.

Joe and Betty grew excited. This guy, it seemed, could deliver on his promise. Sure, the TVs were probably stolen. But what a bargain! The man asked, "So, are you interested or not? Just $300 gets one of these beauties loaded into your car, and you're on your way."

"Okay," said Joe, handing over the money.

"Here, take one of these boxed ones. I don't have any tape to tape up this box."

Joe and the man carried the heavy, sealed box to Joe and Betty's car.

All the way home, Joe and Betty excitedly discussed where they would put their new TV. Once they got home, they didn't even bring the box inside until they had totally rearranged their living room. Finally, they carried their prized purchase inside.

They opened the box, looked inside, and found a pile of tightly packed bricks. Instantly, of course, they knew that they'd been suckered out of $300.

Betty called the police. Three hours later, a detective arrived at their door. The possibility of getting their money back was not good, he told them, but there was a better chance that the man would be caught. "We now know there's someone out there pulling this scam, so we'll keep an eye out," he said.

Chances are the con man got away with it. He is a good con artist. But he's not a great one—he's left the door open to being caught.

An outstanding con artist might pull practically the same con. But what makes him great is that he makes sure that it will never be reported to the police. Here's how he does it: After Joe pays the man and they start loading the TV box into Joe and Betty's car, a voice suddenly shouts: "Police! Drop the box on the ground and put your hands up in the air!"

Joe and Betty raise their hands, frightened. Two cops flash their badges. One of them demands, "Turn around and face the truck. Put your palms against the truck and spread your legs!"

By this time, Joe and Betty are terrified.

The con man speaks to the cops. "What's the problem, officers?"

"We got you this time, Harry. These TVs are hot!" One cop pats down Joe and Betty, while the other puts handcuffs on Harry, continuing, "Who're these two? You got some new partners?"

"Nah, they're only customers. Why don't you let them go?" The other policeman patting down Joe and Betty takes out his handcuffs, ready to cuff Joe. "Come on, guys, you don't want to have to do all that extra paperwork."

The policeman turns to Joe. "Is that true? You just trying to buy this stolen TV?"

Joe nods, "Yes, sir."

"You know that's a crime, don't you?"

Nervously, Betty answers, "Oh, yes, we do, officer. We won't do it again. We promise."

The policeman looks from Joe to Harry, the con man. "You two really don't look like you belong with this clown. Go ahead, get out of here. Consider yourselves lucky."

Joe and Betty quickly jump into their car, driving away as fast as they can.

Later that night, Betty says to Joe, "Honey, that man has our money."

"Yeah, I know."

"Do you remember either of the policemen's names?"

"No. And I don't think we ought to make a big deal out of the money. We were lucky to get out of there without any trouble."

Betty agrees. "Yeah, I guess you're right."

Meanwhile, Harry and the two "policemen" are splitting up the take for another successful night's work—without any worry that any of their marks will call real law enforcement.

CAVEAT EMPTOR

Remember, a con artist can be anyone: your minister, doctor, or travel agent, a loyal employee, business consultant, or janitor, or perhaps, the love of your life. A con artist will play any role in order to win your confidence and trust. So play it smart: Be cautious.

• • •

LESSON

••

The first step in protecting ourselves from swindlers is to understand what makes them tick. Antisocial, amoral, and compulsive, con artists are chameleonlike, ready to become whoever they need to be in order to fleece their prey. Unfortunately, you can't automatically trust people or take them at face value. Listen to your gut instincts and use your good common sense.

••

1. M. Allen Henderson, *How Con Games Work* (Secaucus, N.J.: Citadel Press, 1985), p. 8.

2. Richard H. Blum, *Deceivers and Deceived: Observations on Confidence Men and Their Victims, Informants and Their Quarry, Political and Industrial Spies and Ordinary Citizens* (Springfield: Charles C. Thomas, 1972), pp. 49-50.

3. *Diagnostic and Statistical Manual of Mental Disorders,* 4th ed. (Washington, D.C.: American Psychiatric Association, 1994), pp. 645-47.

4. Gordon Stein and Marie J. MacNee, *Hoaxes! Dupes, Dodges & Other Dastardly Deceptions* (Detroit: Visible Ink Press, 1995), pp. 185-97.

· 3 ·

RELIGIOUS AND SPIRITUAL FRAUD

He was simply charming. I mean usually, when someone is arrested, he is really sullen. But this guy oozed it; he was a charmer. And then you look at him and you think, "Yeah, I could probably be bilked out of money by this guy."

—A deputy district attorney, about a faith healer arrested for fraud

··

THE BLACK MAGIC PRIEST
··

The voice was cool and smooth, like a stream tumbling down out of the mountains. "Y hay gente que esta buscando de hacerle un dano," intoned the man who called himself Dr. Davíd. Translated into English, he was warning his listeners: "And there are people out there who are looking to hurt you."

Hundreds of Latinos in Medford, Oregon, population 53,000, tuned into Dr. Davíd's radio program on KRTA every week. They listened to their transistor radios out in the fields, where they worked the marionberries, the hops, the alfalfa. Later, at home, they crowded around boom boxes in metal-roofed dwellings that contained almost no furniture—nothing lavish except the painting of the Virgin Mary over the sofa. They didn't need any more bad luck in their lives.

Most of them had come a long way to Oregon. They were far away from their homes in Mexico, Guatemala, and El Salvador. Most of them were practically broke. Their backs ached from all the hard labor; their marriages were strained under the stress.

"Estan buscando de verlo un tracasado, un destruido," said Dr. Davíd darkly. "They are looking to cause you catastrophe, destruction."

It sounded horrible—but worse, it sounded true. In the villages where these workers came from, people were fearful of black cats and buzzards. Everyone knew the world swims with dark forces.

"Es peligroso, pero protegeramos de cualquiera mala energia," said the cool voice on the radio. "It's dangerous, but we will protect you from bad energy."

So what if it cost a little money, they thought. Maybe a week's paycheck, but that was all right. Everyone needed a *curandero,* a healer. Back home, such men had often seemed more important than doctors. They gave you herbs when you were sick; they told you what prayers to pray in bad times.

"Por eso," said the voice, "yo le recomiendo usted que venga a mi centro astrologica, la Familia de la Fé." It was an open invitation: "So I suggest that you come to my astrological center, The Family of Faith."

And they did. From January until April 1995, more than twenty people visited Dr. Davíd's small, second-floor office in Medford. They paid $40 for a half hour initial session where they were usually told that their problems were far worse—far darker and more mysterious—than they could have guessed. When Ignacio Ramirez stepped in complaining of a sore back, for instance, Dr. Davíd warned that Ignacio's teen son was destined to be paralyzed in a car crash. And there was only one remedy: Ramirez had to buy—and burn—nine candles made in Rome out of human body fat.

"¿Cuánto me cobra?" asked Ignacio Ramirez. He needed to know how much the candles would cost.

"A hundred and fifty dollars a candle," replied Dr. Davíd.

In all, over a brief four-month period, the citizens of Medford paid more than $20,000 for Dr. Davíd's mystical advice, incense, and candles.

It was all a scam, of course. Dr. Davíd was neither a holy man nor a medical expert. He was just a twenty-four-year-old Colombian youth who'd migrated north with dollar signs in his eyes. His real name was Geovanny Gutierrez-Montoya, and his con was exquisitely engineered to bilk devout Hispanic Catholics.

Catholics in Mexico and Central America practice a distinct faith. Their religion retains echoes of ancient Mexico, of a time when the Aztec Indians thrived. The Aztecs had many gods; they worshipped a sun god, for instance, and prayed to a rain god in times of drought. Similarly, today's Hispanic Catholics worship many saints, each of whom plays a part in everyday life. Every believer has a patron saint to whom he or she is supposed to pray. People glue pictures of Saint Christopher, the patron saint of travel, to their dashboards, and travel to remote churches to gather handfuls of "sacred dirt" when they're ailing. The cosmos, for Hispanic Catholics, is not run by one almighty God. It's far more complex than that. There is magic and miracle and, along with the myriad saints, there is *el diablo,* the devil, among other bad spirits.

Dr. Davíd knew all this, and played on his marks' deeply rooted beliefs. To them, he wasn't just another gringo physician. He was a *compadre*—a Spanish speaker who cared. And when his followers started to find him out, when his "mystical advice" backfired—for instance, when a diabetic woman died shortly after Dr. Davíd advised her not to see a physician—he and his business associate scared their clients into silence. Anyone who squealed to the cops, they promised, would lose his eyesight and his voice.

Maria Swann was seated in Dr. Davíd's dimly lit office. She asked if she could see the human fat candles. Dr. Davíd had told her she should buy four of them—for $900 apiece—so, she ventured, she should at least be able to see them.

Dr. Davíd leaned forward over his desk. He was a thin man, and the mustache on his young face was just a faint, wispy thing, but he was lithe, like a cobra. "I cannot show you the candles because I've already lit them," he crisply informed Maria. "And nobody goes in where they are. Nobody, not even the wind, enters. It's a dark place, very dirty; it smells horrible, eternally horrible. There are worms in there; there are snakes. There are cobras and boas."

Maria said nothing. She was just a meek woman who yearned for a miracle—a woman who wanted to give birth to a son even though her Fallopian tubes had been tied. Or so Dr. Davíd had been led to believe.

In fact, Maria Swann was an undercover policewoman with a camera and microphone tucked inside her blue sweater. For more than two weeks, a dozen people—my camera crew and I, members of the Medford police force, and the INS—had been working with Maria, in the hope of busting Dr. Davíd's swindle.

The work had begun a couple of weeks before, in mid-March of 1995, when Roy Skinner, a detective with the Medford Police, and Detective Sergeant Mark Coffey of Portland finally figured out how they could nab Dr. Davíd. For months Skinner had been frustrated by the district attorney's refusal to prosecute Dr. Davíd. "Freedom of religion," the D.A. said. But then Coffey found the right approach: fraud by deception. Were the candles actually made of human fat? If not, selling them as such was a crime.

Now, it was March 31, and we were across the street from Dr. Davíd's office, listening to Maria and Dr. Davíd from inside a van with tinted windows.

"He says he wants her to make love to her husband with some-one observing," a Spanish-speaking INS agent translated. "Now he's telling her to get two bills, a twenty and a fifty, and make a cross with them. She's got to put some coins to the side and. . . . Now he's saying she's got to get her underwear and her husband's underwear and put it behind the candles. And wait. . . . "

There was only one way this child would come, claimed Dr. Davíd: on her next visit, Maria would have to bring a condom filled with her husband's sperm. The good doctor would treat it—and then he would place it carefully into her womb.

Crosses made out of money? I thought. *Strange rituals involving human sperm?* Where on earth was this guy getting all his ideas? Dr. Davíd called himself Catholic, but really he was faithful only to his twisted imagination.

On the wall of his office, Maria told us, he kept a crucifix bearing an ivory Christ who was, hauntingly, nothing but a skeleton. On a table were a host of bright incense boxes, which he had probably bought at a Mexican *supermercado*. On another wall hung a dark Alchemy poster, the kind you might find in the room of a teenager who spins his Led Zeppelin records backward.

The bookshelves were filled with books like *Corona Mística* (Mystic Heart), *Quiromancia* (Palmistry), and *El Libro Infernal* (The Book of Hell). Inside a glass container, a dead frog floated in murky water. Dr. Davíd had found it, he said, lodged in a woman's stomach. Paintings of the Virgin Mary, plastic skulls, rosary beads, voodoo effigies—Dr. Davíd had borrowed from many sources to achieve just the right spiritual ambiance.

A week later, Maria Swann returned to Dr. Davíd's office. She touched the condom as she knocked on Dr. Davíd's door, making the pearly white liquid undulate inside. Then she laughed. It wasn't sperm in there; it was dish soap. She was going to get Dr. Davíd, she whispered into her microphone before the door in front of her opened. Across the street in the van, we hoped she was right.

Inside, Dr. Davíd led Maria through the ritual that was supposed to get her pregnant. Standing up, he raised his long arms toward the ceiling. "The spirit of grand power," he chanted, "take my body. Take possession of it."

"The spirit of grand power," repeated Maria. "Take my body. Take possession of it."

"You are meditating," Dr. Davíd said a few moments later. "Your mind is blank. You must leave your eyes closed to maintain total concentration. . . . You are going to have a son by your husband. You will feel his body against yours. The spirits will take possession of your body. Do you understand?"

Maria nodded.

"Now," Dr. Davíd continued, "Take that off—the black jacket."

In our van across the street, the witch doctor's voice crackled through the receiver.

"He's telling her to get undressed," said the INS agent.

"Okay," said Roy Skinner, "we've got to go *now*."

• • •

Roy Skinner was the first to burst through the door.

"I'm a police officer. We have a search warrant for the premises."

Dr. Davíd looked up at us, then slumped in his chair. His office—this intricate kingdom he had created—must have seemed invaded by hornets. Eight people had barged in; some rifled through his stuff while others waved their big TV cameras all over the place. In a back room, one of the Medford police officers found a stack of candles—ordinary wax candles. These were the candles Dr. Davíd had claimed were made of human fat.

When Skinner slapped on the cuffs, Geovanny Gutierrez-Montoya—the young man who'd called himself Dr. Davíd—knew he'd been beaten. Led by the cops, he went out the door and down the old stairs with his head hanging low.

In our darkest and most desperate moments, our spiritual and religious beliefs often help us through the day. Because of this, the clergy are, along with doctors and police officers, one of a select group of professions to whom most people defer, simply because of the work they do. Unfortunately, con artists have invaded the clergy just as they have invaded other professions. Worse still, religious con artists are harder to stop than those in other professions. Once an unscrupulous cleric gets a foothold in a congregation, he can insulate himself behind "God's word." There are many examples of crooked holy men getting away with embezzlement, child abuse, sexual abuse, and other hardly charitable acts—while entire congregations turn a deaf ear and a blind eye to their activities.

Consider Dr. Davíd. It appeared he could not be stopped. According to the D.A., the police could not arrest him for fear of violating his freedom of religion. His followers certainly did little to bring him to justice. And when he finally was sentenced, he could only be charged with a Class C felony.

Dr. Davíd spent only two months in jail and was released upon the condition that he would devote six months to help the police nail the con artists similarly scamming the Latino community in

Los Angeles. According to his lawyer, it was unlikely he would pay back the nearly $20,000 he'd been charged with stealing from his followers.

Dr. Davíd broke the law. But perhaps the worst thing he broke was the spirit of his followers. While he walked away from jail a free man, they were out sweating in the fields—poorer by the tens of thousands of dollars they had contributed to Dr. Davíd's crooked coffers.

THE MANY FACES OF SPIRITUAL SCAMS

History is full of religious and spiritual scams and scandals. Religious scams can be found anywhere, but they are a particular problem in the United States. Here, the ideal of freedom of religion ends up allowing all kinds of con artists to get away with their scams. Gurus, cult leaders, swamies, ministers, televangelists—they come in all guises, seeking power and money. The most important piece of advice I can give you: Be aware and wary, especially when you're in an emotionally vulnerable state. That's when you're most likely to fall for a religious con.

MINISTER STEVE: THE CON ARTIST CLERGYMAN

At first, when I lost everything, I wondered how God could have forsaken me like this. But then I realized that it wasn't God; it was a man. Minister Steve is, after all, human just like the rest of us. He knows what he's done. Ultimately, he'll have to answer for his actions, just like we all do.

—Harriet Larson, victim of a con artist clergyman

Con artists are often exceptionally charming, and religious con artists are no exception. Of course, they have an advantage—

most people have a built-in sense of trust toward clergy. A mistaken trust, it sometimes turns out.

Harriet Larson was an elderly widow who, soon after her husband died, moved from Phoenix, Arizona, to Yreka, California. To help get over her grief, she began attending the Yreka First Saints Christian Church, whose minister was one Steve Babcock. Soon her whole life revolved around First Saints. Minister Steve gave her so much personal attention, so much comfort. Some of Harriet's friends even told her that they thought Minister Steve liked her—*really* liked her—an idea that Harriet pooh-poohed, but that secretly thrilled her.

Eventually, Harriet trusted Minister Steve so much that when he told her the church needed money to purchase some land to expand operations, she didn't hesitate—not finding it suspicious at all that he knew she had a big nest egg, even though she had never told him about it. In return for the donation, Minister Steve promised that in addition to church buildings, the church would build a new house for Harriet on the land purchased with her donation. So with that, Harriet Larson wrote a check to First Saints—for $300,000.

In the months that followed, Minister Steve was visibly excited about the church's expansion plans. But he was evasive about where the funding for it had come from and instructed Harriet not to tell anyone about her role in it. Still, she suspected nothing.

And then one day, Minister Steve came to visit Harriet once again. Construction on her house had not begun, he told her, because the church expansion was turning out to be more expensive than planned. In fact, the church had just run out of building money, even before the completion of the planned new church buildings. Was there *any* way Harriet could help?

Even though she was starting to have her suspicions about Minister Steve, she wrote a second check to him, this time for $260,000—the remainder of her estate. After all, he had been so good to her when she'd first come to Yreka in her time of need.

Soon Harriet had almost no money left. She was being evicted from her Yreka apartment. And construction had yet to begin on the new house Minister Steve had promised her. When she turned to Minister Steve for help, he was suddenly very cold. She could live in the barn on the grounds, he said.

That's when Harriet Larson finally got smart and called me. She had seen my news reports on television, she told me the first time we spoke. After talking with her, I began working on an exposé of Minister Steve.

Among other things I found out about the man: He had never told the church board that he had promised Harriet a house on the land purchased with her money. In fact, the original building plans included a barn, and Harriet's name was written inside the structure—to me, proof enough that Minister Steve had intended to defraud her from very early on.

But then Harriet called me again. "Mr. Whitlock, drop the story. The minister says if I go public, he's going to throw me out of the barn, and the other church members will shun me because I'll have turned my back on the church. I don't know what I'd do if that happened. Please drop the story."

Not wanting to risk Harriet's safety, I did drop the story. I had been eager to show the world what kind of man Steve Babcock really was—not a caring clergyman, as he claimed to be, but a self-ish, coldhearted con artist who wouldn't hesitate to bilk a sweet old woman out of her life savings. It saddened me not to be able to do this, but I had to respect Harriet's wishes and her plight.

I did talk with California authorities in the hope that they could somehow help Harriet recover some of the money that had been defrauded from her. Unfortunately, there wasn't enough hard legal evidence to help her. Minister Steve had given Harriet nothing in writing. All their transactions had been conducted verbally.

There was no way, the authorities told me, to prove that Steve Babcock had promised to build Harriet Larson a house or that he had convinced her to hand over her life savings—in sum, no way to prove that Harriet Larson had been defrauded. But if I were on a jury hearing this case, I know who I'd believe.

• • •

TEN PSYCHICS PREDICT TEN FUTURES

These days many people are no longer satisfied that conventional religious institutions can meet their spiritual needs. So they visit psychics and other New Age types. While I'm sure that many psychics are well-intentioned and, in some cases, provide a worthwhile service, I am just as certain that the psychic-help industry is rife with lies, false claims, and misrepresentations. People are paying psychics to predict the future, and they're just not getting what they paid for.

Not long ago I went undercover to visit ten psychics, looking for predictions about my future. The disparity between what each told me was quite telling.

Each psychic began by asking me to cut a deck of cards or close my eyes and think about my problems. But beyond that the similarities among them ended. Each psychic had a different prediction for me. The first nine psychics I saw suggested that I become a stockbroker, a hospital administrator, a car salesman, a builder, a politician, a psychic, an actor, a businessman dealing with resorts, and finally, a bricklayer. The tenth told me to prepare to retire with the money I was going to inherit.

And when I asked one psychic if I should pursue a career as an author or television investigative reporter, she replied, "Perish the thought!"

When asked what my future wife would look like, again they all saw something different. She was going to be blond, redheaded, bleached blond, or brunette, have long, flowing auburn hair, or be a very short woman with pitch black hair.

One psychic predicted that I would have a sex change operation. He was the same one who told me that I had a secret enemy, and suggested that I urinate in a milk carton, write the names of anyone who might be angry with me on the outside of the carton with a felt-tip pen, then place the full carton in my freezer to ward off danger.

And finally, there was the woman who told me, "I talk to my dead husband all the time. We made love last night."

When I went back to the ten psychics and told them that I had recorded their psychic readings, their reactions varied from the defensive to the matter-of-fact to the outraged.

"People who believe this stuff are idiots," one told me.

"I do it for entertainment purposes only."

Another said, "I wouldn't trust what half the people in my business tell you. Most of them are ex-prostitutes, drug addicts, and phonies."

"I worked as a secretary for a while, but psychic readings pay better," another psychic told me.

A more vehement psychic told me that I was the Antichrist for exposing him.

One psychic I spoke to on camera said, "Sure, I give medical advice when the spirits tell me that special potions are needed."

"And do you sell these potions?" I asked.

"Sure, how else are people going to get them?"

"How much do you charge?" I asked.

"Oh, you can see I live quite comfortably."

"How much do you charge?" I insisted.

"I am not at liberty to say."

It was an interesting investigative piece all right. Humorous, in some aspects—but also a bit scary. Some people pay hundreds of dollars for hours of telephone consultations. Others refuse conventional medical treatment and legal advice because of advice their psychics have given them.

Remember: *Caveat emptor.* Let the buyer beware. Psychic readings are for entertainment purposes only.

HOW TO SPOT THE SPIRITUAL FRAUD

Genuine religious leaders, including swamis, ministers, rabbis, and other spiritual leaders, are primarily interested in saving souls and persuading people to follow their teachings. A con artist pretending to be interested in your spiritual well-being, however, will insist on proof of your faith in the form of large gifts to him or her.

Ask yourself the following questions: Is the person extraordinarily charismatic? Do you feel totally swept up in the moment when you're in his or her presence? If the religious leader weren't personally involved in the religious movement, would you still believe in what he or she professes? Is there any secrecy or "us-versus-them" involved? Have you been asked to contribute what you consider a large amount of money? Can you specifically identify where the contributions are going? Your answers to these questions should help you decide if you're being conned.

LESSON

Con artists have invaded the ranks of the clergy just as they have invaded other respected professions. Realize when you're emotionally vulnerable and especially susceptible to those who'll steal from you in the name of religion. Remember Jim Jones? His followers gave everything they owned, eventually giving their very lives at his request. Plan ahead and put limits on your gift giving. Be wary of zealots who promise more than they can deliver.

STREET HUSTLERS, SHILLS, AND STEERERS

They say that you can't cheat an honest man. That's a good one!

> —*Don Quigley-Mason, street hustler and convicted felon*

···

THE PHONY REWARD SCAM

···

The day dawned gray and rainy. Lew Garner was grumpy as he got into his rusted pickup and drove to the Christmas tree lot. He lit his last cigarette as he pulled into the place. Row after row of Scotch pine, spruce, white pine—all looking a bit picked over now, about a week before Christmas. He would be glad when the whole damn thing was over.

The little hut was chilly and damp, as usual. Lew flipped on the small electric heater, which was plugged into a long orange extension cord running from the supermarket next door. His brother-in-law, Paul, had done him the big favor of getting him this job. Now, he was beholden to Paul, an idea he hated. He wished his sister had never married the guy.

The space heater would take a few minutes to warm up the hut, so Lew walked over to the convenience store to fill up his thermos and buy a pack of smokes. There, the Pakistani guy behind the counter made polite, empty conversation as Lew filled his thermos with the burnt coffee.

Just one more week, he thought, *one more stinking week.* He had no idea what he would do for work after that, but at least he would be out from under Paul's thumb—and wouldn't have to drink this sheep dip any more.

Back at the lot, the day's first customer had arrived. A woman, young, maybe thirty, blond, nice clothes, and expensive boots. Not bad.

"Hi," Lew called out across the lot. "Merry Christmas. Need any help?"

"Oh, good morning," she responded. "No, not yet. I'll keep looking."

He smiled and waved, then lit a smoke and poured himself a cup of coffee.

Ten minutes later, the woman knocked on the door of the hut. "Sorry," she said, "but I guess I haven't seen one I really like."

Lew tried to keep her there a while longer. She sure was pretty. And a slow day at the lot could be awfully lonely. "Gee, I don't know what to tell you. I'm pretty sure that we won't be getting any more in before Christmas."

"I guess I'll have to go to a few more lots," she mused. Then, looking down to pull on her gloves, she suddenly gasped.

"What's wrong, lady?" Lew thought she might be having some kind of attack.

"My ring, my engagement ring! It's gone!"

"Were you wearing it? For sure?"

"Yes, yes. For sure. I must have dropped it somewhere here in this lot. Can you help me look for it?"

"You bet. Do you have any idea—"

"No, no. I didn't even know it was missing until right this second. Oh, my gosh, my fiancé will kill me. That ring cost $15,000."

Lew whistled. That kind of jewelry was way out of his league. "Don't worry, we'll find it. I'll start by the fence, you go over by the supermarket, and we'll work toward the middle."

"Okay. But what if we don't find it? I'm so . . . if he finds out—"

"Don't panic yet. Let's start looking."

They looked for a half hour. Lew moved almost every tree in the lot in the process. He wiggled his fingers in every pile of fallen branches and needles. But it was no use. Finally, he admitted defeat.

"Oh, my God, what am I going to do? I've got to be at work in ten minutes," the woman said. She was frantic now.

Frustrated, Lew tried to think of what to do next. "Look, lady, why don't you call me later? I'll keep looking between customers."

"Wait," she answered. "Take my number." She pulled a pad and pencil from her purse, then wrote down her name, Leslie Allen, and a phone number. "Call me if you find it. I'll give you a $5,000 reward if you do."

Lew was staggered. "Gee, Ms. Allen, that's a lot—"

"No, no, it's worth it. I'm terrified of what he'll do when he finds out. The money isn't that important to me."

"I'll call you as soon as I find it."

"Thanks, thanks very much." She walked over to a green Range Rover and drove away.

Lew was amazed. This was not just another day. In fact, it could be just the change in luck he'd been waiting for. With five grand in his pocket, he'd be able to quit this job, leaving Paul high and dry just a week before Christmas. The thought made him grin. Immediately, he returned to the search.

After a while, another customer pulled in.

"Just look around," Lew called to him. "Give me a holler if you find any you like."

"Thanks," the man replied.

A few minutes later, the customer came running to the hut, where Lew was pouring another cup of coffee. He held up a small, shiny object: the ring.

Lew's mouth fell open. Where could this guy have found it? "Mister, I'm sure the lady that lost it will really be happy that it was found."

"Yeah, I'll bet," the man said, starting to walk away.

Lew panicked. That man was taking off with his $5,000. "Please sir, I know who that ring belongs to."

"That's nice. Why don't you give me her name and phone number? I'll call her myself."

"She didn't leave her phone number," Lew lied. "But she did say she'd call me back."

The man stared at Lew. "I'd guess that a ring like this is probably worth some kind of a reward, wouldn't you?"

Lew thought fast. "Probably. But I guess you'll never know who it belongs to."

The man shrugged. "So what? I can always sell it."

"It's got to be worth much more to the person who owns it than to someone else," Lew said, a desperate note creeping into his voice.

The man considered Lew for a moment. "I suppose you have a point." He looked at the ring, then said, "Tell you what. If you front me some money, I'll give you the ring. I'm too busy to try to sell it, anyway. How about $4,000?"

"No, that's too much," Lew said. "I can go up to $2,500, tops. I don't know how much she'll offer—or how much the ring is worth."

The man nodded. "Okay, I guess I can let you have it for that."

Lew wrote the man a check that would clean out his account. Taking it, the man put the ring in Lew's hand and took off. *What a sucker,* Lew thought when he was gone. *He just bargained himself out of $2,500!*

Excited, Lew called the number that Leslie Allen had given him. She wasn't home, so he left a message that he had found the ring and that she could pick it up anytime she wanted. All day, he expected to hear back from her, but she never called.

The next morning, there was a message for Lew. Leslie Allen had called the previous evening, asking that Lew keep the ring safe until she could pick it up. All day long, Lew waited for her green Range Rover to roll up, but she never showed.

Over the next few days, Lew and Leslie continued to trade messages, but she could never manage to get to the lot while he was there.

Soon, Christmas Day came and went.

Well, maybe she doesn't want it after all, he thought. It was the day after Christmas, and he decided to get the ring appraised.

The jeweler looked impressed when he saw the ring. Lew cheered up considerably, thinking, *I might do okay on this deal after all.*

"What do you think?" Lew asked.

"They're making these fakes better than ever," the jeweler said, shaking his head in disbelief.

Lew felt faint. "It's a fake?"

"A nice one. It's probably worth, oh, forty bucks."

Outside the store, Lew rushed to the nearest pay phone, where he called Leslie's number. But instead of her voice, he got a phone company recording. "The number you have dialed is no longer in service. Please check the number and dial again."

Now Lew really felt faint. He hung up and immediately called his bank. The check had been cashed the day he wrote it. Twenty-five hundred dollars, down the drain. Tears formed in Lew's eyes. All his savings, gone. Suddenly, he could see clearly how he'd been duped. The woman had lied to him from the first; the guy who'd found the ring had been in on it, too.

Actually, the woman had told the truth about one thing: She would be visiting a few more Christmas tree lots. Four more that day. And five the next day. At that rate, the two con artists earned $12,500 a day. In just three five-day work weeks that December, they netted nearly $190,000.

I first met Don Quigley-Mason, the man who "found" the ring, at the Federal Correctional Institute at Sheridan, Oregon. Don was a thirty-eight-year-old, pleasant, easygoing con man incarcerated not for fraud but for failing to pay his taxes. I was amazed that he was so willing to talk to me about his life as a con man in St. Louis, Missouri. He and his girlfriend worked a number of cons throughout the year, he told me, but the one they liked the most was the Christmas holiday scam.

When I asked Don what he planned on doing after he was released from the federal penitentiary, he said, "You got to be kidding, man. I'll probably go back to doing what I used to do. Only maybe this time I'll pay the taxes. I've learned my lesson."

THE PSYCHOLOGY
OF STREET CONS

Street cons are the most fascinating of all the cons because they require a tremendous amount of nerve, cunning, and quick-wittedness—and a complete understanding of human nature. Often a street hustler will use accomplices to make sure a mark is hooked. He'll enlist a steerer to locate potential marks and direct them to the confidence game. A shill may pose as a customer to show a mark how easily the game can be won. Con artists will do whatever it takes to dupe their victims into playing their games.

Street cons generally play on two very different aspects of people's personalities. Some, such as the COD scam, in which people pay to take possession of "important" packages for neighbors who are not at home, play on people's sense of trust. Others play on people's sense of greed. The three-card monte con is one of these.

THREE-CARD MONTE

My windfall was burning a hole in my pocket. I just
wanted to cut loose and have some fun, I guess. But
I forgot to bring my brain along this time.

—*Jonas Owings, three-card monte victim*

Three-card monte is a variation on the shell game, in which the player tries to identify which of three shells the pea is hidden under. In three-card monte, the idea is to choose which of the three upside-down cards is the queen.

Walk down Broadway in Manhattan, and you're sure to find a three-card monte game in action. With great manual dexterity, a man standing over a wooden tray manipulates the three cards, inviting pedestrians to bet on which one is the queen. Naturally, a crowd begins to gather. Some instantly recognize the game for what it is. "Let's go. This is a rip-off."

Others inevitably become fascinated with the con's flying fingers, whether they believe in the game or not—street cons are always a good show. When the cards come to rest on the felt surface, someone casually says, "Oh, the one on the left."

The con turns over the card. "Yup, there it is." *Boy, this is certainly easy,* someone in the audience thinks.

The hustler works his magic again. One young man puts a five-dollar bill on the tray and says, "I think it's the right one."

The con man lifts it up; there it is, the queen. "You're absolutely right, sir. I'll match your five dollars."

Next, the same young man puts a twenty-dollar bill down. The con man manipulates the cards, then the young man says, "I think it's in the middle." The con man turns over the card. "Sure enough, sir. You've won again. Here's twenty dollars."

Here, the sucker finally steps forward. This game is just too easy, he thinks. This is like getting free money!

At first, the con artist might allow the mark to win a few times, to bolster his confidence. But then the mark will begin to lose. If the con artist is good, he'll manage to convince the mark to empty his pockets by the time he quits playing. *How can this be happening?* the mark might ask himself. *The game looks so simple. And that other guy managed to win!*

But the mark is mistaken. What he doesn't know is that, through sleight of hand, the con artist can palm the queen whenever he wants, placing it down wherever he wants. There is no chance for the mark to win. He also doesn't know that the guy who played before him—and won—is in on the con. He's the con man's accomplice: a shill. He's there to trick potential marks into playing three-card monte.

The lesson here: Don't play three-card monte. You cannot win.

• • •

THE JAMAICAN SWITCH

*He was such a nice young man and spoke so well,
with that charming Jamaican accent.*

—Dorothy Sparks, after being taken in a Jamaican switch

One of the ugliest street cons is the Jamaican switch.

In this con, the swindler targets a trusting mark with a story designed to elicit the mark's sympathy. In many cases, the con artist says he has just arrived in America from Jamaica. The sole purpose of his journey: fulfilling his late father's dying wish that he donate his father's meager savings, which he carries in a bandanna, to an American church like the one the mark happens to belong to.

When the mark suggests that the newcomer put his money in a bank until such time as he can donate it to the church, the con artist refuses, saying that banks in Jamaica are not trustworthy. Instead, the con artist insists that the mark hold the money. To ensure that the mark takes good care of the money, the con artist convinces the mark to withdraw an amount matching what he has in his bandanna from the bank. That money then goes into the bandanna, too. Then, at some point, the con artist disappears, leaving the bandanna with the mark. When the mark eventually opens the bandanna, it is filled with cut-up newspaper. The con artist has emptied the original contents of the bandanna, and taken off with the mark's money.

There are many variations of the Jamaican switch. Sometimes it's a Russian immigrant who approaches the trusting mark; sometimes a sailor in uniform. Often, two con artists pull the con together. Always, it has the same essential element: a bundle of money carried by a con man in a container or covering that is secretly switched for a similar but empty package.

THE PIGEON DROP

The pigeon drop is another popular street con, one with many variations.

The pigeon drop requires two con artists: one who befriends a passerby (the steerer), and one who acts as though he has just found a wallet full of money on the street. The passerby is the mark, usually a well-dressed person in an affluent neighborhood. Essentially, the con is looking for someone who has plenty of cash in the bank. Clues such as a Rolex watch, a diamond ring, a stylish handbag, or expensive shoes are good signs for the con looking for a "pigeon."

The steerer strikes up a conversation with the mark, getting friendly with him or her. When the second swindler comes up to them with a wallet full of big bills that he's just "discovered," the steerer acts just as surprised as the mark. Since there's no identification in the wallet, and it doesn't belong to any of them, what should they do?

One of the two con artists suggests they split the money three ways. The mark usually says he or she isn't sure whether the money should be split or turned over to the police. The other con artist suggests that his attorney (or banker, financial advisor, etc.) will surely know what to do, and volunteers to take the wallet to him for advice. If he says it's okay for them to split the money three ways, they'll do it. Together, one of the con artists and the pigeon await his return.

When the other con man returns, he excitedly says that his attorney has told him what they should do: the attorney will place the found money in a safe deposit box (or escrow account) for a specific number of days. He'll run an ad in the local paper for the owner, but if no one claims the wallet during that time, the three people can split the money.

The catch: as a show of good faith, each of the three must withdraw matching sums from their bank accounts, placing that money with the found money. Of course, the pigeon is assured, his money will be returned to him even if the wallet's owner surfaces. You can probably figure out the rest.

The interesting thing about this scam is that it plays on both the mark's sense of trust and his sense of greed. And like all the other street scams mentioned in this chapter, it is being perpetrated across America every day.

THE DRUG DEAL CON

In the drug deal con, a mark is approached to invest in a purchase of illegal drugs. The idea is that after buying drugs at wholesale, the purchasers can then turn around and sell them on a retail level—making a mint in the process.

For example, a fellow investigative reporter once confided to me that while in college, she was given the opportunity to put up $3,000 to buy cocaine worth $10,000 on the street. Her contact told her she'd end up with a profit of $3,500 when the cocaine was resold on the street. But after she put up the money and the deal was supposed to have gone down, her contact came back to her and told her that the dope dealer had been arrested at the time of the transaction and the money confiscated. Of course, there really was no drug deal. And she had no chance to recover the money; it would have been more than stupid to go to the police to report a $3,000 investment in a cocaine deal.

SLICK IN A UNIFORM

Not all street cons are performed by street hustlers. It's amazing how easily a uniform, phony badge, or official-looking ID will impress unsuspecting people.

DOOR-TO-DOOR CHARITY SCAMS

In one of the most popular street cons perpetrated across the country, hustlers go door-to-door soliciting donations for phony charities. For one *Oprah* show, I put on a security guard uniform and went door-to-door in a Chicago suburb asking for contributions to the Police Benevolent Association. Without asking questions, homeowner after homeowner put fives, tens, and twenties in my canister in a desire to help the family of Officer Pichunchuck, a nonexistent rookie cop I told them had been killed in the line of duty.

"His widow and three orphaned children are almost destitute because he hadn't been in the department long enough to earn a pension. Anything you can contribute would certainly be appreciated," I said at each door.

Almost everyone I asked contributed to Officer Pichunchuck's family fund. It was such a sad story, my canister filled up in no time at all. My producers and I agreed that it was almost too easy. So we decided to make our task more difficult by soliciting for a cause that people would more likely be able to resist.

"Would you be interested in contributing to our coffee and doughnut fund? We've been running low at our morning roll call and could sure use your help."

Surely most people would balk at that kind of a contribution, I thought. But it seemed to make no difference what I said. People continued to put money in my canister.

Con artists know that if you don a uniform and represent yourself as a police officer, people generally won't hesitate to help. I wasn't even wearing a real policeman's uniform, but still people trusted me. Had I been a real con man, I could have weaseled well over a thousand dollars that day.

THE AUTOMATIC TELLER MACHINE (ATM) SCAM

One evening I stood in front of a local bank in Vancouver, Washington, wearing my security guard uniform. On my chest was a nameplate reading "Lieutenant Whitlock." Around my waist, I wore a gun belt with an empty holster. Attached to the belt: a pair of handcuffs. In front of the ATM, I had placed a magnetic sign reading: "Out of Order—Give Deposits to Guard on Duty."

Earlier in the day, before the bank had closed, I'd taken some deposit slips from the customer counter. Now I had them attached to my official-looking clipboard. Attention to detail is very important in perpetrating cons.

Soon people began approaching the ATM. They couldn't make withdrawals, I told them, but I would be happy to take their deposits. Amazingly, most people trusted me, handing over their checks and cash.

One pharmacy chain employee, a fresh-faced young man of no more than twenty-five, had just collected the day's receipts. In his duffel bag he carried a total of $122,000 in cash, checks, and charges to deposit. I stopped him before he was able to stuff the bag into the night deposit slot.

"It's out of commission, too, unfortunately. Our personnel are working on it inside. I'd be happy to take your deposit."

He agreed instantly, thanking me for the extra service.

Later, I played a variation of this con. This time, I gave out withdrawals of no more than $100 from a bundle of cash I carried.

In return, bank clients agreed to give me their account and PIN numbers. These numbers can be worth much more to the con artist than the $100 in cash he gives away to get them. In all, in one hour more than twenty people gave me all their ATM information. A skilled professional swindler can make millions pulling this scam.

······································
THE BANK EXAMINER SCAM
······································

The phony bank examiner scam has been around for centuries, ever since banks first started doing business in Europe. It works by appealing to good citizens' sense of civic duty. To show Oprah's audience just how this scam works, in 1994 I put together a phony FDIC Bank Inspector ID card and went undercover.

On hidden camera, I stood outside a bank and approached customers before they entered. This time I wore a dark, conservative business suit. "Excuse me, can I have a word with you before you go inside?" I said, again and again. "My name is Chuck Whitlock. I'm with the FDIC. We're doing an investigation on the tellers inside."

At this, my marks were all ears.

"We've had reports that one or more tellers may be embezzling money from depositors like you. If you'll agree, I'd like to ask you to withdraw $100 from your account; then I can see whether the teller you dealt with has debited more than that amount from your account."

Most marks agreed readily, withdrawing the money and returning with it to me, handling the bills by the edges so I could "be sure to get a good set of fingerprints," as I'd directed.

The scam went unbelievably smoothly. If this had been a real scam, I would have made off with more than $4,000 after just four hours of work.

Often, this scam is perpetrated by roaming groups of professionals called travelers. They are extremely well organized and have paid as much as $30,000 apiece to receive specialized training in the bank examiner scam. They learn what to wear to avoid getting caught or identified if they're picked up, as well as the finer points of the scam itself. These groups can net hundreds of thousands of dollars a day. Even the least experienced phony bank examiner can make $2.5 million annually, according to one fraud specialist with whom I spoke.

A STREET CON'S EXPERTISE

The street con artist is an expert in human nature. Most of us want to earn a quick buck and have a little fun doing it. The street hustler is more than happy to oblige.

LESSON
....
Street cons usually invoke our sense of trust and our greed. In order to receive a benefit (greed), a victim is often asked to put up his own money as a show of good faith (trust). Remember: No one gives you something for nothing. If a proposition sounds too good to believe, don't believe it.
....

· 5 ·

EASY TARGETS: ISOLATED, TRUSTING, AND VULNERABLE SENIORS

I perform a valuable service. These old people are lonely, they're dying on the vine. I care about them and I bring excitement into their lives. If one of them gets scared and wants their money back ... well, I've given back partial refunds.... Look, if this was so bad, how come in twenty years in the business I been busted only three times and they never put me away? In the long run, I do more good than bad, I guarantee you.

> —From an interview with Robert, an admitted telemarketing con artist

BOILER ROOM TELEMARKETING SCAMS

When the phone rang, the gray-haired woman put down the magazine, took off her reading glasses, and hobbled across the room. *Maybe it's my dear friend Betty,* she thought as she picked up the phone. Then she remembered: Betty had passed away two months before.

"Is this Marion Porter?"

"Yes."

"Hello, Marion, my name is Robert. I must tell you, this is the best part of my job."

"Oh, why is that?" Marion replied, her curiosity aroused.

"Because I get to deliver wonderful news to you. You are a big winner in our Super Bonanza Giveaway. You're our Grand Prize winner! The prizes you've won include home electronics, a $15,000 shopping spree at your local department store, and a diamond and ruby necklace worth well over $25,000. All told, your prize package is worth almost $100,000! How does that sound to you?"

Despite the excitement she was feeling, Marion forced herself to remain skeptical. "I don't remember entering any contest."

There was a pause, during which she heard what sounded like papers being shuffled on the other end of the line. Finally, Robert said, "Are you Marion Porter?"

"Yes."

"Is your address one-four-seven-three Arbor Avenue in Tulsa, Oklahoma?"

"That's right."

"In the past few months, have you sent away for free samples of skin cream, shampoo, or laundry detergent?"

She thought for a moment, then remembered the skin cream ad in her Sunday newspaper. "Why, yes I did."

"Well, the coupon that you sent in automatically entered you in our contest. And you won."

Marion was speechless. She felt herself blushing, felt the big smile on her face. She'd just won a beautiful necklace! Putting her hand up to her neck, she imagined the cool, smooth feeling of diamonds and rubies against her skin.

"Marion? Are you still there? You didn't faint on me, did you?"

"Oh, no," she stammered, embarrassed at having been caught in her daydream. "Oh, please excuse me, that was rude. I'm just so, so excited! I've never won anything like this before. Please forgive me, and thank you so much."

"You're welcome. But it's my pleasure to be able to deliver such wonderful news to you. As I said, this is the best part of my job. And you sound like you deserve to have won. I can't tell you what a pleasure it is to speak to such a polite, well-spoken lady."

"Well, that's so nice of you."

Again, there was a shuffling of papers on the other end of the line. When Robert spoke again, his tone had somehow changed. "Marion, now that you've won, we have to figure out how we're going to get your prizes delivered to you."

"Well, you have my address."

"That's true, but Marion, as stated in the contest rules, you are responsible for all shipping and handling charges, as well as insurance and all applicable state and local taxes."

"Oh, dear, how much is all that?"

"In comparison to the value of the necklace, it's really a very small amount. It's only $1,000."

"But that seems to be an awful lot of money. . . . "

"Not really," Robert said. "Consider how much the necklace alone is worth. But Marion, I can understand how you might be hesitant to send me the money. If you want to decline your prizes, that's up to you, but I'll need your decision now so I can call the next person on my prize list."

Marion stifled a gasp. He was going to give away her beautiful necklace to someone else! Was she being overcautious? After all, it was only $1,000—and the prize package was worth almost $100,000.

Robert continued, "Marion, I really want to see you get these prizes, especially this beautiful necklace. Look, I think I can finesse the charges, get it down to, say, $900. Will you work with me on this? If you get me a check out today, your necklace will be in your hands this time next week. What do you say?"

Marion considered. She had more than $100,000 in the bank, so $900 for a $100,000 prize package was not such a great risk. Besides, Robert seemed so nice. "Okay, I'll do it. I'll send you the money today."

"That is such good news, Marion. Let me give you my address and express delivery service number. . . . "

When a week passed, Marion was disappointed that her necklace still hadn't arrived. But she decided to be patient and give Robert a couple more days.

The very next morning the phone rang. It was Robert. "Marion, thank you so much for sending your check so promptly. I'm embarrassed to say that your prizes have not been sent out to you."

Poor Robert, Marion thought. He sounded so sad. "That's all right, Robert. I can wait," she said.

"I wish it were that simple. We've run into a problem with the IRS. There's a new federal law that went into effect just two months ago. It seems that they're putting a hold on your winnings until we get a check from you for federal taxes."

Oh, no! Marion was devastated. She wasn't going to get her prizes after all. She held her hand up to her throat; suddenly, she couldn't feel the necklace there anymore. "How much are the taxes?"

"I have it right here." There was more shuffling of paper, then Robert said, "$4,326."

"That's a whole lot of money."

Robert sighed, "I know it is. But Marion, you'd have to pay it to Uncle Sam eventually, anyway. You might as well get it out of the way now."

"Oh, I don't know."

Suddenly, anger entered Robert's voice. "I know exactly how you feel, Marion," he said. "I just hate being jerked around by those pencil pushers! Maybe I'll go ahead and send you your prizes, and to hell with them!"

Robert's burst of emotion startled Marion. But it also made her feel as if he were on her side. She didn't want him to get into trouble on her behalf. "But won't that cause you problems?" she asked.

"I don't care. I'm tired of them taking advantage of me—and you."

"But I wouldn't want you to get into any trouble. And I will have to pay those taxes eventually."

Robert's voice softened. "You're right. It's just that I've had such a hard week dealing with those people. . . . "

On and on he went, pouring out his heart to Marion. The bureaucracies people had to deal with! The unfair taxes they had to pay! Soon it had turned into a long conversation. Throughout, Marion was very understanding of Robert—and he was just as understanding of her. By the time she hung up the phone, she felt she had made a new friend. She sent a check out for the tax money the next day.

A few days later, Robert called to thank her for her check. But he also had some more bad news. Because of the IRS business, some of the sponsors had withdrawn their products as prizes; they would be making cash settlements with her. Unfortunately, she needed to pay a bank origination fee to get that prize money. He felt so bad about the whole mess, he insisted on paying half the fee out of his own pocket. After another long, heart-to-heart talk, she sent him another check.

The next week, Marion received another, similar call from Robert. And the next week, and the next. And absurd as it might sound, Marion kept on writing Robert checks. Why? Well, for one thing, Marion had fallen in love with the idea of winning cash and prizes valued at tens of thousands of dollars. For another thing, she was lonely.

A seventy-eight-year-old widow, she lived alone. Most of her friends were dead or in nursing homes. And Robert was so very kind. Unlike most young folks, he would talk to her for hours. He told her about other prizewinners, seniors like herself, who had bought summer homes or traveled around the world for years on end. He told her that she sounded just like his grandmother. He hadn't known his grandmother very well, since she had died when he was only ten, but she had been a wonderful woman. He asked Marion if she would consider unofficially adopting him as her grandson. They spent so much time talking on the phone that Marion missed Robert if he didn't call her every few days.

After a few months, Marion was jarred back to reality. When she opened her quarterly interest statement from the bank, she saw a sum totaling less than half of what it should have been. It had to be a mistake. Calling the bank, Marion demanded an explanation. The bank officer said to her, "Mrs. Porter, it's all on your statement. Over the last three months you have made over $60,000 worth of telephone transfers to your checking account, leaving you with a balance of $42,975 in your savings."

Marion pulled out her checkbook and added up all the checks she had sent to Robert. She thought she had sent him around $10,000. She was stunned to learn that she had sent him more than $60,000—in just three months!

That's when the FBI entered the picture. Contacted by Marion's niece, Nancy—who had discovered what had happened to

Marion when her aunt phoned her, sobbing, after reading her bank statement—the FBI went to work.

Hoping to record Marion's next conversation with Robert, Agent Candice Smerale asked her if it would be all right if they tapped her telephone. Of course it would, she said. They got a court order, installed the bug on Marion's phone, and waited. Then, on Friday afternoon—just days before the tap was to be pulled—the phone rang. It was Robert, calling from Las Vegas.

"Hello, Marion, it's Robert. Did you get your money?"

"No, Robert. I've been waiting and waiting and I've run out of money and I don't know what to do!" Marion exclaimed.

Robert said, "Marion, I feel so bad about this, but the checks were accidentally sent to the wrong person. He has agreed to send them back so that we can send them to you. Unfortunately, though, he spent $1,700 of the money. That has to be replaced before we can reissue the checks to you, because we have to issue the full amount. That's what the taxes were based upon. Marion, can you send me the $1,700? Can you wire it to me?"

"No, Robert. I'm broke, I don't have any more money," Marion said, beginning to cry.

"Marion, stop your crying," Robert said. "That's not going to get us anywhere. Surely there must be some way you can get the $1,700 down here so that I can send you this money. It's a virtual fortune. Marion, you're like my grandmother. I wouldn't do any-thing to hurt you, would I?"

"No, Robert, I guess you wouldn't. I do have $360 in my bank account."

"All right, Marion, send me the $360. I'll put up the difference so that I can get these checks to you, but then you'll have to pay me back when you get the checks. Would that be all right?"

"Oh, thank you, Robert. I really appreciate that," said Marion, hanging up. With that, the FBI had all the evidence it needed. Because Robert had gotten Marion to send him her checks via private courier services, he could not be prosecuted for mail fraud; but he had used interstate phone lines to scam her. The FBI would be within its jurisdiction to take him down. Armed with a tape of the conversation, the Las Vegas office of the FBI proceeded to raid the offices of International Sweepstakes on Sammy Davis Drive.

There, when they walked through the door, they were greeted with the sight of more than 100 telemarketers working the phones. They closed the place down, confiscating lists naming thousands of people who were over the age of sixty-five and retired, with passive incomes in excess of $50,000. Shockingly, one of the lists named seniors who had been conned by other boiler rooms, and was being used by this boiler room so that these known marks could be conned again. The owner of the boiler room, in making his deal with the prosecutor for no jail time, agreed to disclose where the list of existing marks had been purchased.

Marion turned out to be relatively lucky. She got $10,000 back from the young man who conned her—all the money left from his commissions. In return, he received what amounted to a slap on the wrist as punishment.

WHY ARE SENIORS TARGETS OF CON ARTISTS?

Cons perpetrated on senior citizens are perhaps the most insidious, cowardly cons of all. There are four main types of scams commonly perpetrated against the elderly: telemarketing scams, investment cons (like the ones I'll tell you about in Chapter 15), street cons such as the bank examiner scam and the Jamaican switch, and gypsy home repair crew scams. Perhaps the most prevalent among these are telemarketing scams, which swindle Americans out of an estimated $40 billion annually. According to a recent Louis Harris survey conducted for the National Consumers League, 90 percent of Americans surveyed have been called by fraudulent telemarketers.[1]

The American Association of Retired Persons (AARP) discovered that fewer than 5 percent of the people fifty or older surveyed recognize fraudulent telemarketers as hardened criminals.

Instead, they see these con artists as regular people just trying to make some extra money. Although cons may exaggerrate or mislead others, those surveyed didn't equate the actions to stealing.[2]

If you feel that you or someone you know may be the target of a telemarketing sweepstakes scam, remember the following: All you have to do to keep from being conned is insist that you will pay any appropriate fees at the time any product, check, or service you've been promised has been rendered or delivered—and not before then. If a prize is actually delivered, then verify its value before paying any fees.

Not all seniors are scammed by unknown third parties. Many times, the scammers are the people closest to them. I've investigated stories of sons, daughters, nieces, and nephews who've convinced seniors to sign their powers of attorney over to them, then sold their relatives' assets, leaving the seniors penniless. In other cases, seniors have been scammed by close friends and professional caregivers.

Why are senior citizens so prone to being conned? There are a number of reasons. For one thing, as a group they have a significantly higher net worth than people of any other age. Their investment holdings have matured, giving them years of returns in the bank; their mortgages are paid off, or they've sold the family homestead for a huge profit; their pensions and Social Security give them a steady, substantial source of income. All this makes them ideal targets for con artists.

For another thing, seniors are often emotionally vulnerable. When the kids move away and many close friends die or get sick, seniors often become bored, isolated, and lonely. Then it's easy for a con artist to enter the picture and befriend the senior, quickly gaining his or her trust.

Finally, senior citizens can be less physically equipped to detect con artists. Their eyesight might be poor, so they may be less likely to notice that the con artist claiming to be a policeman is in fact wearing a rent-a-cop uniform; their hearing may have deteriorated, so they can be more susceptible to the con artist who says, "No, Mrs. Johnson, I didn't say the prize you'd receive was in the amount of $10,000. I said it was in the amount of $10."

There are a mind-boggling number of scams against the elderly. Agencies empowered with protecting seniors will often maintain lists of kinds of scams, which can be given out as preventive advice. If you know of any such agency that is not compiling this kind of resource, help them do so! Here are just two of dozens of firsthand accounts that have been told to me:

THE FREE INVESTMENT ADVICE SCAM

This scam came to my attention thanks to one Darlene Coots. A convicted felon, Darlene pretended to be a caregiver to senior citizens. She opened a senior citizens' center in Chicago—a place for seniors to gather for meals, or to play cards or bingo. After gaining their trust, she offered to help seniors with their finances—free of charge. The state of Illinois, she claimed, was paying her to provide these services.

When a number of seniors took her up on her offer, she proceeded to do things like write checks for their bills and balance their checkbooks. Meanwhile, she was gathering all the seniors' important financial papers. And before they knew what had happened, the seniors had lost nearly half a million dollars. Darlene Coots had sold their stocks and bonds, closed their bank accounts—and then disappeared.

Remember: always check out the credentials of someone you might use as a financial advisor. Doing your homework might save you thousands of dollars.

THE TRIPLE-A CON

In this scam, the con artist hangs out at a shopping mall looking for a senior citizen, who he then follows out to the parking lot. When the senior drives off, the con artist follows him in his car. When the senior stops at a stop sign or traffic light, the con jumps out of his car, then knocks on the senior's window, flashing a bogus American Automobile Association (AAA) badge. The con artist informs the senior that he noticed that his or her right rear wheel is wobbling. Then the con offers to fix the problem.

But rather than fixing the problem, when the con artist kneels down with his tools, he loosens the lug nuts, so that the car becomes truly undriveable.

Next, the rip-off artist throws up his hands. He's done everything he can, he says. The only thing to do now is redo the threads on the bolts coming out of the hub. This requires a special, very expensive machine, the con says. He is willing to go back to the office to get it, but the senior has to give him a credit card or a $2,000 deposit for the use of the machine first.

If the senior doesn't have a credit card or cash, the "AAA bandit" next drives the senior to his or her local bank. Money in hand, the con artist then dumps the senior at a local restaurant, assuring him or her that after the repairs are made, someone will return with the car. Which, of course, doesn't happen.

There are a number of variations on this scam. But it's a simple one to protect yourself from. Just remember that as a rule, AAA agents do not go out and stop cars on the street.

FIGHTING SCAMS AGAINST SENIORS

Of all the cons out there, cons against seniors anger me the most. Our elderly should be respected and revered. Instead, it's as if they are walking around with some kind of bull's-eyes painted on their backs. Fortunately, police departments in a number of states have created divisions that deal solely with crimes against seniors. And in Portland, Oregon, and Los Angeles, California, police departments now have special departments manned by veteran detectives who deal solely with financial fraud and abuse against seniors.

One successful community outreach program is the Florida attorney general's office "Seniors Versus Crime Project." In a recent effort, volunteers called people listed on a "suckers list" to warn them that they were potential targets of boiler room operations.

It's great news to hear that some seniors are fighting back, but it's not enough to protect most seniors. We must all do our part. Stay involved in your parents', grandparents', and older relatives' lives. Be ever vigilant: Try to imagine what possible scams could be perpetuated against them and look for clues.

When you visit your older relatives, try to find out what kind of mail they've been receiving. Volunteer to go through their bills and checkbooks to see if they've been running up charges to 900 telephone numbers or writing large checks to unfamiliar, suspicious-sounding companies. And always stay in touch—by phone if you cannot visit.

Seniors are also prime targets for medical quacks; grown children should take the initiative to look in their parents' medicine cabinets for strange potions, lotions, and concoctions. Whenever possible, join your parents when they visit their doctors.

We all need to keep an eye on our senior citizens. Bank tellers should notify their supervisors if a senior appears disoriented or anxious while removing large sums of cash from an account. A con artist may be involved. If necessary, the banker should call a close member of the senior's family and/or the police.

Make sure the seniors in your life don't feel isolated and that they know you care for them. A family's love can go a long way toward helping an older person find the courage to stand up to con artists.

LESSON

••

Because they're often emotionally or physically vulnerable, seniors are ideal prey to telemarketing scams, investment cons, street hustles, home repair scams, and other cons. Stay involved in the lives of the seniors around you and volunteer to help them with their problems. If necessary, have a trusted third party review the financial and contractual dealings of elderly people you care about.

••

1. Mary Jo Marvin, "Swindles in the 1990s: Con Artists Are Thriving," *USA Today (Magazine)* 123, no. 2592 (September 1994): 80.

2. National Association of Consumer Agency Administrators, "New Telemarketing Fraud Message" *NACAA News* 19, no. 10 (August 1996), 1.

PHONY DOCTORS, PHONY CURES

I thought I was stuck with a bum knee, when what I had stuck myself with was a bum. Never again.

—*Unidentified woman who paid for useless radio wave therapy*

....

THE PAIN MANAGEMENT SCAM

....

M r. Whitlock? Chuck Whitlock?" The woman's voice was soft, with a slight Southern accent.

"Yes?" I said into the phone.

"My name is Jane," she said. "Jane Thomas. And I've got something I think you might want to hear about."

Jane Thomas was right; I did want to hear her story.

"I suffer from chronic pain in both my knees," she told me. "I've been to all kinds of doctors looking for relief. I've been to pain management clinics. I've taken pills. I've even tried acupuncture. But nothing seems to work. Every year, the pain in my knees seems to get worse.

"Just recently," she continued, "I heard about a doctor named Mike Minsky. He claims he can manage my pain. Something about radio waves—I don't know, I don't really understand it."

"I see," I said, inviting her to continue.

"I guess I'm calling you because I think he might be a fraud,"

Jane said, "and I'd like you to come to his office with me to check him out."

"That sounds like an excellent idea," I said, hoping that this Minsky was for real, but resigned to the probability that he wasn't.

The next week, I accompanied Jane to Minsky's office, which appeared quite typical. In the examining room, Minsky asked her to remove her pantyhose and lie down on the table so that her knees were exposed. After slipping a ground plate underneath the calf of her right leg, he then placed two electrodes on the forefinger of each of his hands and began massaging her knees, stopping now and then to turn the dial on the standard radio connected by wires to the electrodes. Finally, he stopped at a classic rock station.

"The output from this station is just the right frequency to intercept the muscle mass and bypass the nerve endings, thus eliminating pain and discomfort," Minsky explained to me.

What? Immediately, I was all but sure that this guy was a quack. Tuning in to a rock station on the radio can cure pain? I don't think so. "Could it just be that the pain is somehow camouflaged?" I asked.

"No, no," Minsky said. "Definitely not." He then launched into a speech about changing the molecular structure of muscle mass—mumbo-jumbo that I'd bet meant as little to him as it did to me.

But then, forty minutes later, Minsky took off the electrodes and asked Jane to get up and walk around.

"My God!" Jane said as she strode back and forth in the examining room. "My knees! They feel fantastic!"

"Of course they do," Minsky said, smiling at me.

"What do I do now?" Jane asked excitedly.

"Well, it's $50 for this session. You can pay on your way out. And I'd suggest returning at least three times a month until the problem is gone."

"Oh, I will," Jane gushed. And we turned to leave.

"Are you sure about this?" I asked Jane on the way out of the office. "I still think your pain relief may have been psychological."

But she was too excited about finally finding relief from her daily torture to really listen to me. "Yes, I'm sure," she said.

But then the inevitable happened. A few days later, in more pain than ever, Jane returned to Minsky's office without me. This time, he insisted that Jane undergo his "special" treatment, which ran for $100. But now, Jane's pain only seemed to get worse. Finally, she realized the truth about Mike Minsky's "medicine": It was nothing but a scam. Her knees aching, she left Minsky's office, never to return.

Luckily, this story has a happy ending. Soon after seeing Minsky, Jane Thomas went to an orthopedic surgeon, who referred her to a physical therapist for diathermic treatments. Conventional medicine prevailed where yet another fraudulent miracle cure had failed.

VICTIMS OF MEDICAL CONS

People in the United States spend nearly $1 trillion on health care each year, making the medical industry the largest business in the land. Naturally, dollar amounts that high have attracted all kind of phony health care providers and health care product salespeople to the industry. Experts estimate that the cost of health care fraud is from $100 to $250 billion each year.[1]

Snake oil salesmen have been concocting magic elixirs for years. One product sold in the United States in the late 1800s promised to cure not only baldness but impotency and the common cold. Surprisingly, the state of quackery hasn't changed that much in the last 100 years. In 1997 bogus products promising to cure all that ails you continue to surface and circulate. One, a so-called revolutionary live-cell therapy pill, claims to cure some thirty-nine ailments and diseases while reversing the aging process.

As long as there are desperate people searching for answers and cures, con artists and frauds will be willing to take advantage of them. You don't have to look very far to find someone with AIDS, terminal cancer, or terminal heart disease—to find a desperate person, seeking to live one more month, one more week, one more day. And you don't need to have a terminal illness to be desperate about some aspect of your health. People spend billions each year in the search for cures to nonterminal medical problems: arthritis, obesity, sexual dysfunction, baldness, wrinkles and aging, and so forth. Americans spend approximately $6 billion each year just on bogus diet products.[2] Unfortunately, desperate people are ready-made marks for con artists. And these marks pay. Some are lucky, and pay merely with their cash; elderly Americans spend an estimated $10 billion on quack products and treatments each year.[3] Others are not so lucky. They pay with their health or, tragically, with their lives.

Usually, health care con artists have enough knowledge of medicine and technical language to sound convincing to their marks. Often they have worked in hospitals or nursing homes, or studied a bit of medicine. Or they're ex-doctors, unfit MDs whose licenses have been taken away because of gross malpractice. Sometimes, they're just bad doctors, one step away from having their licenses yanked.

Over the years, I've met or heard about more people who've been victimized by medical con artists than I care to think about.

• There's Lisa Duncan, a woman who was almost killed by an inept plastic surgeon trying to give her breast implants.

• There's Julie Stein, whose doctor poisoned her by giving her toxic breast implants.

• There's Sally Laslowski, a young woman who went to a quack abortion clinic and nearly paid with her life.

• And there's Saul Shapiro, who did not want to use radiation therapy to treat his terminal throat cancer. He was so desperate to find a cure for his cancer that he spent nearly all his family's savings on alternative treatments such as Laetrile, strange teas, and megavitamin treatments. Although some alternative treatments have proven to be valuable in certain circumstances, nothing Saul tried would keep the cancer from taking his life.

• • •

Making all of these cases even more tragic is the fact that in each, the "doctor" either managed to escape, or plea-bargained to receive a slap-on-the-wrist sentence.

······································
THE WEIGHT-LOSS PILL SCAM
······································

A year ago, for a *Hard Copy* television segment, I got to see how easy it is to pull a medical con myself. Calling myself Dr. Charles Whitlock and wearing a white smock and stethoscope, I set up a sales booth at a new-products convention. There, I hawked the Acu-Stop 2000, the fast, easy, and effective way to lose weight—and keep it off. Or so I told my customers. In reality, the FDA had shut down the Florida facility manufacturing Acu-Stop several years earlier, incinerating the devices in its effort to keep them off the market.

What I found out was that people were so desperate to find an easy way to lose weight that they would gladly plunk down $39.99 for the little device I was selling. Attaching this plastic gizmo inside the ear, I told my customers, would block the nerve signals between the stomach and the brain, short-circuiting the hunger impulse.

People ate up my sales pitch—no pun intended. If I had been a real con artist, I could have sold scores of the devices in just one day at the mall. At $40 a pop, they would have brought me quite a bundle.

PROTECTING YOURSELF FROM MEDICAL SCAMS

Medical fraud will be with us forever, I suspect. Desperate people are always going to be willing to grasp at straws, hoping to do everything from losing a few pounds to curing terminal illnesses.

It's unfortunate that the time we're most likely to be confused and desperate is the time we're called upon to make important, sometimes life-or-death decisions. It's essential that you watch out for the quacks and other con artists who are depending upon you to lose your head.

• Always check the credentials of your health care provider. It may seem embarrassing to do so, but you may end up glad you did.

• Call the medical examiners' board of medical quality assurance commission in your state. Ask if the physician has had any formal or informal disciplinary actions taken against him or her. If the answer is yes, explore further until you're satisfied that you've learned all you need to know about the actions.

• Don't be afraid to go elsewhere for second or third opinions.

• Be wary of faith healers. If you're seeking spiritual healing, go in with your blinders off.

• If any doctor or other professional makes unrealistic promises of a cure, run. Miracles can and do happen, but don't bet your life on it. A legitimate healer may be hopeful but should be honest with you.

• Steer clear of products that seem to make unrealistic claims: magic take-off-weight-with-no-effort diet pills, for instance, or new potions that promise to heal everything from halitosis to hemorrhoids.

• Do your homework. Beware of any product or treatment that you can't research. If a doctor or practitioner claims to have a special machine or formula that's not available elsewhere, don't use it.

• Understand what's wrong with you and what your treatment options are. At the same time as an informed patient is more likely to receive good treatment, he or she is much less likely to be conned.

• When you visit your doctor, understand what fees your insurance should cover, and what fees you are responsible for yourself.

• Check your bills. According to Dr. Marc J. Roberts, professor of political economy and health policy at Harvard, 90 percent of all hospital bills are wrong, although not necessarily fraudulent.[4]

LESSON

Desperate people are ready-made targets for con artists, so don't let despair color your ability to make sound decisions about your health care. *Before* you become ill, select a medical practitioner as if your life depended on it, because it might. Always check the credentials of your health care providers. Obtain second and even third opinions when medical treatment is advised. Be an informed patient and learn what your treatment options are. Stay away from products and treatments promising unrealistic or outrageous claims. Be wary of alternative treatments unless all other methods have been exhausted. Discuss any alternative treatments with your doctor *before* you try them. Look into what fees your insurance should cover, and double-check any bills you receive.

1. L. J. Davis, "Medscam," *Mother Jones* 20, no. 2 (March-April-1995): 26-27.

2. Margaret Mannix, "Fat Claims, Thin Results," *U.S. News and World Report* 122, no. 13 (April 7, 1997): 59.

3. Mary Jo Marvin, "Swindles in the 1990s: Con Artists Are Thriving," *USA Today (Magazine)* 123, no. 2592 (September 1994): 82.

4. L. J. Davis, "Medscam."

· 7 ·

WHEN LOVE IS BLIND:
CONNING DESPERATE PEOPLE

*I can't prosecute. It will ruin my standing in the busi-
ness community, and besides, I'm so ashamed of
myself. He told me he loved me, that he was good for
the money, and that if he went back to jail he wouldn't
have the opportunity to make restitution. I guess I still
believe he wants to do that. Do you think I'm stupid?*

—Ginny Spector, victim of a sweetheart con

THE SWEETHEART CON

As soon as Hank Carson walked in the door of her office, Ginny
Spector knew he would become someone special in her life.
He had such a kind smile, and the boyish good looks Ginny just
loved. She had not had a man in her life since her husband died
several years before; but now, for the first time since then, she
could imagine being with someone.

After the handshake and introductions, Ginny got the interview under way. "So, why should I want to hire you?" she asked.

Hank's nervousness was charming to Ginny. "Well," he said, "First
things first: as you know, I've been in prison for the past few years."

It was true; Hank Carson had been referred to Ginny by a local
halfway house job placement counselor. Ginny was gratified to be
doing something to help someone get his life together. If it could
be this man, Hank Carson, so much the better. "Yes," she said.

"Well, that never should have happened. It was all a misunderstanding."

"Really," Ginny said. Suddenly, a hint of distrust crept into her voice.

But when Hank proceeded to tell her the story—that he had arranged to sell three airplanes to three separate parties, receiving down payments from each; but that when his supplier went bankrupt, he had been left with only one aircraft, and it appeared to the authorities that he was trying to sell the same plane three different times—Ginny believed him. The story was too specific to have been made up. Besides, Hank had looked her in the eye the whole time he was telling it.

"And when I realized I was going to prison whether I deserved it or not," Hank continued, "I decided to make the best of the time. In addition to improving my computer skills, I got a degree in business administration while I was there."

With that, Ginny hired him.

On the job, Hank Carson impressed his coworkers. He showed up promptly and worked extremely hard. When one of the travel agents was tied up on the phone, he filled in, taking messages. He performed receptionist duties, helped Ginny with the accounting, and helped streamline the office computer system.

Then, one Friday, Hank asked Ginny to dinner. And she agreed. They sipped Chianti at a fine Italian restaurant, and Hank told Ginny how thankful he was that she was giving him this chance to start over. "Prison was a nightmare," he told her. "Being in there with real criminals . . . it was awful."

"Well, you won't have to go back there again."

"Thank you, Ginny. You're so understanding." Hank paused, staring at Ginny. "You know, you really are a beautiful woman."

"Oh, Hank," Ginny blushed. Her heart skipped a beat.

Over the next months, Ginny started trusting Hank more and more. When he asked her to give him a credit card from one of her personal accounts—he had lost his old card when he had been unable to make payments from prison, he explained, and he'd be glad to agree to a spending limit of only $1,000—Ginny agreed. After all, $1,000 wasn't that big a risk. As it turned out, Hank paid off his charges in full, every month.

Then one day he asked Ginny if she would give him a company

credit card, an American Express card, with an unlimited credit limit. Although she didn't feel completely at ease about it, Ginny agreed. After all, hadn't Hank proved his trustworthiness with the other credit card?

Then, one Friday night after dinner and a movie, Ginny took Hank back to her home, and they slept together. It was wonderful; it was magical. For the first time since her husband died, Ginny began to believe that maybe marriage wasn't out of the question.

The next afternoon, Ginny's phone rang.

"Ginny, it's me, Hank." Hank had gone home first thing in the morning.

"What is it, Hank?" Ginny asked.

"I just got the most amazing news," Hank gushed. "You've got to get over here right away!"

When they got together, Hank told Ginny his news. He had inherited a yacht. The yacht was docked in the United Kingdom, just outside of London, and was valued at $2 million. His uncle had left it to him; Hank showed Ginny a copy of the will. He also showed her a copy of the estate estimate provided by a solicitor in London, on the solicitor's letterhead. Together they celebrated. What good fortune, to inherit a boat worth $2 million!

But there was one small problem: The yacht had to be transported from the United Kingdom to the United States so that Hank could sell it. He had a buyer in San Francisco, he claimed— the friend of someone he sold airplanes to before he went to prison. He showed Ginny a letter from the friend confirming that, indeed, he would buy this yacht for $2 million once it was delivered to San Francisco.

"What do you think, Ginny?" Hank asked. "I've talked to a crew in England, who'll help me bring the yacht across the Atlantic, through the Panama Canal, and up the Pacific Coast to San Francisco. It'll take just two months. But it'll cost $130,000, including fuel. Do you think there's any way you could see your way clear to helping me?"

"I don't know," Ginny said, frowning.

"How about this," Hank said. "If you lend me the money, I'll double it when the boat's delivered and I get my $2 million."

"That's a pretty good return on my money," Ginny said. "A hundred percent, in just two months."

"This deal is worth that much to me," Hank smiled. "*You're* worth that much to me."

Ginny blushed. "You've got a deal," she said, thinking about which CDs and mutual funds she would have to cash out.

Several weeks after Hank cashed Ginny's $130,000 check, he approached her about the yacht deal again. He'd just received a letter telling him he needed to go to England to inspect the yacht and sign the title papers in front of a judge before he could become its legal owner. "Why don't we go together?" Hank asked. "After all, you're in the travel business. We can find a discount airfare and charge the trip to the agency."

Ginny agreed to this plan. But then, just days before they were scheduled to fly, Hank told her he'd gotten another letter. "It looks like this trip could take much longer than I anticipated. It could take a month," he said. "And I know you don't want to leave the office for that long. So why don't I just go alone?"

Disappointed, Ginny drove Hank to the airport and put him on a British Airways flight to London.

When Hank returned, he assured Ginny that everything had gone just fine. Soon he would have the $2 million in hand. Unknown to Ginny, Hank had rented an expensive apartment and begun buying furniture and other items, putting it all on the credit cards Ginny had entrusted him with.

The next month, when the credit card bills came, Ginny was horrified to learn that Hank had charged not only the purchases to furnish his apartment, but also $13,712 worth of expensive hotels, caviar, champagne, and theater tickets while he was in England.

Around the same time, Ginny started having problems with her business's books. Cash had mysteriously disappeared. Hank volunteered to audit the accounting records. When he did, he claimed to have found the missing cash, citing inaccurate ledger entries.

Finally, Ginny began to heed her suspicions. She approached Hank and asked him for copies of the paperwork he'd shown her when she agreed to write him the $130,000 check. When he acted insulted, though—accusing her of not trusting him—Ginny backed off. She was still in love with him, after all.

At this point, Ginny's daughter, Lainie, who was also her partner at the travel agency, decided to play a more active role. Lainie had never completely liked Hank Carson. She didn't like the fact that he'd been in prison, and she didn't like the way Hank manipulated her mother.

So Lainie did a little checking. And she didn't like what she found. For one thing, Hank had made a deal with another travel agency to systematically transfer some of Ginny and Lainie's accounts over to them for a very large commission; they also learned that Hank was dating another woman, who happened to be employed at Ginny's very own firm! Together, they were cooking the books to hide the fact that they were siphoning off business, and splitting the money they made in the process.

The evidence discovered by Lainie, as well as the fact that Hank's yacht never turned up in San Francisco, finally convinced Ginny that she was being conned. So Ginny went to the police. But she didn't sign the fraud report against Hank; she was afraid of both personal and professional embarrassment if her story got out, and she didn't really care about pressing charges on Hank— she just wanted to get her money back, which surely wouldn't happen if Hank was arrested. And, though she wouldn't admit it to herself, even after all he'd put her through, Ginny was still in love with him.

And then Lainie saw me on television. She called me, and I agreed to sit down with her and her mother.

"Well, that's quite a story, Ginny," I said when Ginny had finished speaking. "Do you want me to run it on TV? You withdrew your police report."

"Oh, I don't know what to do," Ginny said through her tears. "I feel so embarrassed, so horrible. I've disappointed Lainie and squandered the money my husband left me. I was so depressed, I tried to kill myself, but I couldn't even do that right. I don't know what to do. Maybe Hank really is going to deliver the money. Maybe you shouldn't do an investigative show about him."

"Mom, what's it going to take to convince you?" Lainie asked.

I interjected. "Why don't I come up to Seattle? We can talk to the district attorney who prosecuted Hank on the airplane deal and to the people who bought the airplanes from him. Let's find out if what he told you originally was true. Then you can make your decision."

Camera crew in tow, we drove to Seattle. There, we interviewed the prosecuting attorney, who told us that Carson was one of the worst con artists she'd ever prosecuted. Then we talked to two of the people who'd negotiated to buy aircraft from Hank Carson. Both were incensed that he had been released from prison. They both thought he should have received life—he had cost them hundreds of thousands of dollars and a great deal of misery.

When we were done, I said, "Now, Ginny, are you ready to file a police report and prosecute Hank Carson? Are you ready for me to expose this bum on TV?"

"Yes, I am," she said.

But the next morning when I got to the news room, there was a voice mail message waiting for me from Ginny. *Please don't run the story. It's my only chance to get my money back.* After receiving a call from Hank, during which he'd begged her not to prosecute and guaranteed that he'd repay her, she'd changed her mind about exposing him. "I think he's going to repay me," she said. "I really do."

Of course, she was wrong. As of the writing of this book, Hank Carson is still at large, and has not repaid Ginny Spector. Most likely, he's moved on—to his next victim.

LOVE IS A VULNERABLE STATE OF MIND

The sweetheart con is one of the oldest cons in the book. And it's easy to understand why. Most people, when they first fall for someone, turn a blind eye to that someone's faults, at least initially. This is the perfect time for the con artist to go to work, getting his or her new lover to agree to things he or she would never do in a more rational state of mind.

Later, when the con has been going on for a while and the mark has started to realize what's going on, it continues for a different reason. By this point, even if the mark no longer loves the con artist, the mark may hope that the con artist will make restitution for whatever he or she has conned the mark out of. The larger the sums involved, the more likely the victim may be inclined to hang on to these hopes.

And this is just what the con artist wants. The longer he or she can string along the victim, the better the chances of getting away with the con. Paper trails get cold, plus it's often difficult to prove fraud when the victim has willingly given the con artist access to bank accounts and credit cards. Statutes of limitation run out. The con artist knows that time is on his or her side.

If you're the victim of a sweetheart con, *don't wait. Take action now.* Call the police and prosecute the con artist!

....
THE CIRCLE OF FRIENDS CON
....

Sometimes, sweetheart cons (like other cons) have more than one victim. Consider the case of one Matthew Cullen. While doing TV investigations, I learned about this handsome—and utterly amoral—charmer and located him with the help of Detective Chris Peterson. Cullen was the kind of guy who always had several women on the line at once—women who were paying to keep him afloat, covering everything from his meals to his rent and utility expenses.

Laurie Linden was one of Matthew's victims. More unlucky than the others, she became pregnant by Matthew Cullen. But at the time she didn't realize that she was unlucky. She and Matthew had made plans to get married, and she was too busy making the preparations.

The Linden family, happy for Laurie, accepted Matthew as one of their own. One of Laurie's uncles contracted Matthew to do a big construction job, paying him a fat advance. Another uncle gave him an expensive set of golf clubs, which Matthew agreed to pay for when his income was more steady—which wouldn't be long, according to Matthew. Laurie's aunt even gave Matthew a couple of pieces of valuable art, which he promised to pay her for in the future.

Matthew Cullen had gotten Laurie to fall for the sweetheart con. But he had also taken advantage of Laurie's friends and conned her family in what is known as a circle of friends con. In this ploy, a con artist uses his relationship with an individual to entice the individual's friends, family, and associates into buying his con. A con artist may entice a respected banker, attorney, community leader, or law enforcement officer into his web in order to promote an investment opportunity to those in the victim's sphere of influence, people who respect and trust the victim. In Laurie's case, by the time anybody realized what was happening, it was too late—Matthew left her pregnant at the altar and her family tens of thousands of dollars poorer.

SWEET REVENGE

Sweetheart cons are not always perpetrated by male con artists on female victims. Sweetheart con artists may also be women. And their victims aren't always men—in other words, heterosexuals do not have a monopoly on the sweetheart con.

Consider the story of Sandra Walker and Judy Quentin. A bisexual who had recently experienced a difficult separation from her husband, Sandra met Judy at the opening of a museum art exhibition. They hit it off immediately. Both were interested in art, travel, dancing, and gourmet food. And Judy was a lesbian.

Soon they started going out. Their relationship deepened in a short time. In five weeks, they were living together in Judy's penthouse apartment. For the next two months, the relationship was absolutely wonderful. Sandra and Judy shared their experiences. They went everywhere together. It seemed as though their relationship was meant to be.

But then Sandra's husband contacted her and convinced her that they should give their marriage another try. When Sandra told Judy she agreed with him, Judy was furious. Still, Sandra went ahead with her plan to go back to her husband. Two days later, Judy called Sandra, telling her of a telephone call that would change Sandra's life.

Sandra had recently filled out an application for a bank loan for her interior decorating business. The loan was for $60,000 and had been granted. Now, Judy claimed, a bank investigator had left a message for Sandra stating that it appeared that the application had been filled out fraudulently.

Sandra was shocked and scared. It was true: She had exaggerated on the loan application. And now, according to Judy, she might be facing criminal charges. For some reason, Sandra never thought to question the message or to wonder why such personal information meant for Sandra would have been left on her answering machine.

Nor did she question Judy's readiness to help: Judy told Sandra that she had already talked to her bosses at the law office where she worked. They had agreed to represent Sandra, and indicated that they could possibly get the matter handled without bringing the law into it. Sandra was asked to put up a $1,500 retainer so that one of the attorneys at her law firm could contact the bank.

To Sandra, this seemed like a prudent course of action. She wrote out the check, leaving the payee line blank as Judy instructed. When it came back from the bank, and Sandra noticed that it hadn't been cashed by the law firm, but rather deposited into Judy's personal account, she shrugged it off.

Several weeks passed, then Judy called Sandra once again. The news wasn't good, Judy told her. The bank had already reported the matter to the local police; the police were seeking an indictment from the district attorney. Still, the attorneys in Judy's law firm felt they could meet with the prosecutor and change his mind before the whole thing became a criminal matter. However, as a favor to Judy, the law firm had already spent an inordinate amount of time with the bank. Now they would require another $2,000 for time and services.

Sandra had already spent most of the $60,000 from the loan on her interior decorating business, on opening a new office and hiring new people. But her business prospects were excellent; she foresaw no problem repaying the loan. What she was really concerned about was this attention from law enforcement and bank fraud detectives. How would this look to her customers, many of whom were business and social leaders?

Once again, Sandra wrote a check. About a week later, a third call came from Judy. This time Judy said that everything was under control, but that she herself had run into some financial difficulties and needed $5,000 desperately.

"I don't have it," Sandra replied honestly.

Judy said it was imperative that she get the $5,000; whatever Sandra had to do to raise the money, she should do it. Judy didn't want to turn state's evidence in the bank fraud, but if she had to, she would.

Sandra understood the implication immediately: Judy was blackmailing her. Judy had been talking to the prosecutor, the police, and the bank fraud detective. She knew all the players. Would she really turn Sandra in, betraying their trust and their friendship? Based on this last phone conversation, there was no doubt in her mind. Sandra had no choice: She paid the $5,000.

Several months passed. Sandra Walker continued to acquire more clients, and her business began to prosper. She assumed that the nightmare was over. But then, just when she was beginning to relax a bit, the phone rang again. It was Judy, after more money. At that point, Sandra made a decision. She didn't care about the consequences. She had to stop the whole thing here.

She called the police department's fraud unit. "I may have to go to jail, but this woman should be in the cell next to mine," she told the police, before disclosing her entire story.

Much to Sandra's amazement, when the detectives investigated, they found that the bank never had known that she had exaggerated on her financial statements. In fact, they were quite pleased with her promptness in repaying the loan. The D.A. had never heard the name Sandra Walker, nor had the police department. Judy's story was a fabrication, a con. Sandra, afraid to have her affair with Judy Quentin become public knowledge, declined to press charges on Judy. The woman she had once loved had cruelly defrauded her, and she was left emotionally and financially drained.

SWEETHEART VICTIMS RARELY PROSECUTE

Many sweetheart con victims are too emotionally attached to the con artist to go after him or her in court. But even if Sandra had pressed charges, there's a good chance Judy wouldn't have been brought to justice. In those sweetheart cons that do make it to court, it can be exceedingly hard to prove fraud on the accused's part. After all, in most of these cases, the victim has freely authorized the use of his or her funds. For this reason, many law enforcement and legal authorities avoid pursuing these cases at all, making it all the more important for you to be on guard against being conned in this way.

LESSON

A sweetheart swindler's motto may well be "All's fair in love and war." Be especially cautious not to expose yourself to financial ruin when beginning a new, intimate relationship. Never disclose your bank account information, Social Security number, or driver's license number to a new friend or lover. Don't lend your money, credit cards, car, or other important personal possessions to anyone unless you're willing to take the associated risk. When a suitor increases his or her demands for financial support, it's a surefire sign that you're being set up for a fall. Keep all personal and financial information private and protected from curious eyes until you're absolutely positive about someone's trustworthiness.

· 8 ·

FRIGHTENING TALES FROM RETAIL

Why should I have doubted who he said he was? He said he was an auditor from headquarters; he had a name badge on. He knew the manager's name and had cash drawers that fit our registers. He was so authoritative; I was scared they might suspect me of stealing, so I did what he asked. It never occurred to me that he might be a con artist.

—*Phyllis, victim of the cash drawer con*

THE CASH DRAWER CON

Phyllis looked at her watch. Just one more hour until her shift was over. She finished waiting on one last customer, then leaned against the counter, glad to have a break. Her shift seemed especially long today; maybe it was because she had worked every day this week, the result of trading days with a coworker. Tony, the skinny, long-legged clerk ringing someone up next to her, made a face at her; she made a face back, being careful not to let the customer see. Behind her, she heard the outside doors open. Turning, she watched a man wearing a plain pinstripe suit and conservative tie come in, carrying what looked like a stack of cash drawers.

As he got closer, Phyllis saw that he was wearing a name tag that said "Chuck Whitlock, Internal Auditor"; it was royal blue, the store's color, and sported the store's logo. Instantly, she straightened up.

"Hi. I'm Chuck Whitlock. With headquarters, in the accounting department," I said, motioning to the cash drawers I carried. "I'm auditing the store today. Is Jim around?"

Now, this wasn't a spontaneous visit. I was undercover for *Hard Copy,* trying to pull off the cash drawer con. I had done a little homework by visiting this store the week before to see what cash registers they were using. Then I had purchased a few cash drawers to fit their RBG model KZ320 registers—for less than $100 each.

Next, I had stopped by a local name tag company to pick up a royal blue tag, on which I'd duplicated the company logo as best I could. And then I had filled the drawers with starter money: two twenties, two tens, two fives, ten ones, and rolls of pennies, nickels, dimes, and quarters.

That morning, I had phoned the store. With little effort, I had learned the manager's full name and the fact that today was his day off, and that Doreen, his assistant manager, would be in charge. I had also dispatched my cameraman, Brian, to the store, where he managed to set up his camera without suspicion by telling the employees that he was filming a training tape for headquarters.

Now, standing in front of Phyllis, I took a quick glance down one of the store's aisles. Good; the camera was set up and rolling. And there was Brian, concentrating very hard on some items on a shelf farther down the aisle, trying to blend into the woodwork.

"Jim's not here. It's his day off," Phyllis said. "Should I get Doreen? I think she's on break." Her hand moved to the intercom microphone.

"No, no, that's okay," I said quickly. "You don't need to bother Doreen. I was supposed to meet Jim. I'll call him tomorrow, and tell him the audit results then." Now we were working from my script. Looking at my watch, I added, "You know, I'm running late and I'm really pressed for time. I'm going to audit the registers first, so why don't you take this starter drawer, and I'll take your drawer. This store's been short a significant amount of money for some time and we need to pinpoint where the problem is, if it's a record keeping problem, equipment problem, or a people problem—if you know what I mean." I lowered my voice a little, as though we were conspirators.

"This is a surprise to me, Mr. Whitlock," Phyllis said nervously, quickly ringing up a zero sale and opening the register. "My drawer always balances when *I* count it." As she pulled the drawer out, I waited, thinking that she might still get smart, and call Doreen, the manager, the home office—someone. *Come on, Phyllis!* I found myself thinking. *Don't trust the suit, the name tag.*

But Phyllis just went right ahead and put the drawer on the counter in front of me. Then she asked, "I guess you want all the checks and charge slips, too, right?"

"Just give me everything, Phyllis, so I can do a complete audit."

Phyllis scraped all the large-denomination bills and checks off the bottom of the cash register, double-checking to make sure she got everything.

"Thanks. And here's a drawer for you," I said, handing her one of the cash drawers I was carrying. As she fit the drawer into her register, a customer walked up.

"Go ahead and wait on her," I said. "We're done for the moment."

Now I turned to Tony, the young man at the register next to Phyllis. "Tony, you probably heard what I just told Phyllis. Let me change your drawer as well," I said.

Tony obediently switched drawers with me. Like Phyllis, he seemed a little nervous, as though trying hard to please. *They're afraid of the guy from headquarters—the auditor,* I thought. *Of course, I didn't accuse anyone of stealing—but I told them there were shortages, and I'm counting their drawers. No wonder they're willing to please.* As if to confirm this, the third cashier, Henrietta, was ready with her drawer by the time I got to her, a bright but somewhat nervous smile on her freckled face.

I smiled back at her as she stacked her drawer on top of the other two. Then I said, "Thanks, guys. Go ahead and wait on those customers, and I'll do my work."

With that, I turned and walked toward the door, full cash drawers under my arm. I sort of hesitated in the doorway, waiting for someone to shout at me, to tell me to stop. *Stop, thief!* But nothing of the kind happened. So I walked over to my car, took a deep breath—no matter how often I do these scams for TV, my heart rate always seems to go up a bit—then unlocked the door and put the drawers in the back seat. *That was too easy,* I thought. So I decided to push the envelope even further.

Back inside, I noticed an electronics display off to one side. My eyes settled on a large carousel watch display, fastened to the counter by a locked cable.

"Hi," I said to the clerk, a pretty blond named Karen. "I'm Chuck Whitlock with the audit department. I'm doing an audit of the entire store. Since I was coming here, headquarters asked me to bring this watch display back. You'll get a new one tomorrow with more watches and back lights and all the bells and whistles. You'll really like it."

"Sure, no problem, Mr. Whitlock," Karen smiled, unlocking the cable.

I looked around and noticed a key-cutting machine. *It's portable and it's valuable,* I thought to myself. "Hey, Tony, want to give me a hand with this?" I called to one of the first clerks I had dealt with.

Tony, who had been watching with interest from behind his register, nodded and came over. Together, the three of us walked out to my car, Karen carrying the watch display and Tony the key-cutting machine. I opened the trunk and they happily loaded the loot in my car.

"Thanks a lot, guys, I really appreciate it," I said.

"You're welcome," they chimed before turning to walk back to the store. As they walked, Tony gave me a glance over his shoulder, and I thought, *Is he finally getting smart? Will he finally do something to stop me?*

I decided to wait in my car a few minutes before doing a reveal. *Plenty of time to drive off without anyone getting my license plate number,* I thought. Five minutes later, I took the cash drawers and the watch display back out of the car, and returned to the store. *Can't carry it all; I'll send Tony out here for the key machine,* I thought.

Inside, I identified myself as Chuck Whitlock with *Hard Copy,* telling the clerks they'd just been conned. Their mouths fell open in shock—literally. They hadn't suspected for *one moment* that I wasn't an auditor.

Karen said to me, "Mr. Whitlock, I don't know what to say. I want to be in law enforcement some day. I should have at least suspected you."

"Why didn't you call someone? Or ask for ID?" I asked.

They all exchanged glances. Henrietta said, "I guess I just believed you when you said you were from headquarters. And when you said the drawers were short, it scared me. I knew that if they sent an auditor down it must be serious, that they probably suspected one of us. Especially if they were counting drawers before a shift change."

Phyllis said, "I should have called Doreen. She would have known what to do." She paused for a second, then added, "Next time, I will."

THIEVING SHOPPERS

Retail stores make a huge effort to combat crime. They employ high-tech security systems, electronic surveillance, even plain-clothes security guards posing as shoppers. All at a very significant cost. Con artists, however, always seem to stay one step ahead, just as I was able to hoodwink trusting employees by my brazen display of confidence and authority. But there are other ways retail cons are executed as well. Here are just a few.

RETURN RECEIPT RETAIL CONS

Often, con artists take advantage of the fact that customer service is extremely important in America. If a consumer possesses a receipt, or even just a product that a store sells, that store is usually willing to refund money or issue a credit.

Consider the case of Mary Ellen Roseman. She looked like any other shopper at her local discount department store. She pushed a cart around, consulting her list as she shopped. But the whole time, Mary Ellen was working a scam. Her technique: after making a legitimate purchase, she would empty her new items into the trunk of her car. Then she would return to the store, acting like she'd forgotten to make a certain purchase. She'd systematically fill her shopping bags—which she'd managed to sneak back into the store in her purse—with items identical to the ones she'd dumped in her trunk. Then, with her bags full of merchandise, she'd just walk to the customer service desk, original receipt in hand, and return the items for cash.

······················
THE TAG SWITCH
······················

In recent years, this con has largely been rendered ineffective due to the use of bar codes. But not every retail business scans bar codes at the register. And even if the fraud is caught at the register, little can be done to prove that a price tag has been changed fraudulently. The con artist can simply insist that a product had been mistakenly tagged—that when he picked up the product, it already had the incorrect price on it. Some stores will even honor the incorrect price, not wanting to lose business over what might be a genuine mistake on their part.

The "Kmart cons," Janet and Lester Marshallton, specialized in—no surprise here—ripping off Kmart department stores. Traveling around the country as part of a ring, they'd apply false bar code labels to merchandise, buy it at reduced prices, then return the merchandise for full credit later.

They were smart enough not to go to the same store twice. A couple of times, when a cashier knew the correct price of the merchandise, they explained that it must have been mismarked, and left the store. Some cashiers even honored the incorrect price after the Marshalltons insisted the merchandise had been advertised and marked at that price, so they were legally obligated to sell it at that price.

The scheme fell apart when Janet Marshallton tried to return merchandise to a Kmart outlet. A sharp clerk spotted a zip code that wasn't in sync with the local address on Marshallton's check, and asked her to repeat her address. As store manager Tom Trevers said, "She couldn't even remember the phony address."

THE REWRAP

A con artist will buy a CD or software, unwrap it, remove the product, re-shrink-wrap the container, and return it for a full refund. The box or container does not look as though it's been opened, the person has a receipt, so there is no reason for the store clerk to refuse.

THE DOG-FOOD BAG SCAM

> *I'm really not a bad person. I would have stopped stealing, except that I kind of got addicted to it. . . . The stores supposedly make tremendous profits, so I didn't think they'd miss a few things. And it was fun, in a way.* —Renee Albert, retail con artist

There just isn't enough money to pay the bills this month. Renee Albert looked over at her kids, sitting at the dinner table. The two teenagers ate three huge meals every day, snacked in between—and still they were always hungry. Renee didn't know what to do. She had been laid off work this month, and it had been her salary that paid for most of the food. Her husband, Bill's, salary barely managed to cover the rent, utilities, clothing costs, and car payments.

"Hey, how's things?" Bill said when he got home from work, giving her a kiss. He went immediately to the fridge. "I thought we had some beer."

Renee bit her lip. There wasn't any more beer left. Not only that, she only had about $30 in cash to feed them for the next week. Taking a deep breath, she told him everything she was thinking about. About why there was no beer. About all their debts. About the fact that they could never afford to go on vacation.

It was a conversation that many married couples have had. But unlike most of them, Renee and Bill Albert were willing to break the rules to help solve their problems. That night, they came up with a scheme to get free food—and lots of it.

The next day, Renee went to the local supermarket. There, she paid about $50 for a smallish load of groceries. But when she got home, she was able to load nearly $200 worth of groceries into her refrigerator and cupboard. How had she done it? It was simple. The night before, she and Bill had emptied the dog's food from its bag, leaving a nearly imperceptible knife-slice near the seam at the bottom of the bag. Renee had then sneaked the bag into the supermarket, placed it on the bottom rack of the cart, and filled it with steaks, fish, chicken breasts, and so on. And so, for the price of one 40-pound bag of dog food, Renee was able to take home some of the most expensive items in the store.

This went on for about two weeks. And then, the tenth time Renee tried her scam, she ran into trouble.

This visit started out like all the rest. As she shopped, she stuffed meat, cans, and other items into the dog food bag. The only things in the cart she would have to really pay for were inexpensive vegetables.

At the register, as usual, Renee smiled at Norman, the assistant manager. But then, as the clerk was scanning Renee's merchandise, Norman abruptly said, "Are you a breeder?"

"Excuse me?" Renee said.

"Are you breeding dogs?"

Renee laughed. "Of course not. Why do you ask?"

"Because I see you in here all the time, and I've noticed that you buy a lot of dog food. I don't know how many dogs you have, but my three German shepherds don't eat that much food together. So, I was just curious."

To Renee's horror, he bent over and tugged on the bag. Because it had been folded and unfolded so often, it tore very easily, exposing her booty. Renee looked up at Norman, helplessness in her eyes. She knew she'd been caught. In the final analysis, all those groceries would prove to be pretty expensive.

THE FAKE GIFT CERTIFICATE CON

A couple of years ago, I was asked to perpetrate a retail fraud for *The Maury Povich Show*. After considering the various types of retail fraud that could be demonstrated on camera, I decided that the one that would have the biggest impact on viewers was one that had recently been committed by a Phoenix, Arizona, con artist, who had taken in $3,000 in half a day by selling phony gift certificates at a grocery store.

After printing up some authentic-looking gift certificates with a local grocery store's name on them, I stationed myself in front of the store. As shoppers came out with their groceries, I walked up to them with a smile and said, "Hi, need some help with that?"

Walking through the parking lot with each of my marks, I continued, "I've got a great offer for you. How would you like a $100 gift certificate good on your next visit to the store—for only $50?"

"What's the catch?" several customers asked.

"All you have to do is answer three survey questions," I said to them. I then proceeded to ask them how often they shopped at the store, if they took advantage of sales, and if they would recommend the store to others, all the while using my trusty clipboard to record their answers.

To those customers who were wary enough to ask why the store would in effect give away $50 like this, I laughed and said, "The store's profits have been phenomenal this year. And we're one of the largest chains in America. We can afford to give something back to our customers; this is an advertising ploy. At the same time, it allows us to find out how we can be of better service to you."

The con worked; shopper after shopper took me up on my generous offer, handing over $50 in the process. Some customers even convinced me to sell them more than one certificate.

FRAUDULENT RETAILERS

There are two basic categories of retail scams. In the first, the retailer is the victim. The con artist can be a crooked employee, or else he is someone posing as a company inspector—as I did—an outside contractor, or an innocent consumer. In the second, the consumer is the victim. The person or outfit offering items for sale is the crook, and the consumer is the innocent. Between these two categories, retail cons are perpetrated almost every minute of every day.

COUNTERFEIT MERCHANDISE

Not long ago, I did a show with Geraldo Rivera in which I showed how even some very legitimate stores end up selling counterfeit goods. It's not uncommon, I showed, to find everything from counterfeit Rolex watches to counterfeit Levi's being sold in retail stores from coast to coast. Some counterfeit products are sold deliberately, by unscrupulous businesspeople trying to increase profit margins by offering inferior goods at designer-label prices; others are delivered to retailers by unscrupulous wholesalers and distributors.

SALE MERCHANDISE SOLD AT FULL PRICE

A more subtle technique to con consumers is to offer merchandise on sale, while "forgetting" to code the sale price into the computer. When the merchandise's bar code is scanned, the original price, not the sale price, is charged. This often goes unnoticed by the customer, particularly when he or she is purchasing more than one item. To avoid being taken in this manner, check your receipts.

THE SOLD-OUT LOSS LEADER

In the highly competitive retail industry, stores will do almost anything to attract customers. One method is to offer particular items at a tremendous discount. This ploy gets the consumer into the store. But if the sold-out loss leader ploy is being used, the sale items will all be sold-out. The idea, of course, is to get the consumer to buy other, full-price products while in the store. Rather than falling for this, ask for a rain check on sold-out items.

COMMON JEWELRY SCAMS

Con artists have been known to use laser beams to bore holes in low-grade, flawed diamonds, then to fill up the holes with glass—making the diamonds look flawless to the untrained eye. In addition to stiffing consumers in this manner, con artists use this technique to scam insurance companies, making claims for the theft of diamonds far in excess of what the stones are really worth. Another common jewelry scam is the quality misrepresentation, in which the con artist stamps "18-karat gold" on a 14-karat or gold-plated piece, for example.

REWRAPPING OUT-OF-DATE PRODUCTS

Misrepresentations aren't made only on high-ticket items. While doing a special report on retail fraud, I happened to stop at the meat department in a local grocery store. There, I noticed that some packages had expiration dates that had passed. One package of meat had three tags, each one pasted on top of the last.

"I'm Chuck Whitlock with *Hard Copy*," I said to the butcher. "Can you tell me why this package of meat has three labels?"

He nodded. "Sure. When we come in every morning, the first thing we do is check expiration dates. We remove the old cellophane and labels, then rewrap the packages and put a new date on them as long as the meat is okay. This one should have been rewrapped, not just relabeled." He took the package from me.

"How many times do you rewrap and redate meat?" I asked.

He shrugged. "Till the meat sells."

"Have you had spoilage that you know of?"

"I don't think so."

I don't think so. I thought that was an interesting response. I wonder just how many grocery stores pull this same scam: rewrapping and relabeling meat whose expiration date has passed. It's impossible to know for sure.

GETTING TAKEN FOR A RIDE

No area of retail is safe from con artists. Car owners seem to attract more than their fair share of fraudulent ploys.

A few years ago I did a *Hard Copy* show in Las Vegas, exposing automobile fraud. During my investigation, one reputable electronics repair shop owner told me about a certain car alarm—"a good value," he called it—that could be purchased in auto parts shops for about $15. But when I went out and visited used car dealers, I found several who had installed this alarm on the cars on their lots, and were charging up to $500 for it.

As part of the same investigation, I decided to go undercover and visit a number of auto mechanics.

CAR MECHANICS, GOOD AND BAD

Now, we've all heard stories about how mechanics can fleece their clients—but none of them really prepared me for what was to come in my foray into the automotive repair world in Las Vegas.

To begin our test of mechanics, I unplugged the map sensor in a 1991 Cadillac that had previously been certified to be in top mechanical condition by a master mechanic. The map sensor is a small electrical part used in diagnosing what's wrong with the engine; it should have been a quick, easy, inexpensive procedure to detect the problem and plug the sensor back in.

But again and again, seemingly reputable mechanics told me that the problem with my Cadillac lay elsewhere. One local garage wanted to charge me $298 plus tax to fix a variety of ailments, including the Caddy's fuel system and cruise control. A

Las Vegas Cadillac dealership gave me a repair estimate of $72 to fix the problems it found, and ended up charging me $180 in parts and labor—and when we looked at the engine afterward, the master mechanic working with me told me the dealership had not even touched the areas of the engine it claimed to have fixed! When I brought this to the attention of the service managers, they refunded the difference to me on camera. Montgomery Ward charged me for a part the mechanic said he never installed.

I added a twist to the investigation, taking the California plates off the Cadillac and replacing them with local Nevada plates, then having a different driver take the car back to mechanics I'd already visited. Sure enough, when it appeared to be a local vehicle, the Cadillac was diagnosed as having even less expensive problems than before.

Only one mechanic treated me in a manner I considered totally honest and fair. "The wire on your map sensor came loose, so I plugged it back in," he said. "No charge." A few weeks later, I received a photocopy of a newspaper article in which the mechanic accurately reported that he was the only one in Las Vegas to have passed the *Hard Copy* honesty test. It was free publicity for him—and he deserved it.

··
GAS STATION SCAMS—FILL IT UP?
··

Gas stations are another place the consumer can be fleeced. When you pull into a gas station, how often do you look at the pump to make sure that you're paying the same price as the station has advertised? How often do you wonder if you're actually getting the amount of fuel that the meter says you're getting?

With these questions in mind, for another TV assignment, I decided to see how easy it would be to pull off a gas station scam. With a station owner's permission, I donned an attendant's uniform and manned the full-service island. As part of the scam, we had the owner of the gas station change the prices on the full-service pumps to well above the advertised price.

As people pulled up to the full-service island, I filled their tanks, cleaned their windshields, and checked their oil. The results were amazing. Not one person realized that he was paying too much for his gas. And again and again, I managed to scam my customers in other ways, as well. In some cases, I squirted oil under the car, then showed the driver that something appeared to be leaking from his engine; most drivers I did this to drove straight to the service bay for a repair estimate. Other times, when checking the oil I short-dipped the stick. I showed customers they were low on oil, then charged them for quarts I only pretended to add to their engines.

Now, I'm not exactly well versed in auto maintenance. My camera crew had quite a few laughs watching me fumbling with hood releases and searching for dipsticks. And a couple of times, I had to enlist the help of the owner, who was in the office, to open a hood or run a credit card charge through. So imagine what a skilled con man, someone with a better understanding of cars and service station procedures, could do to rip you off at the pump.

KEEP YOUR GREED IN CHECK

How to keep yourself from being taken by retail cons like those described in this chapter? Keep your greed in check. Don't be tempted by the promise of something for nothing. If you can resist the promises of that pot of gold at the rainbow's end, you'll shield yourself from the advances of most con artists. Combine this with the awareness that retail is rife with cons, and you'll become the retail con man's worst nightmare: an impossible mark.

Remember me and my friendly, polite demeanor as I have conned the public at large. Don't expect criminals to broadcast their profession. Expect them to be smooth and amiable, even well-dressed. The more you think that a con artist could look and act, well, exactly like me—or even you—the wiser you will be, and the less chance there is you will be victimized.

LESSON

....

Both retailers and customers can be victims of scams, so beware. Check the price of your merchandise and double-check all transactions. Find out a company's return policy before purchasing expensive items; many states have no laws that compel a merchant to give store credit, make refunds, or make exchanges unless the merchandise is defective. Never allow a merchant to record your driver's license, Social Security, or credit card number on your check; if they insist upon it, pay by cash or credit card, or shop somewhere else. Be wary of deals that appear too good to be true.

....

· 9 ·

INSURANCE AT A PREMIUM

Not in my nineteen years of driving have I ever seen such recklessness. I mean, I couldn't stop, I just couldn't. Every time I slowed down, the cars ahead of me slowed down. Now that I think of it, it felt like a setup.

> —*Bob Muller, in a statement to the California Highway Patrol*

....
THE BULL AND COW SCAM
....

When the sun finally dropped below the Coast Range, Bob Muller pulled his sunglasses off, slid them into their case, and rubbed the bridge of his nose. It had been a tiring few days of driving. At least he didn't have a double or triple trailer load; but even just one load was bad enough. He had started in Seattle, making stops to off-load and on-load again in Portland and Eugene. The driving rain and construction had slowed him down, then an unexpected late spring snow had closed the pass over the Siskiyous for a few hours. The heavy cloud cover had given way to sunshine in California, but now that he had reached the valley floor, the road was crowded with drivers speeding past him at 90 or 100 miles an hour.

A careful driver, Bob had a perfect driving record with the company he'd been with for about nineteen years now. Sighing, he ran his fingers through his rapidly thinning hair. He was relieved that this long drive was coming to an end. He couldn't wait to get home to his three kids, ages fourteen, twelve, and ten, and his wife, a nurse at a local hospital. He was tired of talking to her on a cellular phone. His thoughts turned to his retirement, and he chuckled to himself; he'd have to find a good hobby to keep himself busy and out of the house.

From an on-ramp on the right, a brown car merged into traffic, pulling in behind Bob. An older model, American-made car, it carried a driver and three passengers. When the car pulled into the left lane, Bob eased up on the gas so it could pass him. The car sped forward, then swerved directly in front of him. Swearing softly to himself, Bob applied pressure on the brakes so he wasn't right on its tail. *What in the world is that driver thinking? The way some people drive . . .*

A few seconds later, another car, a red Z-28, quickly passed both Bob and the sedan. But for some reason, it stayed in the left lane. *Jerk,* Bob thought. *Another lane hog who won't move over to the right.* And then the Z-28 was followed by a blue Ford van, which stayed right next to Bob in the left lane.

What was going on? Bob didn't like being hemmed in, so he eased up a bit. But when he did, the van on his left also slowed down. Then, suddenly, just as they were passing an exit, the Z-28 quickly accelerated, zoomed in front of the brown car, and sped off the freeway, barely making the off-ramp. As it swerved across the right lane, the driver of the brown car, directly in front of Bob, slammed on his brakes. Bob reacted quickly, but his truck was too loaded down. There was just no way he could stop in time.

And with that, Bob became the latest target of a staged car wreck—of a con called *el toro y la vaca* (the bull and the cow), also known as swoop and squat. In this case, the driver of the brown car had been planning to get in an accident from the moment he pulled in front of Bob. With the help of his partners in the van and the Z-28, he had done just that.

The bull and cow is a common scam on the West Coast, perpetrated by well-organized rings: These can rake in millions of dollars by filing multiple medical claims for "victims" like the driver and passengers of the brown car. Often, dishonest doctors, lawyers, and auto repair firms are part of these rings, helping exploit the system for profit. According to a recent study by the Insurance Research Council, an incredible 36 percent of all bodily injury claims associated with auto accidents appear to involve some element of fraud.[1]

In Bob's case, though, the scam didn't work. Bob was lucky: He wasn't seriously injured, and his immaculate driving record, combined with an eyewitness account, helped clear him of criminal charges. The passengers in the backseat of the brown car were not so lucky. One died immediately in the wreck; the other sustained permanent injuries. And because the case reeked of fraud, Bob's insurance company did not have to pay any medical claims.

INSURANCE SCAMS

When it comes to insurance fraud, staged auto accidents are just the tip of the iceberg. According to the National Insurance Crime Bureau (NICB), insurance fraud is one of the most costly white-collar crimes in America, ranking second only to tax evasion.[2] Industry experts estimate that 25 percent of the $200 billion paid out annually in property/casualty claims are phony.[3] And while most people wouldn't think to steal, often they won't hesitate to exaggerate an insurance claim. According to the Insurance Research Council, an estimated 10 percent of American adults say it's all right for someone injured at home to fraudulently claim their injury is work-related to collect workers' compensation benefits.[4] The NICB estimates that the total cost of insurance fraud may exceed $100 billion per year. Ultimately, the insured pay the price for insurance fraud: The average American household pays an extra $200 in premiums each year to make up for fraud losses.[5]

Often insurance scams include the participation of doctors and lawyers. These crooked professionals help defraud insurance companies by overbilling, billing for unnecessary services or services not rendered, and making fraudulent medical diagnoses. Medical mills—doctors and lawyers who make a practice of defrauding insurance companies—play an especially large role in workers' compensation fraud.[6]

Insurance scams generally fall into one of four categories. Auto insurance scams, like the bull and cow, aim to defraud auto insurance companies. The other types of insurance on which con artists often make fraudulent claims include homeowner's insurance, health insurance, and business insurance.

AUTO INSURANCE FRAUD

According to the NICB, an estimated 15 percent of all reported auto thefts are attempts to defraud the insured's insurance company.[7] There are a number of ways to perpetrate this type of fraud. A claimant may report his car stolen, collect the insurance settlement, then sell the car for an additional profit. In a variation of this, others claim the theft of their cars after taking them to chop shops, which disassemble automobiles and sell the parts. Some con artists register and insure cars that don't exist, then file theft reports and insurance claims.

Other con artists go to outrageous lengths to perpetrate auto insurance fraud. In one case, a woman hired a contractor to dig an enormous hole in her yard, in which she then buried a BMW she'd claimed had been stolen. Her scam was exposed only when the man who'd dug the hole noticed that it was not for a swimming pool, as he had assumed, but that something had been buried in it, making him rightfully suspicious.

HOMEOWNER'S INSURANCE FRAUD

One method that many con artists use to defraud insurance companies is arson. Consider the case of Harry and Alice Goddard: After removing all of their valuables from their suburban home, they torched the old wood-sided split-level. To give themselves an alibi, they made sure they were seen on the way out to the symphony well before the fire broke out.

But then the insurance adjustor went to work. During her investigation, she uncovered evidence that supported her suspicion that the Goddard house fire had been a case of arson. The Goddards had managed to get their valuables out of the house before the fire, for instance. They were deeply in debt; any insurance settlement would save them from going under financially. And finally, they had a history of bogus insurance claims, including a house fire five years before that resulted in payment to them even though there had been evidence of arson.

This time, the Goddards got caught—unlike the thousands of others each year who manage to collect on bogus claims. According to the National Fire Protection Association, during one recent year there were close to 85,000 structural fires either proven to be deliberately set or of very suspicious nature. The result: more than $2.3 billion in property loss.[8]

BUSINESS LIABILITY INSURANCE FRAUD

I was so worried about the little boy and saving my business that it never entered my mind that it might be a scam. —Innis O'Malley, toy store owner

Because people often believe that businesses have unlimited amounts of resources—or at least very deep pockets—nuisance lawsuits against businesses are commonplace. Unfortunately, people are right in thinking that many businesses, unwilling to go through the expense of defending themselves in court, will settle even frivolous suits. As a result, businesses are hit every day with everything from phony slip and fall claims to phony workers' comp claims. In fact, workers' comp fraud is the fastest growing type of insurance fraud. Why? The payoff to claimants can be huge. Most states require a 100 percent payment of medical and rehabilitation expenses for employees injured on the job, and up to two-thirds wage-loss benefits while the claimant is unable to work.[9] Of course, phony claims raise insurance premiums for businesses to the point that some can no longer compete. The end result for the consumer: higher prices for goods and services.

One method that con artists use to make fraudulent claims is the yank-down technique: intentionally pulling merchandise down from shelves onto themselves.[10] After their "accidents," these con artists claim that the merchandise had not been stacked properly by the employees of their victims' businesses, and so the businesses are liable for any injuries sustained—which are often greatly exaggerated. Some con artists even take this scam a step further, training their children to play a role in the scam.

Like Mark Jolson. Jolson had two sons—identical twins. But because of a childhood accident, one was permanently mentally retarded. Jolson's scam: He would take the son who was not mentally retarded to a toy store. There, he would stage an accident in which his son seemed to be injured. Later, he would take his retarded son to the doctor, claiming that he was the one who had been in the toy store accident. Next, he would claim that his son's brain damage had been caused by the accident involving improperly stacked merchandise.

Mark Jolson was caught only through the diligence of a talented insurance investigator. The investigator, Susan Lowery, visited the Jolson home unannounced. There she saw the handicapped son's twin brother frolicking, carefree, happy, and healthy, in the backyard. Immediately, she knew something was fishy—and further investigation quickly revealed Mark Jolson's con.

HEALTH INSURANCE FRAUD

Health insurance fraud is rampant in the United States. One insurance scam operation that I learned about, in Birmingham, Alabama, netted several million dollars over seven years. For this scam, con artist patients would obtain duplicates of legitimate X rays from cooperative doctors, then use them to bolster phony claims of industrial, auto, or personal injuries.

One scam was halted only after an eighteen-month undercover sting operation in which undercover investigators went to suspect clinics and were diagnosed with soft tissue injuries, even though all were physically fit. The result: grand jury indictments of seven medical doctors, a chiropractor, and twelve health care workers on charges of offering kickbacks or falsifying insurance claims.[11] In one investigation in Texas, officials charged more than 100 individuals, including doctors and lawyers, in a huge fraud scheme involving falsified claims for injuries and vehicle collisions. In a recent Arizona investigation, doctors and lawyers numbered among twenty-five people charged with a variety of fraud counts. NICB investigators reviewed nearly 300 claims worth more than $12 million after searching twenty-one different offices.[12] Organized fraud rings mean big business.

MEDICARE FRAUD

As part of my award-winning investigation for *Inside Edition* that was mentioned in Chapter One, I learned more than I really wanted to know about the extent and insidiousness of this type of fraud. Many nursing homes, medical supply companies, and clinics routinely exploit senior citizens to defraud the Medicare system. Some overcharge for treatments and supplies; others give treatments that are utterly unnecessary, often painful, and at times even dangerous.

What makes this especially disgusting is the fact that fraud and mismanagement are threatening to destroy the Medicare system. Medicare was designed to help the elderly and infirm; but in another decade, it may no longer exist.

If you are a Medicare patient—or even if you're just a concerned American—you should take part in the fight against Medicare fraud. Pressure your legislators to pass laws that deal harshly with Medicare fraud. If you're a patient, be an informed consumer. Ask questions about your treatment; pay attention to what's been prescribed to you.

If you're the friend or family member of a Medicare patient, go out of your way to monitor the patient's health affairs. And no matter who you are, if you believe you or someone you know is being cheated or lied to by health professionals, make sure to bring your beliefs to the attention of law enforcement authorities.

LIFE INSURANCE FRAUD

I'm worth more dead than alive.

—Ted Clarke, to his wife after a financial reversal

If you were to watch too many Hollywood movies like *Double Indemnity* or *Body Heat,* you might think life insurance scams were an everyday occurrence. While they're not as common as that, they do happen. In some cases, a man or woman—alone, or with the help of an accomplice, often a lover—will murder his or her spouse to collect on the victim's life insurance. In other cases, the con artist will fake his own death, then share the insurance payment with the named beneficiary.

Take Ann and Ted Clarke, for instance. In recent years, their marriage had been rocky at times—like all marriages. The biggest problems came when Ted cheated on Ann. But all that was in the past now, Ann thought. She and Ted were in love; they wouldn't do anything to hurt each other. Everything seemed to be going just right in their lives.

Until one day, when Ted came home with bad news—very bad news. The stocks that he had purchased a few months before—with their savings, and against Ann's better judgment—had tanked. Ann and Ted were now broke, for all practical purposes.

"The only money we have is our home equity and life insurance values," Ted said. "I'm worth more dead than alive."

Ann was devastated. All they'd worked for was now gone. Then Ted had an idea. If he faked an accident and disappeared for a while, his life insurance policy would pay out. Then, some time later, he could return to live with Ann.

After Ann and Ted discussed it, long into the night, they made a pact to go ahead with Ted's plan. Ted would fake his own death, then disappear. Ann would collect on Ted's life insurance policy. And some time down the road, when it seemed safe, they would reunite to enjoy a new life in Florida.

During the next week, Ted methodically laid the groundwork for his death. He had a wild idea: to steal a body from a funeral home he had worked in. With the set of keys he still had, he would sneak into the funeral home and steal a corpse. When the funeral home couldn't find one of its bodies, Ted was sure the owner wouldn't publicly admit it.

When everything was ready, Ted drove off in the new BMW that he had bought and fully insured. The next thing Ann knew, the police had phoned to tell her there'd been an accident. The police said the body inside the BMW was completely burned; but certainly, it was her husband. Numbly, Ann agreed.

Eighteen months after the funeral, Ann finally received a phone call from Ted. He was in Kansas City, living in an apartment and using an alias. Soon, they would get together again.

Ann was overjoyed. Ted was safe; their plan had worked. They had succeeded in scamming the life insurance company. But as it turns out, this is not simply the story of a successful life insurance con. When Ted contacted Ann again, he told her to sell the house, then send him a check, written to his alias, in the amount of the proceeds of the sale plus the amount of the life insurance settlement.

At this, Ann got suspicious. After doing some checking, she discovered that Ted had reverted to his old womanizing ways. In fact, he had married a much younger woman in Kansas City, and had conceived a child with her. At that point, she realized that Ted had no intention of reuniting with her. What had been simply a life insurance scam had become a double scam—with Ann as the second victim. Livid at Ted's betrayal of her, Ann picked up the phone and reported the scam to the insurance company.

• • •

UNFAIR INSURANCE INDUSTRY PRACTICES

So far, all I've talked about are scams perpetrated to defraud insurance companies. But insurance scams are not limited to crimes against insurance companies; insurance companies have also been caught treating clients unfairly. For example, in a dispute about deceptive sales practices, Prudential Insurance Co. of America agreed in early 1997 to settle a nationwide class-action suit that alleged that Prudential agents persuaded policyholders to purchase life insurance policies that were more expensive than the ones they already had. The settlement covers 10.8 million policyholders, but critics of the settlement feared that the complexity of the claims forms would deter unsophisticated policyholders from seeking restitution. If the 700,000 who've indicated they plan to seek restitution follow through, it could cost Prudential $1.6 billion, an average of $2,300 per claim.[13]

And then there was the well-publicized case in which Allstate agreed to pay an unprecedented $1 million fine to settle charges brought by the California Department of Insurance for the way it mishandled claims after the 1991 Oakland and Berkeley Hills fires.[14]

INSURANCE FRAUD AFFECTS US ALL

Stories like these understandably incense the public. The average insurance client pays his premiums on time; he deserves fair treatment from his insurance company. If, as sometimes happens, he files a legitimate claim for an auto accident, burglary, or fire, then finds himself the subject of an investigation by an antifraud unit, of course he's going to be incensed. If, after paying premiums on time for ten, fifteen, or twenty years, he suddenly has his insurance canceled when his house catches fire or he has a car accident, of course he's going to be irate. But this does not justify fraud on the part of the insured—no matter what insurance con artists may say to explain away their actions.

The net result of insurance fraud is that all of us are being defrauded, in the form of the higher premiums we must pay because of it. If insurance fraud continues to go unchecked, premiums will become so high that most clients won't be able to afford insurance. As it is, an increasing number of drivers don't buy automobile insurance or are underinsured because they say they can't afford the coverage, and many physicians have been forced to leave private practice because their liability insurance premiums are unaffordable.

The insurance industry is now working to fight fraud through the National Insurance Crime Bureau (NICB), which through NICB Online assists nearly 10,000 law enforcement officers and insurance investigators in identifying fraudulent insurance claims. The NICB has also set up an insurance crime hotline number, 800/TEL-NICB, allowing callers to report all forms of insurance fraud.[15]

The American Insurance Services Group is also building a database of claims, and insurance companies are beefing up their investigations units. The number of states with formal insurance fraud bureaus has climbed from eight in 1990 to twenty-eight.[16]

If you know of the perpetration of an insurance fraud, it's in your best interest—and society's—to report it.

LESSON

••

Insurance fraud costs all of us who are insured. Beware of crooked professionals who try to entice you into schemes to defraud insurance companies. Don't exaggerate or fabricate insurance claims; you may be charged with fraud. Report suspicious claims and accidents to the authorities.

If your insurance company isn't treating you fairly or you encounter problems dealing with your agent, contact your state's insurance commissioner.

••

1. National Insurance Crime Bureau, "Insurance Companies Crack Down on Con Artists seeking to Exploit Soft Tissue Injury for Hard Cash," *Spotlight on Insurance Crime* 1 (1997): 7.

2. NICB, "Insurance Fraud: The $20 Billion Disaster," *Report the Ripoff.*

3. Susan Adams, "The Strange Case of the Dangerous Intersection: Computers Are Helping Insurance Companies Track Down Phony Claims. Good News for the Average Motorist," *Forbes* 158, no. 13 (December 2, 1996): 122-24.

4. NICB, "Fraud on the Job: Workers' Compensation Fraud," *Report the Ripoff.*

5. NICB, "Insurance Fraud: The $20 Billion Disaster."

6. NICB, "Fraud on the Job: The Schemers and the Schemes," *Report the Ripoff.*

7. Western Insurance Information Service, "Insurance Fraud: Who Pays?" (4/95).

8. *Ibid.*

9. NICB, "Workers' Compensation Fraud."

10. NICB, "Fraud in Homes and Businesses: Bodily Injury Insurance Fraud," *Report the Ripoff.*

11. NICB, "Insurance Fraud: The $20 Billion Disaster."

12. NICB, "Fraud on the Road: Putting a Dent in Staged Collisions," *Report the Ripoff.*

13. Leslie Scism, "Prudential Restitution Could Top $1.6 Billion," *The Wall Street Journal* 136, no. 105 (May 30, 1997): A3.

14. Martha Groves, "Allstate to Pay Record Fine in Handling of Fire Claims," *Los Angeles Times* (December 23, 1992).

15. NICB, "Proactive Fraud Detection," *Report the Ripoff* (5/1/96).

16. Adams, "The Strange Case," p. 122.

·10·

THE GREAT PYRAMIDS: PYRAMID SCHEMES THAT WOULD STUN THE PHARAOHS

They say that if it seems too good to be true, it most likely is. I know that, and my wife knows that. So how did we fall for this thing? Was it the gold?

—*Victim of a pyramid scam who wishes to remain nameless*

ALL THAT GLITTERS IS NOT GOLD

One night, while sitting in my office preparing for that night's five o'clock newscast, I received an intriguing phone call. "Is this Chuck Whitlock?" the deep male voice on the other end asked.

"Yes it is. Can I help you?"

"My name is Norman Henderson. I'm a carpenter who's had some tough times lately. I've been in and out of work because of an injury I got while building a home two years ago. Recently, I was introduced to an outfit called Gold Corp. and invited to become a distributor. They told me my financial worries would soon be over if I paid the $1,500 start-up fee. All I had to do was bring in two additional people, and I would earn $4,500 back on my initial $1,500 investment, in a combination of gold bullion and cash."

Henderson paused, and I told him to continue.

"Well, just now, I talked to one of the owners, Jonathan Ford. Mr. Ford said I couldn't get a refund of my money even though I wasn't able to add additional people. And that's something they promised us at the meeting at the hotel a couple weeks ago, when I joined. And I'm really upset. I think I've been defrauded."

So do I, I thought. "I'd like to talk to you. I think there's a real story here."

The next morning at eleven o'clock, my camera crew and I arrived at Norman Henderson's house. He lived in a small tract house, about 1,100 square feet, that was maybe twenty-five years old—the kind you might find in any lower-middle-class neighborhood. That Norman had not been doing so well lately was obvious from the shape the place was in: sagging porch, chipped paint, faded furniture. There was no way this guy could afford to lose $1,500.

"Oh, hi, Mr. Whitlock. It's a pleasure to meet you. Come on in," he said politely. He was about thirty, with long, dark brown hair and brown eyes. And he seemed depressed.

Inside, I asked Norman to tell me his story from the beginning.

"Well, a month ago, a cousin of mine called and told me she was a distributor for this Gold Corp., an Indianapolis-based company. She was already making a fortune, she said, and since I was unemployed, she knew that I would probably want to get in on the action, too. She invited me to come as her guest to a meeting at a local hotel a couple of weeks ago. So I went. And it was amazing. There were probably a hundred people there. There was so much excitement. One of Gold Corp.'s national sales managers was even there.

"He told us that Gold Corp. sold gold, jewelry, and sacred icons. Then he showed us their catalog; it looked great—very attractive. The gold almost jumped off the page. All I had to do to become part of their team, they said, was put up $1,500 in cash. They didn't want a check and they didn't accept credit cards.

"Anyway, they told me that all I had to do was bring in two additional people, and when each of them paid the $1,500 start-up fee, I would get a $750 commission on each, in gold bullion. Then, each time I brought in an additional person, there would be another $750 commission. At the same time, I could make even more money as a distributor, selling the company's gold jewelry and these one-of-a-kind sacred icons."

Norman paused, shifting his weight a little. Obviously, his injuries still caused him discomfort. Sighing, he continued. "I was excited. I figured that, between my neighbors, friends, relatives, and old coworkers, I could bring in as many as 50 or 100 people. If I brought in 100 people, that would be $75,000 in commissions. And to me, Mr. Whitlock, that's all the money in the world.

"That should have made me suspicious, I guess, but it didn't. Everybody in that room was up, enthusiastic, and I guess I just got swept along in the excitement."

Later that day, after finishing my interview with Norman, I checked up on Gold Corp. by calling the Better Business Bureau of Indianapolis, Indiana, as well as the Indiana attorney general's office. From them, I learned that hundreds of people had been complaining about being defrauded by Gold Corp., and that the FBI had just confiscated all its records and closed its headquarters temporarily. "It's a Ponzi scheme," the attorney general's office told me. "An elaborate one, but nevertheless, a Ponzi scheme." You probably know this by another name, the pyramid scheme.

When I went back to Norman with this information, he was shocked by what I told him, and wanted to get back at Gold Corp. for taking advantage of him. As soon as I suggested it, he agreed to get me into the next Gold Corp. recruiting meeting. Activity was still going on even in the face of the FBI raid at headquarters.

The next Tuesday evening, I drove Norman to the local hotel where a Gold Corp. representative was scheduled to speak. Afraid that I'd be recognized because of my TV appearances and barred from the meeting, I disguised myself by wearing a fake mustache.

Inside, I took a seat in the rear of the room.

Soon Linda Chapman, the Gold Corp. representative, began her presentation. An attractive blond of about twenty-six, she was very articulate. She told a wonderful story about the company's founders and its success. With pride, she told us that the company now had assets in excess of $100 million. Gold Corp., she said, was in the business of selling gold and jewelry for below-retail prices. Gold Corp. could do this because, unlike jewelry stores that you walk into off the street, it didn't have huge markups. There were no stores to run, so there was very little overhead. And because Gold Corp. had so many representatives throughout the United States, it didn't even have to inventory its products. It could buy and ship within just a few days, leaving inventory responsibility to the manufacturers. Together, these factors made for lower prices for the merchandise sold by Gold Corp. distributors.

Linda Chapman was a spellbinder. Every eye was on her as she worked her way through her spiel. She was poised, confident, and totally credible. Between that and the fact that people are attracted to gold because of its intrinsic value, I could see why so many people were becoming Gold Corp. investors.

But then Linda moved to the next stage of her presentation. Using elaborate charts, she explained how a distributor came into the company at one level, then worked his way up based on how many other people he brought in. That was the catch, the telltale sign. There was no getting around it. This was a pyramid scheme, doomed to collapse and take a lot of victims with it.

Suddenly I began to feel sorry for the people around me. If they took part in this scheme, they would almost certainly lose money. I knew that as an investigative reporter my job was to report the news, not make it, but I couldn't help but want to protect them from what amounted to a complex con. Fifty minutes into the presentation, I made my move.

Standing up, I said, "Ladies and gentleman, my name is Chuck Whitlock. I'm with KGW television, here in Portland, and I believe this is a pyramid scheme. I believe that all the things that Linda Chapman has told you, with a few exceptions, are untrue. First of all, I doubt that the company can have very many one-of-a-kind sacred icons. Second, I don't see how they can promise you five ounces of gold to cover your $1,500 commission, since the price of gold fluctuates. What if gold were to double in value? Would you still get five ounces, or just two and a half?

"I believe that the rungs of the ladder Linda showed us are indicative that this is a pyramid scheme. Apparently, many law enforcement agencies agree. Gold Corp.'s records were confiscated and headquarters shut down just a few days ago, and I believe the principals are going to be indicted for operating an illegal pyramid scheme."

The reaction that followed shocked me. The audience was mad as hell, but by and large, it was not mad at Linda—it was mad at me!

"Who allowed him in here?" one woman shouted.

"We're not interested in anything you have to say," a man in a sweat suit said firmly.

I pleaded with them. "Can't you see that all they're doing is taking your money? You'll get nothing in return!"

For the most part, my words fell on deaf ears. A few people got up and left, but most stayed—and most of those were busy trying to shout me down. These, I figured, were distributors who had brought guests to this presentation. They saw the commissions from these new victims disappearing right before their eyes, and I was the culprit. I was the one who was exposing the scam, so *I* was the bad guy—not the real crook, Linda Chapman.

I left, knowing that at least I had warned everyone in the audience that this was likely a pyramid scam.

The anger toward me continued the next night, when, after broadcasting my suspicions about Gold Corp. on the five o'clock news, I was besieged by protesters claiming that Gold Corp. was not a pyramid scheme but a legitimate multilevel marketing organization.

Eventually, though, my suspicions about Gold Corp. were confirmed. A judge ordered the company to cease and desist its operations. Its owners were indicted for mail fraud and operating an illegal pyramid scheme. No matter what its distributors wanted to believe, the fact was that Gold Corp. was a pyramid scheme— in other words, a fraud.

• • •

PYRAMID SCHEMES: THE INFAMOUS CHARLES PONZI

In 1919, an American named Charles Ponzi created one of the first highly successful pyramid schemes. After serving time for forgery, Ponzi figured out a way to take advantage of the fact that postage rates varied greatly from country to country. He reasoned that one could buy international postal coupons in a country where postage rates were low, redeem them for stamps in a country where rates were high, then sell the stamps for cash, pocketing the difference between what he'd paid for the coupons in the first country and what he'd made selling the stamps in the second.[1]

In fact, doing so was illegal. But Ponzi didn't care, because he had no intention of actually acting on his concept. Instead, he used this "foolproof" method for making money to attract investors. For a small investment, Ponzi promised his investors a 100 percent return in 90 days. In the first month, he persuaded fifteen people to invest a total of over $800. The next month, attracted by the dividends the first investors had received, seventeen more people put in another $5,000. By the fourth month, Ponzi had 110 investors, who had entrusted almost $29,000 to his care. And just two months later, he had no fewer than 20,000 investors, who had committed the unbelievable sum of $10 million. Of course, that was a fortune. Quickly, Ponzi's scheme attracted a lot of attention, including that of law enforcement. For his crimes, Ponzi ended up spending five years in federal prison.[2]

And ever since, any pyramid scheme in which the original investors are paid off by succeeding recruits has been known as a Ponzi scheme.

HOW A PYRAMID SCHEME WORKS

But what exactly is a pyramid or Ponzi scheme? Simply, it's an illegal scam in which large numbers of people are recruited to pay money to the few people who began the scheme. These new members then recruit more new members; each new participant pays for the chance to advance to the upper levels of the pyramid and profit from payments of newer participants at the bottom levels. A diagram of the organization looks like a pyramid: broad at the base, where the many new recruits are, and narrow at the top.

Most victims of pyramid schemes are fooled into believing that they are buying into riskproof investments or legitimate business opportunities.

Some pyramid promoters try to disguise their schemes to look like multilevel marketing operations. Multilevel marketing is a lawful, legitimate business method in which a network of independent distributors sells consumer products. To take on the look of a multilevel marketing company, a pyramid scheme may feature a line of products, claiming to be in the business of selling the products to consumers. However, little or no effort is made to market the products. Instead, money is made primarily through recruiting. Often, recruits are pressured to purchase large and costly amounts of inventory when they sign up. This is called front-end loading.

For example, to become a distributor in a pyramid scheme, one might be required to purchase $5,000 of virtually worthless or hard-to-sell products. Of this money, a little goes to buy the product, the recruiter might receive a $2,500 commission, and the remainder is divided between those levels of distributors above the recruiter in the pyramid. When there are no more new members to be found, the cash flow grinds to a halt. Because the company's products are all but impossible to sell, those on the bottom levels of the organization are stuck with no way to recoup their initial investment.

Pyramid promoters are masters of group psychology. At recruiting meetings, they try to create a frenzied atmosphere in which peer pressure and promises of easy money play upon people's greed and fear of missing a good opportunity. A pyramid recruiting meeting is like a pep rally sweetened with the aroma of fast and plentiful cash.

Promoters often hold thousands of dollars in their hands, wear expensive jewelry, or drive up in a brand-new Mercedes. All this is part of a show meant to convince attendees that this business opportunity will lead to imminent success. Meanwhile, pyramid company cheerleaders discourage thoughtful consideration and questioning. It is difficult to resist this kind of appeal unless you recognize that all Ponzi schemes are doomed to collapse.

HOW TO RECOGNIZE A PYRAMID SCAM

The best way to avoid a pyramid scam is to know how to distinguish it from a legitimate multilevel marketing income opportunity. In a legitimate multilevel marketing opportunity, the upfront investment is usually minimal. The aim of the company is to make it easy for a distributor to get started. Your success should be based upon the sale of products and services, not solely on recruiting new people. The aim of a legitimate company will be selling to customers and establishing a market.

The tactic of robbing Peter to pay Paul is ever present in a pyramid swindle. Pyramid schemes make nearly all their profits on signing new recruits. There is little or no emphasis on product sales except as a means of recruiting. If you're told that you should act immediately to get in on the ground floor or risk missing the boat, the implication is that people joining later will be left holding the bag.

Remember: Pyramid schemes are illegal. Even if you're not at the bottom of a pyramid, you run the risk that the scheme will be shut down by the authorities—in which case you might be subject to fines and/or imprisonment, or be required to return all monies received through the scheme.

LESSON
....
Learn how to differentiate a legal multilevel marketing business from an illegal pyramid scam.

Unlike a multilevel marketing opportunity, in a pyramid scam little or no effort is made to market products; the emphasis in a pyramid scheme is primarily on recruiting others. You can be prosecuted for your involvement in a pyramid scheme even if you're not one of the original perpetrators. Before you invest, contact your state attorney general's office if you suspect the opportunity might be a pyramid scheme. Remember that all pyramid scams are doomed to collapse and may take you down, too.

••

1. John Steele Gordon, "As Old as the Pyramid Scheme," *American Heritage* 45, no. 7 (Nov. 1994): 18.

2. *Ibid.*

·11·

So You Want to Be in Pictures? The Lure of Celebrity

This is pathetic. I wouldn't hire one person in that entire room as a model.

—Joan, owner of a professional modeling agency, at a modeling magazine cattle call

MAKE BIG MONEY: NO EXPERIENCE NECESSARY

Wanted: Models, all ages, for major talent agency search. No experience necessary. Photographs helpful but not required. LD Associates. Red Lion, Ballroom. 6:00 p.m. Wednesday.

The ad caught Lisa Allen's eye. "No experience necessary," it said. Many of the ads she had seen before said "Only those with experience need apply." Quickly but carefully, she tore the ad out of the paper. Leaving newspaper scattered in her wake, she rushed out of her room to find her mother.

Kathy was just getting dinner started when Lisa burst through the door of the kitchen, her blond hair flying, her face lit up in a huge smile. "Look, Mom, they want models with no experience! Can I try out?" she said, showing her mother the ad.

Kathy took the ad and read it silently. She knew that Lisa's dream was to make it in the entertainment industry. Lisa had been in school plays since she was in elementary school—never in the lead role, but she always got a part. She knew how excited Lisa must be by this ad. Still, she wasn't comfortable with something about what she read. *No experience necessary.* There was a catch; there had to be.

"I wonder how much it costs?" she mused aloud.

"I've got some savings," Lisa volunteered.

"That money's for college," Kathy said sternly. A hurt look came over Lisa's face.

Her mother considered her for a moment. It seemed harmless enough to let her go see what this was all about. And they weren't asking for money yet. And if they did ask for money, Kathy had some put aside for emergencies—in case the water heater went out, for instance, or her twelve-year-old car needed to be repaired. Perhaps it would be worth giving her daughter the chance to do something she really wanted to do.

"Okay, honey, we might as well go to this meeting and see how much it costs. No promises, though," she said.

"Thanks, Mom!" Lisa said, grinning with delight.

When they sat down to dinner, Kathy was still thinking about the newspaper ad. It seemed that it should be harder to get a modeling agency to look at just anyone. And yet, here they were, advertising in the newspaper.

"Maybe I could support you," Lisa said, a faraway look in her eyes. "You could leave that stupid secretarial job and travel to photo shoots with me. Paris, Milan. . . ."

"Let's not get carried away," Kathy said, suddenly concerned by how much stock Lisa had set in this ad.

After dinner, Kathy rummaged through her purse and found a phone number she'd written on a scrap of paper a few days before. It was a scam hotline she'd seen on the local NBC station. For some reason, it seemed like a good idea to give it a call.

That's when I entered the picture. When Kathy called my scam hotline, I listened to her story and agreed to check out the modeling agency that had placed the ad. "Maybe it's a legitimate business," she said, "but Mr. Whitlock, I just don't feel good about it."

When we finished talking, I went to work. First I called the local Better Business Bureau to see if LD Associates had any complaints filed against them; there were none. Then I contacted Gloria Cedar, the owner of a legitimate talent agency that had been in business for more than eighteen years. I figured that Gloria, with her experience in the industry, might know something about LD Associates. And I was right; according to Gloria, the modeling industry was fraught with scam artists, and this Phoenix-based company in particular had a bad reputation.

The next day, I called Kathy and told her what I had learned. And we agreed that it might be a good idea for me to accompany her and Lisa to the LD Associates' talent search at the ballroom of the Red Lion Inn.

That Wednesday night, my cameraman, my friend Ed, his daughter Stephanie, and I went to the casting call, where we met up with Kathy and Lisa. Arriving half an hour early, we were surprised to see at least 200 people already standing in line. A lot of girls, it was apparent, shared Lisa's desire to make it as a model. Many were so made-up—expensive gowns, elaborate hairdos—they looked like they were on their way to the Academy Awards. Intimidated by this display, Lisa gave me a stricken look; I tried to reassure her with a smile.

The attendant at the registration table looked as though she had once been a model herself. She was tall and slender, with prominent cheekbones, heavy mascara and eye shadow, and dark lipstick on her full lips. A short maroon skirt and high heels showed off her long legs. Compared to her, most of the girls waiting to get in seemed short, overweight, too awkward—in other words, totally out of place.

When my cameraman and I moved to follow Lisa and her mother inside, we were approached by a stout, bearded, middle-aged man with wavy black hair. He told us in no uncertain terms that the media was not welcome at the meeting. Luckily, I had anticipated this, and sent Ed and Stephanie in. We backed off without protest, awaiting Ed's return.

Forty minutes later, Ed and Stephanie emerged from the ballroom. Ed estimated that there had been about 300 aspiring models on hand to listen to the thirty-minute pitch. The bearded man, Ed told us, had been the speaker. According to him, LD Associates regularly published a magazine which it sent to every modeling agency in the country, which had already led to great success for many of the models in it. The bearded man had also talked about the glamour and excitement of a modeling career—the world travel, the fine clothing, the riches and public acclaim.

The bearded man had also made it clear that not everyone would be accepted for inclusion in the magazine. When Ed told me this, I recognized it as the old sales technique called the country club close. In order to be a member, you have to qualify, the salesman claims—causing people to go out of their way and even lie in order to qualify and thus feed their egos. The bearded man stressed that it cost money to photograph the models and distribute the magazine; as a result, LD Associates would understandably have to charge a fee to those models included in the magazine. Finally, he had told the audience that all those who made the cut would receive a call from his Phoenix office within ten days.

After the presentation, the candidates had been asked to file slowly past the bearded man. As each candidate walked past him, he'd asked one or two questions. "Why do you want do be a model?" Or, "Are you willing to travel?" As the candidates spoke, he recorded his impressions of them on note cards. Within an hour, every candidate had gone through this process—all 300 aspiring models.

My curiosity piqued, I obtained the names and phone numbers of about twenty candidates exiting the ballroom. Telling them who I was, I made plans to contact them in a week or two, to see just how many LD Associates had contacted—and how much they'd been asked to pay for inclusion in the magazine.

Two weeks later, all twenty had been called back; so much for the magazine's selectivity and exclusiveness. Each had been told that inclusion in the magazine would cost $500, without photography. If they didn't already have modeling photographs, the magazine would be happy to provide them—for an additional $225 for black-and-white, or $425 for color. Of course, color photos were strongly recommended, because they would give modeling agencies a much better feeling for the aspiring model's skin color, hair color, and total look.

Most of the twenty people that I contacted said they were going to pay to be included in the magazine. One young woman bragged that when she told all her friends she'd been chosen, they had been "so jealous." Another told me that the magazine would be sent to Paris and Tokyo, where there aren't enough models to meet local needs. "Wouldn't it be exciting to model in Paris or Japan!" All in all, it sounded like a wonderful opportunity—*if* it was legitimate.

I called Gloria and told her what I had learned. She told me that when she received magazines of the type distributed by LD Associates, she didn't even bother to thumb through them; instead, her secretary threw them straight into the garbage. Representatives of other agencies told me essentially the same thing. One owner in particular, Joan, was incensed at the way companies like LD Associates took advantage of people; angrily, she told me that she would bet that *not one* of the people in the LD Associates magazine would get hired by a modeling agency.

Next, I phoned Kathy. When I told her what I had learned, she said that she had suspected something fishy about LD Associates from the very beginning. Luckily, after the presentation at the Red Lion, Lisa had agreed with her that it probably wouldn't be worth it to spend the money necessary to be included in the magazine. I congratulated her on having raised such a wise young woman.

A week later, LD Associates held a photo session at a local hotel, at which people from the area who'd been selected for inclusion in its magazine could have their modeling shots taken. I was there—along with Joan, the talent agency owner who'd been so upset at the tactics of companies like LD Associates. We stood outside the Meridian Room, checking things out.

While my cameraman tried to get shots of the photo sessions going on inside—interestingly, the photographer was the same bearded man who'd given LD Associates' presentation at the Red Lion Inn—Joan and I talked to people coming and going. Some who'd finished their photo shoots told us they were quite pleased with the setup here, and looked forward to getting the modeling jobs that would surely result. But one woman, a pretty redhead, wore a grim expression as she exited the Meridian Room. She had just demanded her money back.

"I have some modeling experience," she said. "And I know a scam when I see one."

Originally, she had thought LD Associates was a legitimate agency that just happened to have a magazine. After paying her money, though, she had learned that they were not an agency at all, but strictly a magazine publisher.

"Did they give you your money back?" I asked her.

She nodded. "Yes. Especially after I raised my voice a little and threatened to expose them as frauds!"

More representative of the people inside was the father who was using his rent money to pay for the photos. His fourteen-year-old daughter really wanted to become an actress, and modeling would be a good place to start.

After a while, Joan went into the Meridian Room and looked things over. "This is pathetic, Chuck," she said when she came back out. "I wouldn't hire one person in that entire room as a model. They're all too short or too plain-looking. Not one meets the minimum requirements. Don't these people understand that models have to meet certain measurement requirements? That they have to be at least five feet seven inches tall? That they have to have a certain distance from ankle to knee, from knee to hip, in order to qualify as professional models? That there are certain physical attributes required before one can even be considered?"

She was so upset, she said, that at one point she couldn't help herself, and had told one woman waiting in line to take her daughter home—to leave without paying, that there was no hope that her daughter would ever get a job as a model. Joan had tried to say this as kindly as possible, because she knew that her words would shatter the girl's fragile hopes, her dreams of becoming a famous model, a celebrity. And while the daughter had started to cry, her mother had thanked Joan. She was a single mom, she explained, a waitress earning minimum wage; she had taken a loan on her car in order to come up with the required money.

Eventually, my cameraman and I went into the Meridian Room. The photographer—the bearded man—recognized us; but this time he didn't ask us to leave.

"Can I help you?" he asked.

"Yes," I said bluntly. "How many agencies actually receive the LD Associates magazine?"

"Gee, I don't know, offhand. I can tell you in a couple of days when I return to the home office, if you want to call me then."

"How many people in your magazine actually get jobs?"

"Gee, that's a good question. I don't know. You'll have to ask the people in the magazine," he said, turning as though to go back to shooting photos.

But I wasn't finished with him. "But the only number in the magazine is *your* number, so wouldn't you be the one who knows which agencies are calling which people in your magazine?"

"Well, you might think that, but it's not really true. I just don't have any idea at all."

Now his eyes were beginning to dart around to see if anyone in the room was getting impatient because of the wait, so I said quickly, "When I talked to the Ford Modeling Agency and other modeling agencies in New York and locally, I was told that these model magazines are a big scam, that the real modeling agencies don't even use them; they throw them away. Is that true?"

"Well, they're entitled to their opinion. I think we provide a really good service. People like to see their pictures in our magazine."

"And how many magazines do you print?"

"Gee, I really can't say." He wet his lips nervously.

I said, "In order to report this fairly, I really need some straight answers from you."

At this he began backing away from me; pulling his card from his jacket, he said, "Perhaps you can call me later. I'll be happy to help you then. As you can see, we're busy processing people and I need to get back to work."

"Yes, I can see that," I said. "But I have one more thing I want to talk about. We have an expert outside; she came into the room earlier. She said she couldn't find one person here that she would hire as a model."

The bearded man shrugged. "Well, she's entitled to her opinion, too. If you'll excuse me, I need to go back to work now."

Before going ahead and airing the story about LD Associates, I followed the bearded man's suggestion and tried to get in touch with him to learn his side of the story. But every time I called the number on his card, I got an answering machine. No one returned my calls. And LD Associates' Los Angeles address turned out to be nothing more than a mail drop.

In the end, our piece on modeling on KGW-TV received a tremendous public response. I got a number of telephone calls from parents and young people who had been bilked in similar scams. I can only hope that others learned to avoid scams like this from the telecast.

THE LURE OF CELEBRITY

Becoming a high-price model—or any other kind of show business star—is about as difficult as winning the lottery. Probably one person in a million has what it takes to become a world-famous fashion model. Oh, there are plenty of jobs for catalog models, for commercial models—but even those are for the most part given to the very best models, or don't pay that well. So the next time someone tells you that you're a great singer, actor, or model, and wants money in order to help you, beware.

When considering a career in modeling for yourself or for your child, take a few Polaroids and go to a reputable, long-standing modeling agency or two. Ask them if they would like to represent you. If they tell you they're not interested, you should probably listen to them. The one thing that every legitimate modeling agency wants is to find models who meet the industry's standard requirements. They don't have time to waste. They're not going to sell you videos, photo portfolios, placement in talent directories, or courses in manners or poise; but if you meet the requirements, they *will* hire you. That's how they stay in business.

Whenever we want something in life—regardless of what it is—there will always be con artists who will try to convince us they can sell it to us. For many of us—especially for the young—the biggest dream of all is to make it in show business. Every day, we see or hear our favorite celebrities—Tom Cruise on the big screen, Pearl Jam on MTV, Cindy Crawford on the covers of *Vogue* and *Cosmopolitan.* Their lives seem bigger than ours, better than ours. Of course we dream about being like them. And those dreams are exactly what con men—and women—prey on.

SO YOU WANT TO BE A ROCK 'N' ROLL STAR

Are you willing to pay what's necessary to be a star?
—Henry Rock, Henry Rock Records

Modeling is not the only field in which con artists take advantage of innocent victims. Other industries attract con artists and swindlers as well. The recording industry, for instance.

Michelle Moreland possessed a wonderful singing voice. More than anything in the whole world, she wanted to become a Christian gospel singer. Since she had begun singing in the choir five years earlier, she had not missed a single practice or Sunday service. A devout Christian, she loved her music almost as much as she loved her faith.

So when she found an ad in the paper inviting Christian gospel singers to contact Henry Rock Records in Nashville, she couldn't help but get excited. A record company advertising for Christian singers! She had always assumed that to break into the business she would have to travel to Los Angeles. She'd never had enough money to do that; the idea of going to LA also frightened her a bit. Before she lost her nerve, she grabbed the phone and called the 800 number.

The receptionist who answered had a slight drawl. "Henry Rock Records, can I help you?"

"Yes, my name's Michelle Moreland. I'm from Boise, Idaho, and I'm responding to the ad I saw in the newspaper. I'm a Christian gospel singer."

"I'll put you through to Henry Rock. One moment please," the receptionist said.

Michelle held her breath as she waited. Within seconds, Henry Rock was on the phone. "Hello, Michelle from Boise. I placed the ad because I needed talented people to cut records. Are you good?"

"Yes, Mr. Rock, I'm very good. People tell me all the time that I should cut a record."

"What kind of experience do you have?"

"I've been singing for five years in the church choir, doing lots of solos. I've also had some voice training. My teacher says I shouldn't waste my talent."

"Well, that sounds just great. Have you ever cut a record before?"

"No, I've never cut a record."

"That's not a problem. Listen, can you send me a demo tape of your singing? It doesn't have to be studio quality or anything. Just be sure that I can hear you singing over the background music. If I think you've got what it takes, I'll get you in to do a real demo to send to music producers, so you can sell records and make us both a lot of money."

"I'm singing a solo this Sunday; I can tape that if you'd like," Michelle said.

Her fingers tightened around the receiver as she waited for Henry's response. She really wanted to do this.

Finally, Henry said, "That would be fine. Here, let me give you my address. Send the tape out as soon as possible; I'll get back to you right away."

That night, thrilled at the prospect of finally making it as a singer, Michelle visited her good friend Helen. When Michelle asked Helen to record her that Sunday, and told her why she was asking, Helen was almost as excited as Michelle. She offered to borrow her brother's tape recorder, which had a good microphone. To make sure they'd get the best sound possible, Michelle agreed that she should buy some high-quality tapes.

On Sunday, Helen sat in the front pew and waited for the music to start—her cue to start recording. Finally the music began. And everything seemed to go well—Michelle sang beautifully, and the tape recorder worked without a hitch.

After the service, Helen and Michelle rushed to Michelle's house. They said nothing as they listened to the tape, then hugged each other after it was over. It was good! "This is it—your start to stardom!" Helen exclaimed, as Michelle addressed the Federal Express envelope to Henry Rock Records, Nashville, Tennessee.

Two days later, Michelle was sitting at home, nervous and anxious, when the phone rang.

"Michelle, Henry Rock. Got your tape. You're fantastic! Listen, I want you to cut a record. We'll have to get you to Nashville so we can get you into a recording studio with professional musicians. Can you come down here next Monday?"

"Yes, no problem, Mr. Rock," Michelle said. *I can take a couple of vacation days, or even a sick day,* she thought. *I just have to go do this!*

"Great," Henry continued, "Okay, now I need to commit the band and the studio time. Why don't you go ahead and send me a cashier's check for $3,500. And as soon as I receive that, I'll get a recording contract drawn up for you to sign when you come in. You're a big talent, Michelle, and I want to represent you. I charge 20 percent, the going rate, okay?"

Michelle hesitated. "Mr. Rock, you know, $3,500 is an awful lot of money for me. I'm a nurse's aide—that's almost two months' salary."

Henry's voice was firm. "Well, if you want to make it in this business, young lady, you're going to have to make an investment—not only in time, but a little bit of money. For a career in music, $3,500 is nothing, believe me." He sighed, then added, "But if it's too much, I understand."

Watching her dreams vanish before her eyes, Michelle quickly said, "Oh no, no, please. I'll find a way to get the money. Can you give me a couple days?"

"Well, okay. Man, I never do this, but you're good! Get the money together and FedEx a check to me. As soon as I get it, I'll get the band and studio scheduled. You've got great talent, Michelle. Don't let this opportunity pass you by."

"Oh, I won't, Mr. Rock."

Within days, Michelle had raised enough money to pay Mr. Rock. By putting her student loans on forbearance and borrowing a couple of thousand dollars from her father—who was happy to give her the money to pursue her dream, even though it made up most of his savings—she could now write a check for $3,500.

When Michelle arrived in Nashville, Henry Rock's assistant was waiting for her at the airport gate, holding a sign with Michelle's name on it. The assistant sure stood out in the crowd. Her short blond hair had two streaks in it, fluorescent green and neon pink, and jutted out in all directions as though she had stuck her finger in a light socket. She also had a nose ring and a small ring in her eyebrow, and her tank top exposed her belly, showing off a tattoo of a lizard. *Well, that's show biz for you,* Michelle thought, feeling like a small-town hick in her conservative loafers, slacks, and denim jacket.

When they pulled up to the recording studio, Michelle's mouth practically fell open. It was a big, impressive glass building. She didn't see the name "Henry Rock Records" on the sign outside, but the assistant had mentioned in the car that Henry Rock owned various companies. As they entered, Henry Rock, who had been sitting in the lobby waiting, welcomed Michelle warmly. He was with two other people, one of whom held a guitar. They both had hair past their shoulders—longer than Michelle's. The musicians, she guessed, and she was right.

"Hi Michelle, I'm John," one of them said.

"I'm Rock, no relation to Henry Rock. I'm Rock Jones, he's Henry Rock," the other one said. He and Henry laughed; obviously this was a running joke between them.

In the studio, the musicians tuned up while Henry had Michelle put on the headphones and approach the microphone. She was a little nervous, but Henry said encouragingly, "This is the easy part, Michelle, just give it your best shot. You can do this."

Soon they began. Michelle sang one song after another, growing more confident with each song. *Why, this is easy,* she thought to herself.

Less than three hours later, Michelle had recorded ten songs. "This is fantastic, Michelle, we're done!" Henry said. John and Rock congratulated her on a great job, telling her she was a real professional. Michelle accepted their praise modestly, but inside she was jubilant.

That night at the Holiday Inn, she went to bed thinking about singing her songs to large church congregations all over the country. Perhaps someone like Billy Graham would even notice her, and she'd get to go on crusades all around the globe, singing the gospel! And she couldn't wait to pay back her dad; she'd give him a big return on his loan. She'd double his money—no, triple it!

Four days later, back home in Boise, Michelle received a call from Henry Rock. "Have you sent out the tapes?" she asked enthusiastically. "Does anyone want to make a record with me?" Cutting short her questions, Henry told her that the demo tape sounded great, but that the really big companies wanted a more professional tape. Because he had her voice on tape, it wasn't necessary for her to travel back to Nashville, but she would have to send an additional $2,000 so that he could enhance the music and make it more marketable. If she couldn't come up with the money, he was sorry, but he would have to drop the entire project.

Michelle was heartbroken. She could barely respond, and when she did, her voice was full of emotion. She wanted so desperately to cooperate with Henry, but she told him that another $2,000 was out of reach. Henry listened to her, then said, "Well, perhaps I can get by with only $1,500. But that's the absolute minimum, Michelle. I'm sorry."

As Michelle hung up the phone, she thought about the money she had already borrowed. She couldn't stand the thought of asking her Dad for more money. Then she thought of her car, an older model Toyota. Oh, she would hate to part with the car, her only transportation. But if she made it big, she'd get another car—a new car! Maybe it was God's will that she pay a higher price for a greater reward. Quickly, before she could change her mind, she rushed down to the used car dealer.

With the money she got for the car, she was able to send a $1,500 check to Henry Rock. Two days later, she called to confirm that he got it; he had. Then, two weeks passed with no word from Henry. Three weeks; still no word. Then a month.

Finally, Michelle could wait no longer. But when she called Henry Rock Records, she found out that the line had been disconnected, and no forwarding number noted. She started to panic, then thought of John, the musician, who had handed her his card in the recording studio.

"Hi, John. This is Michelle Moreland. Do you remember me? I'm the Christian singer who recorded with you last month."

"Oh, hi. What's up? Need a musician?"

"No, I'm just trying to locate Henry Rock. His number's been disconnected, but I thought perhaps you might have another number for his studio."

"His studio?"

"You know, the one where we did the recording."

John snorted. "That's not Henry's studio. That's an independent studio. Henry doesn't have anything to do with that place. He was just renting the studio for the afternoon. He was renting me, too, kind of. The studio hires me out to anyone who needs me."

Thanking John, Michelle hung up. With a sickening sense in the pit of her stomach, she called her dad, who after calming her down made a few phone calls, and discovered the truth about Henry Rock. According to the Better Business Bureau in Nashville, more than 100 complaints had been made about Henry Rock. And according to the Nashville police, he was under investigation for fraud. Michelle, it was suddenly obvious, had been scammed.

Even though he's a fraud, Henry Rock will probably escape the long arm of the law. He did provide the studio for Michelle, and he did cut a record with her. Basically, he did what he said he would do, so fraudulent intent might be difficult to prove. Only if he had promised Michelle a record deal in writing would

Michelle have a chance of successfully proving that Henry Rock had defrauded her.

Michelle is still in Boise, singing in her church choir and working a second job to pay off her debts. She still dreams of singing for a living, of becoming a star—but now, she realizes that celebrity doesn't come easily.

YOU CAN SING YOUR HEART OUT

Even if you've been told you're talented and have won accolades before, there is no guarantee that you'll find success. There are many talented individuals in the world. In order to become successful, you first need a good agent whose accomplishments you're able to verify. If anyone tells you that he or she can guarantee you fame and fortune for a fee, don't believe it.

LESSON

The lure of celebrity is strong, and con artists know that some people will pay almost anything to get their big break. First and foremost, be realistic about your talents and abilities. Seek the opinions of experienced professionals before you allow the stars in your eyes to blind you. If someone wants a large sum of money to help you or promises to land you a big contract, beware. Before accepting any offer, check out the person or company thoroughly, starting with the state attorney general's office and the Better Business Bureau. Before signing a contract, have an attorney who specializes in entertainment law review the terms and conditions.

·12·

RISKY BUSINESS

I fell for it because I wanted to be successful. I never checked out his credentials, never questioned his motives. I learned the lesson of a lifetime.

—*Sandra P., after losing her $10,000 investment in a bogus business scheme*

··

THE PROMISE OF EASY MONEY
··

From my place at the dais at one end of the Business Opportunity Convention, I looked out over the crowd in front of me: 100 people, all of them staring at me in rapt attention. I was wrapping up a speech on how to avoid becoming a victim of business opportunity fraud.

"Take your time making a decision to invest even a relatively small amount of money in a business opportunity. Don't ever let anyone pressure you into making a quick decision. It's important to fully investigate the company in question, so be prepared to do some detective work. This means calling the Secretary of State in the state in which the corporation is domiciled to see if it's registered, calling your state Franchise Board and the Federal Trade Commission that have jurisdiction over business opportunities, and calling your attorney general's office to find out if the company has been cited for illegal or questionable activities.

"Every day, businesses are started that make their money by selling business opportunities in the form of licenses and franchises. Some of these marketers offer legitimate business opportunities; others, unfortunately, are in the business of fraud.

"But you can't stop there. Get the company's financial statements for the past three years; make sure they've been audited by a reputable accounting firm. Ask for business, bank, and customer references, then check them out. But retain your skepticism: The references could be friends, or worse yet, accomplices.

"It should go without saying, but it bears repeating: Before you enter into any business arrangement, make sure to get everything in writing, and have your attorney and financial advisor go over every aspect of the deal.

"Simply put: Some opportunities are only opportunities for con artists to rip you off. Be skeptical; don't believe everything you hear."

When I finished speaking, I opened the floor to questions. Although I received a number of inquiries, one man in particular, a tall guy with a completely bald head, persisted until he had all of his questions answered. I felt pleased that my speech had sparked such enthusiasm and intelligence in this man and the audience as a whole.

Finally, the question-and-answer session over, I left the dais. Slipping into a small room off the auditorium, I quickly donned a disguise: gray wig, mustache, and black horn-rimmed glasses. Then, before the audience had a chance to leave, I walked back into the convention hall and assumed my place behind a sales booth in the back.

The audience members didn't know it, but I was testing them, on camera, for *Hard Copy*—attempting to see just how much of my lecture's content they'd really absorbed. Behind me, there was a sign reading "Platinum 1000: The lightbulb that never burns out. Buy a franchise today!" Of course, there was not actually any such product as the Platinum 1000; I was pulling a scam.

"Come on over and let me show you the lightbulb that *never* burns out! The Platinum 1000 is made with a special titanium filament, to which my company has the exclusive patent rights," I said, thinking I sounded more than a little like a circus ringmaster.

Like eager kids, many of the people who'd just listened to my speech stopped to ask questions.

"Wow," one woman exclaimed. "What's the business deal?"

"It's simple. Give me a check for a $1,000 deposit, sign a distributing contract now, before anyone else comes along, and I will give you the city of Vancouver, Washington, exclusively. You can pay the balance of $5,000 over the next two months."

"I think I should have my attorney and wife look over the agreement, but it sure sounds great!" said one man. I couldn't believe it—it was the same tall, bald man who'd asked me such intelligent questions a few minutes before. *Were you really listening to me?* I thought.

"That's great! It's phenomenal!" I gushed. "The only problem is that I can only allow one exclusive distributor per city. So if the next guy who comes along decides to lock up the opportunity, you'll lose." *Okay, guy,* I thought. *Remember what I said about quick decisions.*

But he didn't. "Will you take a check?" the man asked.

"Sure," I said.

"Where do I sign?" he asked, his smile huge by now. It was incredible—just minutes after hearing about how to avoid business opportunity fraud, here he was acting as though he'd been asleep during my speech.

In all, ten people from my audience ended up buying a Platinum 1000 franchise—each of them for the same "exclusive" rights to the Vancouver market. One man even paid me the full $5,000 fee. If I had been a real con artist, I would have walked away with $14,000.

Why did this happen? Why were all of my warnings about business opportunity fraud ignored? The answer is simple: Unless they are eternally vigilant, most people can't help but be attracted to the promise of making easy money. And by offering people the chance to make millions of dollars for a relatively minimal investment—which is surely what would have resulted had the Platinum 1000 been for real—that was exactly what I was promising.

• • •

CORPORATE SCAMS

The business world is rife with opportunities for con artists. Some, like my phony lightbulb business opportunity, are perpetrated by businesses. Others are perpetrated on businesses—by customers, employees, and phony contractors.

In the end, of course, both kinds of scams end up costing all of us: legitimate businesses, business opportunity fraud victims, and innocent consumers—who end up paying the costs imposed by corporate scams in the form of higher retail prices or lesser retail product quality. And sometimes the price of business fraud is even higher—resulting in business failure or employee layoffs by businesses that can no longer afford to keep them on payroll.

....
KING OF THE BANKRUPTCY CON
....

*I've gone bankrupt at least thirty times and my
credit is great!*   —Morris Shane, businessman
                                         and con artist

One of the most common cons perpetrated in the business world is the bankruptcy con. Relatively easy to pull off, it results in the loss of billions of dollars annually in the United States.

Morris Shane was the king of the bankruptcy con. A resident of Florida, Shane seemed to most people to be a sincere, personable guy. But in his fifteen-year career, he formed bogus corporations and perpetrated the bankruptcy con at least thirty-two times.

His modus operandi was to form a company—often with a name similar to that of a well-known company—and begin ordering merchandise from suppliers. Initially, he would order just a small amount of merchandise. For example, he might order a small number of computers, maybe two or three, paying for them immediately. Then he would order five or six; again paying for them immediately. Then, after establishing himself with his supplier, he would call and ask for discount terms.

The supplier's sales department, anxious to make a sale with a fast-paying customer, more often than not would be happy to allow a discount in return for quick payment. So Shane would order perhaps ten computers, paying at his discounted rate within ten days. With each subsequent order, he would increase the order, always paying on time.

Then one day, Shane would tell his supplier that he had received a substantial order from one of his customers. He would need 250 computers, but he would need thirty-day terms for the order because it was so large. Because he was now recognized as a good credit risk, the supplier would have no reason not to ship the larger quantity of computers as requested.

Upon receipt of the large order of computers, Morris Shane would sell the machines at wholesale to a distributor. Then he would declare his company bankrupt, listing his trusting computer supplier as a creditor, which indeed it was—thus avoiding paying the supplier for the computers it had shipped to him. In the process, Shane would walk off with hundreds of thousands of dollars.

Morris Shane perpetrated this con repeatedly. Since he did it with a new corporation each time, there were never prior complaints against his company with the Better Business Bureau or the attorney general. The shipments that he avoided paying for were made to his corporation, not to him personally, so his personal credit remained intact; in fact, his TRW credit report was phenomenal. He showed a high income. He showed quick payment for all of his personal debt. He showed that he owned a house worth more than a million dollars, mortgage-free. He drove a nice car, always making payments on time.

So again and again, companies mistakenly believed there was no reason not to extend credit to Morris Shane's corporations. By taking advantage of U.S. bankruptcy laws in this manner, Morris Shane ended up bilking thousands of suppliers out of millions of dollars.

• • •

THE TRASH AND DASH SCAM

This scam was first brought to my attention by Detective Mark Coffey of the Portland Police Department. An example of a scam perpetrated on businesses by a contractor, the trash and dash begins with the con artist claiming to be a legitimate janitor. Once he's gained access to a business's offices, the con artist can make off with office equipment and other company assets, including corporate checkbooks, ledgers, etc.

To show how easy this scam is to pull off, I attempted the trash and dash on a Wilsonville, Oregon, company. Wearing a janitor's uniform and a phony photo identification badge on my pocket, I boldly walked into the company's front office. When she saw me, the receptionist waved me through to the back offices. Next, I stopped to ask workers where the utility closet and bathrooms were—and no one thought to check that I was who I said I was.

When the offices emptied at the end of the day, I proceeded to pick up laptop computers, diskettes, ledgers, calculators, telephones, and other office equipment. I even found the corporate checkbook in the controller's office, and customer records in the sales office. *How easy it would be for someone to blackmail this company if they had this information,* I thought.

This scam works because, to most people, janitors and maids are all but invisible. When I revealed who I was, employees at the Wilsonville business wondered if they would have even thought of the janitor I'd played as a suspect after they discovered the theft. Even if they had, they weren't sure if they'd have been able to even describe me to the police. It was a real eye-opener; in the future, they said, they'd be much more careful of strangers washing windows or doing janitorial work.

THE COMPUTER REPAIR SCAM

Detective Coffey also introduced me to the computer repair scam. Like the trash and dash, this scam is perpetrated by an outsider entering a company's offices, ostensibly to conduct legitimate on-site business.

Not long ago, I tried this scam with the help of my friend Martin Anderson, a business owner eager to see how susceptible his employees would be to con artists. Taking off my jacket and tie and pulling on a sweater, then donning my trusty gray wig, I set to work. If I hadn't been doing this kind of thing for so long, learning again and again how readily most people can be scammed, I would have been shocked by the results.

Again, as in the trash and dash scam, I was able to get my hands on all kinds of expensive office equipment and invaluable office records. But that was just the beginning—this time, I gained even greater access to proprietary company information. How? By learning the passwords to key employees' computer systems. When I asked a secretary for the password to one vice president's computer, for instance, she gave it to me without hesitation.

The next day, when the office equipment was discovered missing, my friend Martin told his employees he'd call the police. Instead, he called me; and now pretending to be a police detective, I returned to the office. Remarkably, no one recognized me—even though my computer repairman disguise had consisted of nothing more than a wig and some casual clothes. And not one of the office employees could give me an accurate description of what the thief had looked like. A couple of them even started arguing about whether he had been taller or shorter than me!

Currently, computer repair cons, janitorial scams, and various office creeper scams are being perpetrated all over the United States, by corporate espionage agents as well as sophisticated con artists. Based on the responses of 325 U.S. companies, the American Society for Industrial Security (ASIS) reports that theft of trade secrets and other forms of corporate intellectual property climbed 323 percent between 1992 and 1995. Three-quarters of the thefts involved company insiders. ASIS estimates that such breaches of security, which oftentimes go unreported or are undetected, cost American businesses $2 billion a *month*.[1] Many companies lack even basic written corporate security policies and procedures.

So take an extra-hard look the next time a janitor or repairman enters your workplace—and don't give strangers or employees access to information without checking that it's okay to do so first.

EMPLOYEE SCAMS

According to the Small Business Administration, dishonest employees account for an estimated 66 percent of all retail theft, with pilferage and embezzlement ranking as the most common methods used.[2] On average, theft by employees costs American companies over $120 billion annually. Estimates for the year 2000 place the cost at $200 billion.[3] Nationwide, employee theft is at an all-time high. Even employees who lead otherwise law-abiding lives seemingly don't hesitate to take tools, supplies, and finished goods from their place of work.

When employees conspire to defraud a company, the company is almost helpless to prevent the crime. While it is easy to put electronic gadgetry on retail products to catch would-be thieves, it is difficult and time-consuming to catch dirty employees.

THE PHANTOM SUPPLIER

There are a variety of employee scams besieging American businesses. One con artist recruited by the Mafia while doing time, Jonathan Weis, assumed the identity of a man named Allan Lucas, a recently deceased corporate executive, after getting out of jail. In his new and highly respected identity, Weis proceeded to get a high-power job at another corporation in a different part of the country.

There, he instructed the purchasing department to buy supplies from a new set of suppliers. These suppliers required payment in advance, but offered much lower prices than the company's regular suppliers. What the company didn't know was that the new suppliers were actually phony outfits run by the Mafia. When the supplies it had ordered were not delivered, the company realized it had been conned. Its checks had all been cashed, the suppliers' phone numbers had been disconnected, and Allan Lucas had disappeared without a trace.

THE PHANTOM EMPLOYEE

The phantom employee con is another scam targeting businesses. In this con, the perpetrator opens bank accounts under a variety of fictitious names, then infiltrates the target company's payroll system, adding the fictitious names to the payroll—and having the phantom employees' paychecks deposited directly to the phony bank accounts. Interestingly, this was the con Jonathan Weis was working when he was finally captured.

PHONY COMPANIES

THE YELLOW PAGES SCAM

Many businesses place ads in yellow pages across the country. So it's not uncommon for a company to receive yellow pages invoices from a confusing variety of local telephone companies. Enter the con artist, who scams companies out of cash by sending them phony yellow pages invoices.

Typically, the yellow pages con artist convinces his targets that they're being billed for new local business-to-business yellow pages ads identical to those already running in the regular yellow pages. By sending tear sheets showing the ads that the scammer claims will be run in the business-to-business pages—usually just copies of the targets' ads already running in regular yellow pages—he makes it easy for his targets' accounting departments to consider his invoices legitimate. And since the Walking Fingers logo isn't trademarked, including it lends an air of credibility.[4]

Especially hard hit are restaurant operators; about 21 percent who advertise in Yellow Pages directories are familiar with bogus Yellow Pages schemes. The Yellow Pages Publishers Association estimates that $500 million a year is collected by con artists in these scams.[5]

Big business, indeed.

THE PHONY REFUND CHECK SCAM

Many companies—major airlines, hotel chains, and the like—often send out refund checks, which are usually produced on a laser printer. Knowing this, one con ring in Minneapolis recently set up a scam to take advantage of these companies—making millions before being caught. First, the con artists would book travel on airlines, paying by checks in excess of what was due for the tickets—causing the airlines to have to send them refund checks. If a ticket cost $200, they would pay $225, thus receiving a refund check for $25.

Since the kind of paper used to print the refund checks doesn't absorb laser printer ink, the con artists were then able to remove information like the amount or the payee's name from the checks. Next, they would scan the checks into their computer system. At that point, they could then print blank checks from the companies they'd scammed—filling in whatever payees' names and dollar amounts they wanted.

If an original check included the words, "Do not cash for more than XX dollars," and gave a specific amount, the swindlers would make the check out for exactly that amount. If the check stated that larger amounts required two signatures, they would simply obtain an annual report from the company they were scamming, scan the executive signatures included therein into the computer, and bingo! A check with two signatures!

These con artists would have been thwarted if their targets' checks had not come right out and stated the maximum amounts the checks could be cashed for, or the amounts above which the checks required multiple signatures. Here, once again, we can see that businesses and their employees are often woefully unaware of the ways in which they can be scammed.

CORPORATIONS ARE EASY TARGETS

Companies may be attacked by their employees, suppliers, customers, competitors, and partners. Although checks-and-balances systems are helpful to protect companies, con artists frequently find ways to thwart these systems. It's important to develop policies and programs that prevent and deter fraud, not just correct the problem after they've occurred. Make loss prevention a priority and teach employees to be alert, cautious, and suspicious. Do business with new suppliers only after their existence and reliability have been verified. Since many security problems are internal, employee references should be checked carefully prior to hiring. Conduct periodic account audits using internal and external auditors.

Wise consumers carefully select the companies with which they do business. Ask friends for references. Check out businesses through the local Better Business Bureau and the department of corporations in your state. You can contact the attorney general's office in your state to see if the company has been cited for illegal activities.

LESSON
....

It's essential that you really know who you're dealing with in business, whether it's an employee or a vendor. Make sure your company has the proper security procedures in place to avoid undue risks with your money, property, or valuable information. When investing in a business, take your time and do some detective work. Insist on current, audited financial state-

ments and have your accountant review them. (If you don't have an accountant, get one.) Contact the secretary of state in the state where the business is domiciled to see if it's registered. Call the state franchise board, the Federal Trade Commission, Better Business Bureau, and the state attorney general's office where the company resides to see if there are any citations for illegal or questionable activities. Ask the principals for permission to obtain credit reports on them and their company; if they refuse, find another business venture. Have an attorney who specializes in business law review all agreements before you sign.

••

1. H. Garrett DeYoung, "Thieves Among Us: If Knowledge Is Your Most Important Asset, Why Is It so Easily Stolen?" *Industry Week* 245, no. 12 (June 17, 1996): 12-14.

2. Council of Better Business Bureaus, *How to Protect Your Business from Fraud, Scams, & Crime* (Englewood Cliffs, N.J.: Prentice Hall, 1992), p. 172.

3. "Mistreating Workers Boosts Employee Theft," *USA Today (Magazine)* 124, no. 2611 (April 1996): 6.

4. Amy Zuber, "Businesses Pointing a Furious Finger at Bogus Yellow Pages," *Nation's Restaurant News* 31, no. 19 (May 12, 1997): 3-5.

5. *Ibid.*

·13·

BREAKING THE BANK: IS YOUR MONEY SAFE?

He used my credit card with my picture on it! He wouldn't look like me if he put on a wig, makeup, and a dress!

—*Cheryl K., disbelieving credit card holder*

A CASE OF MISPLACED CONFIDENCE

I walked through the record store, flipping through the racks of CDs by bands I'd never heard of: Pavement, the Wu Tang Clan, the Reverend Horton Heat. I know I'm not a kid anymore, but my utter ignorance of what was hip and what wasn't among the recordings I was looking at made me feel practically ancient. Where was Elvis Presley when I needed him? Finally, I just grabbed a CD from one bin, and one from another, until I had about ten or twelve of them.

At the counter, the clerk took my selections. After studying them, he looked at me with a puzzled expression.

"You like Death By Metal?" he asked, fingering the ring through his lower lip. *Go ahead, say it,* I thought. *An old guy like you?*

"Uh, sure. Their last album was a real disappointment, so I'm hoping this one is better."

His eyes lit up. "You have their first CD? I'll give you forty bucks for it."

Uh-oh. "Uh, well, no. I'd really like to keep it."

He raised an eyebrow. "You just told me you didn't like it."

I coughed and cleared my throat. "It's like this," I said finally. "Even though I don't, uh, the music isn't that great, I have to keep it for my collection. *Nice recovery,* I thought.

He seemed satisfied. "Yeah, I can respect that."

Soon, he had totaled up the price of the CDs: $140.

"How do you want to pay for these?" he asked.

I whipped out a credit card. "This okay?"

"You bet. Good as gold."

Taking the card, he ran it through his register. Then, as he handed it back to me, he glanced at the picture on it. Then at me. Then at the picture. *Yes!* I thought. *Finally, a wary clerk!*

The credit card he held belonged not to me, but to my friend Cheryl. According to her credit card company, the photo on it was meant to ensure that only she could use it. The clerk didn't know it, but right now my camera crew was filming him. We were about to see just how fraudproof these new cards really were.

Finally, the clerk made his decision. He handed me the slip to sign. "If you change your mind, the forty bucks is firm," he said, stuffing the slip and the CDs in a bag and handing it to me.

Later that day, my cameraman and I tried our scam out again. We went to a nice restaurant for lunch, better than the usual quick-in-quick-out place—the kind of place where you could run up a bill.

Lunch was great. My cameraman had veal, I had pasta, and we split a bottle of Oregon wine. The bill came to about $70. When the waiter gave it to us, I made a great show of letting him know I'd be paying with Cheryl's card.

"Yes, indeed, I'll pick up the check here. My credit card. You do take this one?"

"Of course, sir, we take all major credit cards."

"Allow me to inspect the bill," I said imperiously. I wanted to make sure this guy remembered me. "Is this wine the one we were billed for? It wasn't the best, and I don't want to pay too much for it."

"If you weren't satisfied with the wine, sir, I can have the manager speak with you." The guy was really being nice and helpful.

"The manager? I think not. Well, I'm sure this is all correct. Take it away, my good man!"

The waiter returned very quickly with the credit card slip for me to sign. He left the credit card sitting there on the table, Cheryl's picture showing. Amazingly, he did not even mention that I was not the attractive brunette in the photo.

All day, this pattern continued. I made purchase after purchase in store after store, paying for everything with Cheryl's card. Each time I used it, I made a great show of flourishing the card. I did not attempt to hide the picture; in fact, I practically made a fool of myself to make sure people noticed both it and my own smiling face as I handed them the card. I had a number of stories committed to memory and all ready to go if anyone asked me why I was using a card that obviously wasn't mine. The woman in the picture was my wife, my girlfriend, my sister. But no one asked me—not one person.

After the story aired, I spoke to a man whose credit card displayed a photo of his dog. It was enough to make me think about going back to using nothing but cash.

BANK FRAUD TAKES MANY FORMS

Banks may be the most con-vulnerable institutions in the United States. In the not-too-distant past, bank owners and boards of directors merely had to worry about robberies, employee embezzlement, check fraud, and customer fraud. A crooked loan officer might grant a loan to a noncreditworthy associate for a kickback, for instance. Or a loan applicant might defraud the bank by exaggerating his earnings. Today's banks still have to worry about these things. But now, they also have to be concerned about credit card fraud, ATM fraud, wire transfer fraud, automatic debit scams, and attempts by con artist hackers to take advantage of every computer system they design.

Cons on banks run the gamut from the very simple, such as basic check fraud, to the exceedingly complex and creative. Years ago, a con man named Frank Abagnale walked into a bank to open an account with a $100 deposit. The teller gave him temporary checks for the new account, and instructed him to use the blank deposit slips on the counter until his arrived in the mail. Taking a large stack back to his room, he encoded his new account number with magnetic ink onto all of the blanks. The next day, he returned to the bank and placed the deposit slips back onto the counter. In one day, his account was credited with almost $40,000, because every deposit made that day using the counter deposit slips went directly into Frank's new account.

Today, thankfully, Abagnale runs a legitimate business teaching banks and government agencies how not to be defrauded.

....
CREDIT CARD SCAMS
....

Among scammers, credit card con artists are often the most difficult to locate, investigate, and prosecute. For one thing, the employees of stores they victimize usually have no idea a crime is being committed as they ring up sales on the scammers' stolen credit cards. Second, they tend to patronize stores where minimum-wage clerks haven't been properly trained in stopping credit card fraud. And finally, when a card they're using is refused by a store's credit card verification system, they can usually just walk out of the store before the authorities arrive, and before anyone can really memorize how they look.

The number of methods used by con artists to defraud credit card companies is astonishing. Some con artists pay willing waitresses and clerks to give them credit card information. One waitress in Boston, Massachusetts, made $100 each time she gave a particular con artist information on a new American Express Platinum card—name, number, and expiration date. She was making far more each day by selling customer's names and credit card numbers than she was making every *month* as a waitress.

Many con artists go to outrageous lengths in their search for credit cards, credit card applications, statements, and receipts. Office creepers invade offices, then wander around searching for unguarded purses that might contain credit cards or checkbooks.

Some con artists specialize in Dumpster diving for precious financial information at homes, retail stores, and banks. As these con artists can tell you, it's amazing what gets thrown away.

And other con artists steal new or replacement cards from the mail. (Thankfully, this is being rendered ineffective by new credit card company practices such as making the credit card holder call the company to verify certain personal information before the credit card will be activated.)

Some fairly sophisticated con artists make it a practice to actually call homes from whose mailboxes they've just stolen credit cards. When a con artist finds a credit card in a mailbox, he already knows his mark's name and address. If the mark has a listed telephone number, the hustler, calling as a bank employee, requests verification of important data such as the mark's Social Security number and mother's maiden name. Most card holders are not suspicious when they receive a phone call like this; after all, who else but the bank could know their name and credit card number, and that they were about to be issued a credit card?

A word to the wise if you receive a phone call like this: don't volunteer information about yourself over the phone. Let the caller give you the information he wants, for you to confirm or deny. Better yet: don't provide him with *any* information. Simply hang up the phone, call the credit card company or bank yourself, and ask if someone there just called you.

BANK FRAUD THAT'S AUTOMATIC

The greatest bank robber of the twentieth century was Willie Sutton. He robbed banks because, as he said, "That's where the money is." It's still true, only now you don't need a gun. You don't even need to be near the bank itself. —A bank manager, after a major ATM loss

In recent years, banks have become plagued by automatic debit fraud. Nowadays, many bank customers have their home mortgage payments, auto payments, and other monthly obligations automatically deducted from their bank accounts. The customer signs an authorization for this with the creditor; the creditor submits the authorization to the depositor's bank, and the bank automatically makes payments from the depositor's account to the creditor. While this may be convenient, it also allows con artists access to depositors' money by submitting unauthorized automatic debit requests to their banks.

In one version of this scam, the con artist requests authorization for a small automatic debit from a customer, then increases the debit amount when the authorization form is given to the bank. Because bank statements generally go out monthly, it may be a month or more before the victim notices that the amount automatically withdrawn from his account far exceeded what was authorized.

A popular ATM fraud is the cash-back deposit con. For this con, the con man starts by opening a checking account with the minimum initial deposit. In the old days, this con was fairly labor-intensive: the con artist would have deposited money to his account in a series of small checks, and waited for each check to clear before withdrawing money from the account; only after establishing himself as a good customer would he have asked for cash back on his deposit of a bad check.

These days, the con is much simpler: open an account, then deposit a bad check to an ATM; since the ATM immediately credits some or all of the amount of the check to your account, you can then withdraw the maximum cash back from that check that the ATM will allow. Repeat this procedure enough times, and you'll be making a more-than-decent living. One gang in Cincinnati, for instance, managed to take banks for up to $5,000 per day each via this method—for a total of more than $100,000 over the course of a few months.[1]

CHECK-WRITING SCAMS

Check-writing scams are a classic means of defrauding banks. In its simplest form, a con artist pays for items and services using bad checks—getting away with the scam either because he's using stolen checks, or has opened a checking account using an alias, or because he leaves town after passing the bad checks.

There are other, more sophisticated scams as well. "Kiting" checks has been going on since banks first began to operate. To run a check-kiting scheme, a swindler starts by opening a checking account. Next, he or she opens another account at another bank, using a bad check from the first account as an initial deposit. Then the con artist opens a third account, with a bad check from the second—and so on. Kiting works because of the two-to-four day "float" between banks, the amount of time it takes for a check to be returned and processed by any bank.

Some of the more complex check kiting rings open up checking accounts on both the East and West coasts of the United States, or even in different countries, so that the float can be extended to seven to ten days. Some swindlers have floated as much as $100,000 at a given time. But at some point, if the con artist doesn't know when to quit, kiting will catch up with him. Unfortunately, though, even if he's caught, the check kiter will probably only spend a few hours in jail, then will be free to continue his scamming in another city.

Another favorite technique of today's con artist is to go through mailboxes to find bill payments. When he finds one, the con artist removes the check from the envelope, then "bleaches" it by placing it into a diluted bleach solution. While the pre-printed portion of the check remains unaffected by this process, the pen ink on the check—the amount of the check, the signature, etc.—is erased. Some con artists can even manage to get all the handwritten information off the check except the signature, using a special apparatus resembling a developing tray for photographic film. And voilà—the con artist now possesses a signed blank check.

Finally, bad-check scams can be incorporated into other scams—for example, the sweetheart scam. Consider the story of Christian and Edgar. Deeply in love—at least as far as Christian could tell—these two men moved in together. They shared everything—including a checking account. Unfortunately, though,

Edgar turned out to be a bad-check-passing con artist—and when he skipped town, Christian was left not only with a broken heart but also a financial mess to clean up, caused by his ex-lover's fraudulent ways.

Many check-writing scams would not work if retail merchants spent a bit more time and effort on security measures like double-checking the check writer's identity or requiring a check-cashing card. Yet even with ultravigilant security, check-writing scams would probably persist. Some retail merchants would still probably be conned into accepting bad checks, for fear of offending regular customers. And it would still be nearly impossible to stop the con artist who holds a stolen driver's license or credit card bearing the same name as that on the stolen check he's trying to pass.

ON-LINE BANK SWINDLES

A good computer hacker can easily gain access to a bank's computer system, or to a depositor's system and account. Once the hacker is in, he can quickly and quietly cause thousands of dollars to be transferred to his own account. In the second case, for example, the hacker can easily make it look like the legitimate depositor is directing the bank to wire funds to the hacker's account. The bank has no way of knowing that it is the hacker authorizing the transfer, not the customer.

Consider the case of Herman Pickles. One of the first computer nerds, Herman helped a big California bank integrate ATMs, which were new at the time, into its computer systems. But Herman didn't just take a paycheck for his work; he also took home a briefcase full of individual account access codes, and knowledge of ways around the systems' security safeguards.

When his job at the bank was over, Herman began to systematically rip off its depositors. Taking only a small amount from each account he entered—a technique known as salami slicing—he slowly and secretly managed to transfer more than $3 million, over an eight-month period, to a Swiss account. After transferring that money to a Russian bank, he proceeded to purchase a collection of diamonds—which he then sold in Belgium for $4 million, for another million-dollar profit.

Ironically, Herman Pickles was caught for his crimes only when the mob entered the picture. The mob, it seems, had somehow learned just how he had come by his riches. And when Herman refused to pay off the mob to keep quiet about what it knew, the FBI was soon made fully aware of everything illegal that Herman Pickles had done.

CON ARTISTS V. BANKS: THE CONTEST CONTINUES

Every year, banks continue to improve their security systems—implementing checks and balances, asking for passwords or codes, and using other safeguards to protect accounts. But enhanced security systems only serve to challenge hackers, inspiring them to perform ever greater system-cracking feats. High-tech scams, it seems, are destined to be the wave of the future.

LESSON
....

In this high-tech world, it's getting harder than ever to protect your money and private information. Never provide your account numbers, PIN, Social Security number, or other personal information to anyone unless you know the individual and have verified that he or she really has a need to know. Reconcile your checking, savings, and credit card accounts each month; if there's a discrepancy, contact the issuer immediately. Never lend your credit cards to anyone and keep track of them. Make a record of when your cards are expiring and take note of the time of month when you usually get your financial statements; since con artists often steal financial statements to get account information, call your card issuer if you haven't received your statement. Shred all financial records before throwing them in the trash.

••

---

1. *ATM Crime and Security Newsletter* 7, issues 1–3, (January–March 1996): 10.

·14·

IT'S BETTER TO RECEIVE THAN TO GIVE: CHARITY CONS

Cast thy bread upon the waters, brother, and it shall come back to you twofold. Praise God!

—*Theodore Dewitz, fund-raising swindler*

....

PRAISE GOD AND PASS THE PAYMENT

....

Jim Harriman first heard the name Theodore Dewitz soon after he started his new job as controller at a small Christian Bible college in South Carolina. Shortly before retiring, Merlin White, the outgoing controller, sat him down to go over some key files. Opening the drawer labeled "Fund-raisers," Merlin pulled out Dewitz's file.

"Now Mr. Dewitz, he's one of the best fund-raisers this college has ever had," Merlin said emphatically, handing Harriman the thick file.

Adjusting his reading glasses, Jim opened the file. In it, he found a list of checks written by the college to Dewitz's company. In the columns next to that list of checks, other larger dollar amounts had been recorded—except in the space next to the most recent check paid to Dewitz.

"The first column is what we paid Mr. Dewitz," Merlin said. "And the second the amount he raised with our funds."

Jim studied the document in his hands. Check 8088, written by the college, was for $1,000; one month later, Dewitz had sent back a check in the amount of $2,000. Check 8105 was for $3,000; Dewitz's check of a month and a half later was for $6,000. And so on. The dollar amounts grew larger and larger, while the time that Dewitz took to raise funds with each payment from the college got longer and longer. The last check written by the college—in the amount of $35,000—had gone out six months before.

"We're expecting a return payment on that last check fairly soon," Merlin said. "Normally, the check arrives before we even think about contacting Mr. Dewitz."

Over the next few weeks, Jim tried to learn as much as he could about the college's financial procedures, at the same time getting to know some of the administrators and staff. And then Merlin White retired, leaving Jim in charge of financial administration. Merlin's retirement party lasted for hours, and during it, the college gave him an engraved watch in appreciation of his long years with the school. As he watched, Jim hoped he would have as warm a farewell when it came time for him to retire.

Back at work the next week, Jim got busy making sure he was on top of all the files Merlin had left him. The first one was the Dewitz file. He spent half an hour looking at the file, checking the amounts and the dates. Then, because something seemed not quite right about it, he called an old friend, Art Norton, who worked at another Christian college, to see if he had ever heard of Dewitz.

"Yes, we've used Dewitz before," Art said. "But the board decided that the delay between the payments was getting to be too long. They got anxious and pulled out. Against my recommendation, I must add. It takes time to raise that much money; I don't know how Dewitz pulled it off, but he did."

"Confidentially, Art, he's got $35,000 of ours. I'm a little nervous about it," Jim said, wondering just what it was about Dewitz that made his old friend so favorably disposed towards him.

"I'd be nervous, too, but why not just give him a call?"

"Good idea," Jim agreed.

When he dialed the number for Dewitz's headquarters in Stamford, Connecticut, Jim was connected with Austin Bolt, Dewitz's controller. Bolt told Jim he would look into Jim's concerns about the college's $35,000, then call him back.

Days passed. When Jim finally phoned Dewitz's company again, he was told that Mr. Bolt had been hospitalized with a major illness, and that unfortunately, Mr. Dewitz was out of town. No one else in the office could help Jim with his questions.

Starting to worry about the outstanding $35,000, Jim tried repeatedly to reach Theodore Dewitz. But Dewitz was never there. And when he tried to learn more about when Dewitz would be making the payment he owed the college, Jim repeatedly ran into excuses instead of information. During one conversation, an accountant told Jim the office's computer had contracted a virus, and they had had to erase the entire system; it would be at least another week before the system was back on-line.

Another week went by. Then another. Finally, wracked with worry, Jim called the attorney general's office in Connecticut. Not surprisingly, Theodore Dewitz was under investigation.

But before Jim could do anything about the situation, he was asked to sit in on a board meeting that had been called with very little advance notice. There, one of the board members stood and spoke. "Jim, I think it's time for the board to tell you something you won't want to hear. Last night, Theodore Dewitz called us with a fund-raising opportunity that was too attractive to refuse. We decided right then to go ahead and send Mr. Dewitz the $90,000 he would need to complete our new fund-raising effort."

Jim was flabbergasted. "But Dewitz already has $35,000 of our money," he said.

"We know that," the board member replied. "But this new money will generate so many programs."

Jim frowned. "If we get it," he said.

Standing, he told the board what he'd learned about Theodore Dewitz. The board's members were visibly upset to learn that Dewitz was currently under criminal investigation. Finally, it was decided that Jim would get on the next flight to Connecticut to try and track down the money Dewitz owed the college.

The next afternoon, Jim checked into a Stamford hotel. After dropping off his suitcase, he took a taxi to Dewitz's office.

Inside the office, Jim met a young woman, dark-haired and attractive, sitting behind a high counter and staring at a computer screen.

"Hello, can I help you?" she asked in a clipped voice that reminded Jim that Stamford really wasn't too far from New York City.

"Yes. I'm Jim Harriman," he said, producing a business card. "I'd like to see Mr. Dewitz."

She looked at the business card briefly, put it down and said, "You should have called ahead. Mr. Dewitz is not here right now. He's out of town."

"What about Mr. Bolt?" Jim asked.

"He's on vacation," the woman said.

"I thought he was in the hospital."

"He was. He recovered; now he is on vacation," the woman said, emphasizing the words "he is on vacation" as though Jim were a child. She looked at him impatiently, then at her computer. Finally, she sighed and went back to typing.

"Do you know when Mr. Dewitz will be back?" Jim asked.

Without stopping her staccato typing, the woman said, "I have no idea."

"Okay, well, what about the other directors? Surely there's someone I can talk to," Jim said. He leaned forward on the counter, hoping to somehow intimidate this woman. But she didn't even look up from the computer screen.

"Call back and make an appointment," she said in an exasperated voice.

"Can't I make one now?" he asked.

"Call back in an hour. The appointment person is at lunch."

Frustrated, Jim stormed out of the office. Back at the hotel, Jim waited until an hour had gone by, then called Dewitz's office to make an appointment. The woman who answered wasn't much friendlier than the one he'd met in the office, and he wondered if it wasn't the same woman. But at least now he had an appointment with Dewitz, at four P.M. on Thursday, two days away.

Next, Jim called the attorney general and got the names of the church colleges that had filed complaints against Dewitz. Then he spent the rest of the day calling the controllers of those colleges.

"Mr. Dewitz? He was one of our most effective fund-raisers," one controller told Jim. "Until the last time, when we sent him $20,000. We were forced to file a complaint after eight months of trying to contact him. Still, I trust Mr. Dewitz. He's been a little slow on payment this time, but he'll make good; I know he will."

Another told Jim the same basic story. "But there must be some logical explanation for this," she said. "He's just too good a man."

What was it about Dewitz, Jim wondered after hanging up, that makes everyone trust him so much?

Soon Thursday rolled around—the day of the appointment. But when he called to confirm, Jim was told that Dewitz was out of the office; the appointment would have to be rescheduled for the next day. The next day, Friday, the same thing occurred—Jim was told that his appointment with Dewitz would have to be delayed. Finally, on Monday, Jim received a phone call from Dewitz himself.

"Mr. Harriman? This is Theodore Dewitz. Sorry to have inconvenienced you. I've received all your phone messages; I would have responded sooner if I wasn't so busy trying to manage repayment of funds to the organizations that participate in our program."

Dewitz went on to say that the Cayman Islands bank he was dealing with was reluctant to disburse funds to America, but that he was slowly wearing them down with his persistence. He offered his sincerest apologies to Jim. "It was totally unnecessary to have waited for me," Dewitz said. "But now that we'll both be in town, how about meeting with me tomorrow so I can present a check to you for $250,000? That's twice what your college gave me to work with."

"I'd like to meet today, if possible," Jim said.

"Oh, I'm afraid that's not possible. You see, I'm in Kansas City. I won't be flying back until late tonight. Besides, I have to wait until the bank clears the funds to give you the check," Dewitz said.

Dewitz then changed the focus of the conversation, asking about Jim's background. It turned out that Dewitz had attended the same Christian college as Jim, before leaving to follow his real calling: fund-raising.

When Jim brought up some of the colleges that had complained, Dewitz calmly explained that all that was a misunderstanding. His rich, honey-toned voice mesmerized Jim. And the more they talked, the more Dewitz's voice seemed to contain a hint of a Southern accent, like Jim's. Maybe this Dewitz wasn't such a bad guy after all, Jim started thinking.

But when he went to meet Dewitz at the office the next day, it was closed. After waiting in the lobby for fifteen minutes, Jim began feeling panicky. He found a pay phone and dialed Dewitz's office number. It was definitely the right number; he'd certainly dialed it enough in the past week to be sure. But all he got was a phone company recording, informing him that the number had been disconnected, and no forwarding number registered.

At this, Jim became irate. He began walking around the building, seeing if he could locate someone from building management.

"Hi, I'm trying to get in touch with an organization on the fifth floor," he said when he finally found the manager.

"Let's go upstairs and check it out," the manager said.

On the way up, Jim told the manager what had transpired over the last few months. A worried look passed over the manager's face; Dewitz's company, she said, was three months behind in paying the rent. Because they'd been such good tenants until then, the management company had allowed them a grace period.

At Dewitz's office, the manager knocked sharply on the door. When no one responded, she used her key to open the door. "They're probably just taking the day off," the manager said. But when she turned the lights on, she gasped. "They've taken everything!"

Jim and the manager walked through the now empty office. It had been cleaned out. The rented office furniture, the photocopier, supplies, the coffeemaker—anything that could be moved was gone. Horrified, the manager explained that it had all been rented to Dewitz by the building.

Jim packed his bags and went back to South Carolina. Dewitz ended up being indicted four months later; his trial is pending as of this writing. Meanwhile, Jim is left trying to make the most of the remainder of his college's funds. He knows that when he retires, even though it wasn't his fault, he will be known as the one who couldn't save them from Dewitz.

Swindles work best when the intended victim, whether it be a church, a Christian college, or an individual, possesses a certain level of desperation. The greater the desperation, the greater the vulnerability to being conned. If a Christian college is teetering on the precipice of bankruptcy and someone comes forward with a deal that will help it stay afloat, it will in most cases be willing to believe almost anything. Unfortunately, this is something that people like Theodore Dewitz know all too well.

THE CRIME OF CHARITY CONS

In the end, the crime of charity cons is that they deprive such worthwhile charities as the Salvation Army, the American Red Cross, the American Cancer Society, the American Kidney Foundation, and the American Heart Association of funding that they would otherwise receive. Here follow just a few cases where money meant for charitable causes is diverted through greed, guts, and deceit.

THE PHONY CANISTER CON

Cops are supposed to be cynical, but I emptied the change from my pockets every day for two weeks to put in that can. A cornea for a blind kid? Who wouldn't give a few cents for that?
—*Willie Chambers, police officer*

Most of us experience a surge of compassion when we hear about someone who's been struck with tragedy. While this is a good thing, one of the things that make us caring and human, it also opens a doorway through which the savvy con artist can slip.

Often, when someone in a community has encountered a tragedy—a devastating illness or accident, or the loss of a bread-winning family member—other community members will take up a collection to help their unfortunate neighbor get through the tough times. Knowing this, con artists often take up collections that they say will help tragedy victims, but which in reality do nothing more than fatten the scammer's wallet.

Consider, for example, the story of Ronald Cola. A Brooklynite with a sour disposition, he managed to go so far with his con that he even tried to take the officers in the local police precinct for hundreds of dollars.

It began like this: One night while watching the news, Ronald saw a story about how a tourist couple had been helped by donations from New Yorkers after all their money and luggage was stolen from them on the street. Ronald was stunned. At that moment, he came up with an idea: He would tell people that his son had been shot and horribly wounded while an innocent bystander at a gang shooting—even though Ronald was not actually a father.

Ronald proceeded to place canisters soliciting donations for his nonexistent son in businesses throughout the neighborhood. Eventually, one of the canisters made it into the local police precinct house. Ronald was caught only when one of the local cops, deeply affected by the story of his poor, injured son, visited his apartment. There, he quickly learned that Ronald Cola did not have a son, that he lived alone—and that Ronald's story was nothing but a scam. Scattered throughout the apartment were hundreds of the donation canisters, each stuffed with money. Ronald Cola had taken in more than $7,000 in the course of three weeks—a crime for which he would be charged with felony fraud.

DISASTER AND CRISIS RELIEF CONS

When disaster befalls our fellow human beings, it is among our nobler instincts to help—to feed and clothe and shelter those in need, to comfort the sick and injured, to rebuild tragedy-stricken communities, or, in the case of war, tragedy-stricken countries. There is something about a disaster that brings out the best in people. Unfortunately, it also brings out the worst.

During the Persian Gulf War, phony charities suddenly popped up urging Americans to donate money to benefit the troops. Food and other items, the "charities" claimed, would be airlifted to the Middle East, then distributed among the troops. Unfortunately for donors, little if any of their contributions resulted in the distribution of anything to soldiers in the Middle East.

Floods, earthquakes, hurricanes, tornadoes: all of these help fill the coffers of relief organizations everywhere. The problem is, they also help fill swindlers' pockets. After the 1995 Oklahoma City bombing, Arkansas Attorney General Winston Bryant tried to alert the public to this fact. The following advice from Bryant's statement could be taken to heart by those who suffer natural disasters everywhere:

> *The attorney general's office in Oklahoma has identified a group as the one which called consumers promising that if they made donations to help victims of the April 19th Federal Building bombing, they might be eligible to win a cash prize. In another scam, telephone solicitors identified themselves as employees of "Feed America," which the office described as a phony group.*[1]

Don't be fooled by legitimate-sounding charity names. Check to make sure the charity you're donating to is in fact the one you think it is, and not a fake charity with a deceptively familiar name.

I know firsthand how easy disaster makes it for the con artist to score. During the recent floods in the Pacific Northwest, I went door-to-door to homes that had been devastated in the floods, hoping to show my viewing audience how disaster can make people more susceptible to cons. It wasn't hard to determine which homes needed repairs. In some cases, wet carpeting had been placed outside on lawns, to dry in the sunlight. In other cases, mobile homes had been pushed off their foundations by the floodwaters.

I approached these flood victims with a proposition. I could repair their home quicker than other repair firms, for an unbelievably low price, I said—because my efforts were being subsidized by charitable organizations. Overwhelmed with the generosity of the deal I proposed, homeowner after homeowner didn't hesitate to write me a check in advance of any work being done. Of course, I immediately gave them their checks back. Unlike most con artists, I had no desire to see disaster victims become scam victims as well.

PHONY PANHANDLERS

The world is full of panhandlers who make their living through sympathy generated by phony sob stories. There are plenty of panhandlers like the one I met who lives in a nice home in New Jersey but dons hobo clothes and takes the train to Manhattan every day, where he makes his tax-free living—plenty of con artists who spend hours on street corners, sitting in wheelchairs and begging, only to stand up, count their money, and walk away at the end of the day.

For one on-camera con for *Hard Copy*, I pretended to be a minister collecting money to help replace the stolen bells of a church in Guadeloupe. During the con, I noticed a real priest looking for donations down the street. At least, I thought he was a real priest. When I walked over and asked him what diocese he was with, he said, "Beat it, Mac, this is my corner." Another time, a lady in a wheelchair stood up and walked with me in exchange for a $10 contribution.

"Blind" people who can see, "crippled" people who can walk, "deaf" people who can hear—all of these stand on street corners throughout the country, preying on the kindness and sympathy of the generous American people.

• • •

THE MAGAZINE-SALES-FOR-CHARITY SCAM

Do not allow a lack of education or training to hold you back. Travel the country, stay in first-class hotels and earn a lot of money while doing it. Apply today and start tomorrow.   Ad in the classifieds

Not long ago, I was asked to investigate a story about college-age kids trying to earn a little money who wound up owing their souls to the company store. The kids had been hired to sell magazine subscriptions, and directed to tell prospective customers that a percentage of the money paid for each magazine subscription would go not only to one of three legitimate charities, but also toward helping the sales representative through college.

To help me with this investigation, a neighbor's seventeen-year-old son agreed to take a job with the magazine sales crew in question, which had been advertising in the local newspaper. Woody was the young man's name.

Although it was my understanding that applicants to the sales crew had to have proof they were eighteen, Woody was not asked for age verification; he was not even required to fill out an application. All he had to do was agree to travel with other young people, many of them street kids, up and down the West Coast, selling magazine subscriptions. His employer, he was told, would provide housing, food, pay, and a handsome commission on the sale of each magazine subscription.

One week later, Woody completed his third year of high school and joined the magazine sales crew in Portland, Oregon. My camera crew followed the sales crew as it traveled. Also, for Woody's protection, I gave him a cellular phone to use in case of emergencies.

Every day, Woody and the other kids were loaded into vehicles—sometimes nine or ten kids to a van—and driven to a new neighborhood. There, Woody would stop at each home as he walked.

"I'm working my way through college," he would say, as he'd be trained to, whenever someone answered a door. "Part of any money I make will go to charity. More important, part of it will help me get through school. Would you consider buying a subscription to any one of these nationally known magazines?"

With that, he would hand the homeowner a list of magazines: *Vanity Fair, Parade, Newsweek, Computer World, Popular Science, Popular Mechanics,* and so on. Homeowners agreeing to the sales pitch would sign their subscription applications, paying immediately by cash or check. Then Woody would continue on to the next house and the next block. The crews worked from sunup to sundown, every day. At the end of each day, Woody and the other kids would give the receipts to the area manager.

Instead of receiving commissions in the form of cash, the kids selling the magazines received clothing and shoes as necessary, with the rest of what was due credited to them on paper. Meanwhile, the cost of all their food and lodging was being deducted from their credited earnings—at top-dollar rates.

It was tantamount to indentured servitude. The area manager recording the workers' credits and deductions could write almost anything he wanted; and it was only very seldom that he would give the young people access to their own records.

But the kids weren't the only victims of this scam. When we checked back with the customers, one, two, and three months later, few had received the magazines they had purchased. Many had forgotten altogether that they'd even bought subscriptions. "Oh, well, it was for a worthwhile cause," many of them said.

These magazine sales rings, it turns out, are not at all rare. Our investigation discovered that there were several magazine subscription kingpins in the Dallas-Fort Worth area, all living high on the hog.

And from Denver, Colorado, we received reports of sales crews in which youngsters had been beaten and tortured.

Other complainants have reported sexual abuse and prostitution associated with the sales rings.

But few of the rings have been stopped. One reason: Attempts to prosecute sales ring leaders are hampered by the fact that witnesses return home or to the streets when their sales time is over, so there's very little chance for police follow-up.

GIVE GENEROUSLY—AND WARILY

Approximately 70 percent of American households contribute to charities. The average annual contribution per household in 1995 was $1,017.[2] According to the American Association of Fund-Raising Counsel, in 1996, charitable contributions totaled $150.7 billion.[3] There is a great deal of competition for charity dollars by the more than 626,000 charities that the Urban Institute says exist in the United States. To keep the competition clean, most states require charities and fund-raising companies (which, for a percentage of what they raise, will solicit money for almost anybody) to register with them even if their headquarters are in another state.

It's important to make sure any charity you donate to is a registered nonprofit organization. But even when giving to registered charities, there's no guarantee you won't be defrauded. While most registered charities are legitimate, many are borderline-legitimate, at best, passing along only a small percentage of the funds they raise to those in need. The National Charities Information Bureau (NCIB) suggests that no more than 30 percent of a charity's expenses should be devoted to fund-raising.[4]

The NCIB also states that philanthropic groups should spend at least 60 percent of their annual expenses for program activities.[5] If the charity you're thinking of donating to does not meet this standard, consider giving your money elsewhere.

LESSON

Plan your giving in advance before any requests are made. Decide how much you'll donate to your selected charities, and don't let anyone pressure you into giving more than you can afford. Check to make sure you're giving to a real charity, not a fake charity with a deceptively familiar name. Ask for written information on each charity, including an annual report or financial statement showing how their funds are allocated. Pay special attention to what percentage is spent on overhead and fund-raising. Then check out the organization with the National Charities Information Bureau and the Philanthropic Advisory Service. Call the secretary of state's office in your state to see if it's registered. Be very wary of any solicitation from an unknown party over the phone, at your door, or on the street. Don't ever be afraid to just say "No."

··

1. Esther Shapiro, "Tragedy Brings Out Charity and Con Artists Too," Knight-Ridder/Tribune News Service (June 27, 1995): 0627K8390.

2. Independent Sector, "Giving and Volunteering in the U.S." pamphlet. Washington, D.C. (1996): 2.

3. Pamela Sebastian, "Charitable Giving Rises, Thanks to Gains in Personal Income and in Stocks," *The Wall Street Journal* 136, no. 104 (May 29, 1997): A1.

4. NCIB, *Before You Give: A Contributor's Checklist* (1991): 6.

5. NCIB, *Standards in Philanthropy* (June 1996).

·15·

"Guaranteed" Returns on Dangerous Investments

I sacrificed my self-respect when I got greedy and tried to make a fast buck. I almost lost my wife ... you know, she tried to tell me. I should have listened to her before I listened to a scam artist like Jack Downs.

—Ben Reid, after he'd given away his financial independence to Jack Downs

CASH-FOR-CARS CON

Ben Reid eased the flexible plastic pipe through the crack in the back window and sucked the first exhaust fumes into his lungs. The catch in his chest and throat bolted him forward in the seat of the car. As he hacked and coughed, his eyes began filling with tears.

The tears, however, were not from the pain of poisonous gases now searing his lungs; no, these tears came from a pain much deeper—the pain of losing the life and the people he loved. His wife of forty years, Miriam, had recently filed for divorce. His three children were no longer speaking to him. His life savings were gone; suddenly, he and Miriam were deeply in debt. The Reids' credit was now shot. Since he'd been unable to meet the second and third mortgage payments against their home, it was gone, too. And the tiny gardening business Ben had started to supplement his retirement income was now teetering on the brink, because lately Ben had been too depressed to work. His life, which only months before had seemed so wonderful, so spectacular, now looked hopeless—thanks to Ben's greed and bad judgment and the help of a con artist named Jack Downs.

Leaning back in the seat of the car, Ben Reid took another deep drag of carbon monoxide. The second breath was easier. He felt a little dizzy, but not nauseous. He hoped this would be quick and painless. Certainly anything would be less painful than what he had put himself and his family through by sinking everything he owned or could borrow into Jack Downs's luxury car scam.

Out the window of the car, Ben could see the Portland International Airport—PDX. He wondered if anyone on the jetliner now approaching PDX could possibly have messed up his life as much as Ben had messed up his. Would the people on that plane have seen Jack Downs for the con man he was? Would they have listened if the people they loved warned them that Downs's scheme was just too good to be true? Would they have kept on borrowing and mortgaging and scheming, like Ben did, because they were foolish enough to think they could double their money in just days?

He decided they would not have. Nobody in the world could have been so blind, so naïve, so stupid as he, Ben Reid, had been.

Before meeting Jack Downs, Ben Reid had been a happy man. As a retired U.S. customs officer, he received a good pension check each month, which he supplemented with profits from his lawn maintenance business. He and Miriam were by no means wealthy, but they had saved well, investing their money in CDs.

Ben took pride in the fact that they could afford a new car, paid for in cash, every three years. Their modest home was paid for too, so they were able to vacation together while they were still young enough to enjoy the beaches and mountains of their beloved Oregon. Their three grown children and nine grandchildren adored them. Life was good. No, life was *wonderful* for Ben and Miriam Reid. They felt lucky; they felt blessed.

Then Jack Downs entered their lives. One summer afternoon, Ben visited a potential client's house to give him an estimate for maintaining the man's yard. Jack Downs's house was big and fancy, and his land elaborately landscaped; together Ben and Jack agreed on a rate of $125 per month.

With his usual gusto, Ben went to work on Jack's yard, returning once a week. Every time Ben finished for the day, Jack would come out and compliment him on his meticulousness. Pretty quickly, they struck up a friendship of sorts. They both enjoyed sports, and made it a habit to talk over soft drinks before Ben went home.

One day as Ben arrived, Downs was waiting for him on his porch, a big smile on his face.

"Mr. Reid, how's business?"

"Couldn't be better. The wife and I recently paid off our mortgage. We've got lots of savings. I have a nice business with lots of wonderful customers, like you, Mr. Downs. Everything's going really well."

"How are you doing on your investments and bank savings? I don't know about you, but I'm a little disappointed with mine. Three, four percent interest rates on a fixed income, that's not a whole lot of money."

"Yeah, I sure know what you mean. That's why I had to start this business. My retirement and Social Security weren't quite enough. It just didn't give us the kind of retirement life we wanted. Good thing I have a green thumb."

Downs laughed, then said, "Right now I'm making 100 percent on my money with a new business venture I'm involved with. I go up to Seattle and I buy expensive cars—Rolls-Royces, Lamborghinis, and BMWs, wholesale, for cash—and I deliver them to crazy Californians who pay good money for them. I pay practically nothing for the cars—way below Blue Book value. And in California, I can sell the cars at a premium. And the good news is that I don't even have to report it to the IRS—it's all in cash."

"Wow, you make 100 percent return on your money?"

"Yup, every month."

"Wow, that's really—I guess I just haven't done things smart. I've always had to work really hard for a living," said Ben.

"Last month I made almost $300,000. That's how I can afford this beautiful home, my Mercedes. I never have to worry about money again," said Downs.

"Do you suppose that if I gave you a little bit of my money, you could put up some cash for cars on my behalf?"

"Well, you seem to be a pretty upright kind of guy. Sure. How much money would you like to double?"

"I've got to talk to my wife, but I bet I can get Miriam to agree to put up $10,000."

"All right, that would be fine with me. No problem."

But Miriam was not as amenable to this idea as Ben had thought she would be.

"How much do you know about this guy?" she asked when Ben told her about Downs and his plan.

"Oh, he lives in a really nice house, drives a really expensive car. Why don't we just go ahead and gamble $10,000? We have plenty of money in our CDs. We don't have a mortgage payment. I'm making almost that much every two months now. I think it's worth a try."

"Okay," Miriam said, "but it's your show."

Three weeks later, Downs called with good news—Ben had just doubled his investment. Ben was so overjoyed that he got the first speeding ticket of his life while racing over to pick up the money.

"Mr. Reid," Downs said, "Congratulations; here's your $20,000 in cash."

"So," Ben said. "Are you planning on buying more cars soon? Any chance I could get in on another deal?"

"Well, I'll tell you, Mr. Reid, I'd love to help you again, but usually I only deal in large transactions. My minimum transaction is $150,000. The reason is that we have to buy whole car carriers of these luxury cars to take down to California. We can't dabble, can't buy just one or two cars at a time. I just did that last transaction as a personal favor to you. I can't really handle amounts that small anymore."

"A hundred and fifty thousand, huh? I've got that much. And I'd get $300,000 back, right?"

"Exactly. You catch on quick, Mr. Reid. And you're going to get *rich*. I'm going to have to find myself another gardener."

But Miriam hated the idea. Discussing it with her, Ben felt like he was running into a brick wall. A $150,000 investment would wipe out their savings, she protested—they would actually have to borrow some money from his credit union, and maybe a little against the house, to get that amount. It would be a huge, scary commitment for the Reid family—one she wanted nothing to do with.

For the first time in forty years of marriage, Ben Reid totally ignored his wife's advice. He borrowed the money, sold his CDs and, over Miriam's protests, gave Jack Downs $150,000.

When three weeks had passed, Ben called to check on his investment.

"Oh, everything's set," Downs said. "The cars are on their way to California. As soon as they're sold, I'll give you your money. But I'm glad you called. I just heard about an even more attractive deal. . . ."

A wholesaler in Puget Sound, just south of Seattle, Downs went on to say, had a truckload of Rolls-Royces that could be bought for ten cents on the dollar. If Ben wanted to play in this one, he'd have to come up with another $50,000. The good part was that he would get $300,000 back for his $50,000 investment.

Ben did the math in his head: a total return of $600,000 on just a $200,000 investment. He could not believe his good luck! The offer was just too fantastic to pass up. That much money would set him up for life. Even if he only got five percent interest on the $600,000, he'd still net $30,000 a year in income!

That same day, Ben went to the bank to borrow more money against his home. He took out a second trust deed. Only a month before he'd had no mortgage; now he had two.

Several weeks later, Ben phoned Jack to find out when he could expect the proceeds from his investments. Downs assured him that it was just a matter of time, that there had been some complications. There had been a theft of some of the cars in transport, he said, and one of the buyers had gone bankrupt after taking possession. But not to worry, Jack assured Ben, everything would be straightened out.

But every time Ben called him after that, Jack had another excuse. And then Miriam found out about the scheme Ben had bought into and hit the roof. Rushing to Downs's house, she demanded repayment of their money.

"Talk to your husband," Jack Downs told her. "It was his decision to make the investment. And by the way, this investment is somewhat illegal. Ben got involved because he could avoid paying taxes on it, since it's all done in cash. I don't mean to be intimidating, but if you report me for anything, I might have to turn Ben over to the IRS."

Miriam Reid felt trapped. She didn't know it, but this was a technique often used by con artists to blackmail their victims into silence. On the way home, Miriam thought about what Ben had gotten them into. Financially, she and Ben were ruined—at a time in their lives when they would never be able to regenerate their savings. Social Security and Ben's pension would never be enough to keep them afloat with all these new loans against their property.

Not long after that, the Reids sold their home to pay off the debt, moving into a mobile home. That's when Ben tried to kill himself. Only the actions of a quick-thinking passerby managed to save him. The thought of losing Ben rattled Miriam to her senses. She decided not to divorce him. And in desperation, she called the Portland Police Department's Fraud Unit, where she spoke to Mark Coffey.

When he interviewed Ben, Detective Coffey found him to be truthful. Jack Downs, on the other hand, not only had a prior arrest for fraud, but gave the detective the name of a nonexistent company when asked where he had bought cars. This information was enough to convince the district attorney's office to issue a warrant for Downs's arrest, on charges of felony fraud. At the invitation of Detective Coffey, my camera crew and I agreed to go along for the arrest.

But first we had to develop a strategy, a way to get Jack Downs out of his house, where he would be easier to arrest, and where we could get him on videotape. We decided that Detective Carolyn Wooden-Johnson would drive my Lexus to the front of Downs's house, where she would tell him that she'd been referred by a friend, and that she had a car she wanted to sell him cheap.

It worked. Downs came right out of his house and down to the street. However, as Detective Coffey, my camera crew, and I ran along some hedges to get a better view, Downs saw us and bolted for his front door. But Detective Wooden-Johnson tackled Downs before he could get back inside. Downs was read his Miranda rights and taken into custody. He pleaded no contest. Posting bail that afternoon, he agreed to appear in court for sentencing 60 days hence. After rescheduling the court date a couple of times, he finally just skipped bail.

Today, Jack Downs is supposedly traveling in gypsy con artist circles, using the same fraudulent cash-for-cars scheme that Ben had fallen for on new victims. It has been over a year since his arrest in Portland.

Meanwhile, Ben and Miriam Reid are left with the bad memories of this terrible time in their marriage. They live in a mobile home; two of Ben's three children still refuse to talk to him. Ben did not lose his life, but he did lose his life's savings. And even worse, he lost his self-respect.

INVESTMENT SCAMS

Law enforcement officers specializing in fraud hate phony investment cons. Why? Cops hate it when they can't get enough evidence together to arrest a crook, or when someone they've arrested eventually goes free. Unfortunately, both of these things happen far too often where phony investment con artists are concerned.

A few years ago, posing as a legitimate financial planner, Paul Rourke swindled Joan Stewart by convincing her to invest her mother's life's savings in jojoba plants—guaranteeing her a 200 percent return in a year. When Paul took her money and fled, Joan used a private investigator to track him down in Boise, Idaho.

Even though she has located him, Joan has yet to see any of the money she invested with Paul Rourke. The reason? One of the big problems facing prosecutors in securing a conviction against people like Paul Rourke is in proving that there was actually an *intent* to defraud in the first place. Were Joan and her mother victims of Rourke or were they just people who made a bad investment? Was Rourke a con man, or just a stupid businessman?

Unless the authorities can come up with legally binding answers to these questions, answers to prove that Paul Rourke had intended to defraud Joan Stewart from the very beginning, Joan will probably never see her money—and Paul Rourke will remain on the streets free to perpetrate his next con.

Investing wisely is a smart thing to do. Just remember: When somebody offers you a deal that seems just too good to be true, it probably is.

GOLD FEVER

It's a modern day gold rush—without all the back-breaking work, claim jumping and heartache of the 1850s. —From Gold Resource Corp.'s sales brochure

The stock market wasn't the only market that boomed in the 1980s. For a while, the market in gold also experienced a big bull run. And just as some con artists flocked to the stock market to victimize innocent investors, so did others flock to the gold market.

A bull market is an amazing thing. Lost in their greed, in the exciting delusion that their investments can't help but grow, people let go of their sense of financial reality. Tom and Edward Heathman learned this first-hand as the proprietors of Gold Resource Corp. Every day during the height of the bull market, their shop would fill with people mad with gold fever, all of them thinking just one thing: Buy gold. Buy it now; buy as much as you can.

What all those investors didn't realize in their frenzy was that the Heathmans were just as irrational and greedy as they were. Dissatisfied with just their commissions on sales of gold, over time the Heathmans became involved in a variety of scams.

First, they engaged in what seemed to them a win-win bending of the rules. When customers called in to order gold, the Heathmans would order the gold from their suppliers. If the market went up in the week it took for the gold to be delivered, the Heathmans would turn around and sell the gold to the investor who'd ordered it at the new, higher price—pocketing the difference between what they'd paid for the gold and what they'd sold it for, in addition to any commissions they made on the transaction. Because the market was relentless in its upward climb, and their clients seemed to make money on their investments no matter what price the Heathmans charged them for gold, there was no need to feel guilty about it. Never mind that the practice was illegal.

Then the Heathmans became more greedy. To feed his new cocaine habit, Edward, the older brother, displayed Styrofoam bars he'd painted gold to convince investors to keep pouring money into the Gold Resource Corp. offices.

Finally, the market peaked, and began an inevitable decline. Struggling to make payments on his own substantial investments, at this point Edward Heathman went from being the con artist to being the conned. First, he invested in a Nevada mine—only to learn, after his money disappeared, that gold nuggets supposedly found in the mine had been planted there by the swindlers.

In a final attempt to grab some gold somewhere, anywhere, Edward funded a gold exploration project off Alaska's coast. But the crew stole the gold, sank the ship, and disappeared.

The lesson of this story: don't lose your head or become greedy when investing, like both the Heathmans and their clients did. Remember: the offer that you seemingly can't refuse is most likely the offer you absolutely should refuse.

BOGUS REAL ESTATE DEALS

Have you seen this place? It sells itself. The view of the Columbia River adds 20 percent to the price of similar land without the view. It's too bad that this creep never really owned what he was selling.
        —*David Stegner, original owner*
                of land used in a scam

Possibly the oldest form of investment scam is the real estate scam. We've all laughed about the investor greedy and stupid enough to hand over money believing he's been sold the Brooklyn Bridge; we've all heard the stories about people who go to visit their new "gorgeous beachfront property," only to find they've been sold a worthless plot of swampland by a real estate swindler.

One such real estate swindler was Tom Stephens. With just a single pretty parcel of land on the Columbia River in Washington state, he managed to sucker a group of eager investors out of hundreds of thousands of dollars.

I first met Tom Stephens through a neighbor, Sam Bricker. A financial planner, Sam is naturally suspicious of investment opportunities that sound too good to be true. When he was approached by Stephens with a real estate investment opportunity that didn't sound possible, Sam contacted me. "Claims he's a doctor," Sam said. "But he sure doesn't look like one."

Not long after that, posing as an investment-minded entrepreneur, I went with Sam to meet Tom Stephens. Sam was right; he didn't look like a doctor. A tall, husky man with a sun-wrinkled face and dirt under his nails, he claimed to us that he owned a big piece of property near a town called Longview. According to Stephens, while the land was worth a couple million dollars, he owed only $700,000 on the property, leaving him with $1.3 million in equity.

Stephens continued, telling us his plans for the property. "I've subdivided the property into eighteen lots," he said. "And I'm ready to develop the land. As a matter of fact, I've already sold two of the lots—at $90,000 apiece."

He said that he already had all the permits necessary to develop the land, and that the road improvements necessary to develop the land would be paid for by the people he had bought the land from.

"Sounds great," I said.

"It is," Stephens responded. "The only problem is that I've run out of the money I need to do some well work on the property, so I need to market the lots now. If you can put up $300,000, I'll give you the second trust deed on the property. The development company I bought it from has the first. Then there'd only be a million dollars owed on the property. And it's worth $2 million, so your investment would be fully collateralized. I'll give you 25 percent interest on your money—$75,000—plus $10,000 for each lot I sell."

I did the math in my head. "Wow! That'd just about double my $300,000 investment!"

Stephens nodded. "That's right."

"If I decide to do this," I said, "who do I make the check out to? An escrow account? An attorney?"

"Make it payable to me," Tom Stephens said.

Right then, I knew for sure that he was scamming me.

I agreed to seriously consider the deal, then Sam and I left. Immediately, I started checking this Tom Stephens guy out. I did a title search on the property in question; I did a criminal background check on Stephens. Right away, my suspicions about his crookedness were confirmed. In fact, there were already three trust deeds on the property—not one, as Stephens had claimed. In addition, there were liens totaling $600,000 on the property.

In all, there was more than $2 million owed on the property. Even if the property sold for $2 million, there was no way that he could ever have paid my $300,000 back. The property he was offering me as collateral on my investment, which he claimed would have an equity value of a million dollars, was in fact worthless as collateral—already, more was owed on it than it was worth. Tom Stephens was a financial con man.

I proceeded to learn more about Tom Stephens. He was not a doctor. In fact, when I inquired about "Doctor" Stephens at the hospital where he said he worked, I was told he used to clean the labs but had been fired a year earlier. However, posing as a doctor helped him sell his land scheme. Already, I learned that 15 people had given him their money, between $25,000 and $35,000, as down payments. In return, they had been promised lots on the subdivided property, and in two cases, houses built on the lots. He had even conned a woman who thought she was his girlfriend, Mary Hatfield, never telling her that, in fact, he was already married.

After interviewing most of his victims, I went to confront Tom Stephens on camera. But he denied everything, covering his head with a coat as he got into his car. And my story on his scam never made it to the airwaves. When law enforcement authorities came into the picture, Tom Stephens ended up falling through the cracks in their bureaucracy, and eventually disappeared; I have not aired his story to protect law enforcement's pending case against the man.

As I write this, as far as I know, Tom Stephens is somewhere out there, free to continue conning trusting investors. It's an unfair resolution to his story—and, unfortunately, an all-too-common one, when it comes to phony investment con artists.

INVESTING: WORDS TO THE WISE

Savings and investments are the foundation of smart financial planning. Almost always, safe investments grow steadily over time; they are not ways to get rich quick. Remember the first rule of investing: risk is commensurate with return. The greater the possible payoff of an investment, the higher the risk that the investor will lose some or all of his money. And in a world where even solid blue-chip stocks can tank during a market downturn, imagine how risky other less common, more exotic investments can be.

Before you invest, you should always check out the investment opportunity with the experts. Visit a CPA, an attorney, or a certified financial planner; fill him or her in on everything you know about the opportunity. If he or she tells you not to invest, *don't*.

Also, avoid putting too much of your money into any one investment. Why? If the investment bombs, you're stuck—just like Ben and Miriam Reid. If you don't put all of your eggs in one basket, it's much less likely that they'll all break.

Finally, be aware of the tendency of cons to take advantage of bull markets. When the stock market exploded in the 1980s, all of a sudden there were countless new stock brokerages around. Many of these specialized in penny stocks; and some of these fraudulently lost their clients' money on worthless investments they'd assured the clients would bring huge returns—pocketing a sizable commission on each ill-fated investment.

LESSON

The greater the possible payoff of an investment, the higher the risk, so don't act precipitously. Always do your homework and check with the experts first. Anyone can claim to be a financial planner, so be careful. Contact the Securities and Exchange Commission (SEC) to make sure the party selling stocks and bonds is registered. Call the National Association of Securities Dealers (NASD) to see if there are any complaints against the broker or financial planner. Whenever possible, deal with a major company such as Merrill Lynch, Smith Barney, or Dean Witter Reynolds. Be wary of promises of huge profits and fast gains.

•16•

THE CON ARTIST OF THE FUTURE

The day is coming very fast when every cop will be issued a badge, a gun, and a laptop.[1]

> —Charles Rinkevich, Director of the Federal Law Enforcement Training Center near Brunswick, Georgia

··

PULLING A CYBER-CON
··

It was eight-thirty A.M. when Danny O'Neal unlocked the front door to International Data Processing Linguistics Corporation (IDPLC) and went inside. After turning on the lights and getting the coffeepot going, he made his way back to his office.

Since it was the day after Thanksgiving, there would be a skeleton crew in the office today. Danny would be the day's senior manager. At twenty-three, he sometimes felt a bit young to be the senior design specialist for IDPLC, but it was gratifying to know that his talents were appreciated.

Soon the front door opened, and Danny heard conversation echoing through the empty offices. In a few moments he recognized the language as Spanish. That would be Ralph, Esther, and Georgie, the morning health care operators; IDPLC ran a twenty-four-hour Spanish-speaking hotline for a California HMO.

Danny unpacked his briefcase and got organized. Currently he was working on a multilingual CD-ROM for a local software manufacturer. He was just getting up from his desk when Georgie appeared at his door. Originally from Lima, Peru, she had come to the States on a full scholarship to Stanford. Now she was in charge of Spanish language customer service for IDPLC.

"Hey, Danny, who's been screwing with our stations?" Georgie asked.

"What do you mean?"

"Come on, I'll show you."

Danny followed Georgie over to the workstations. There, it was obvious that someone had been through the office, tampering with the equipment. All the monitors and PCs had been pulled away from their normal positions. *What happened here?* he thought.

Then he remembered. "There were a couple of computer maintenance guys in here late Wednesday, cleaning the keyboards and dusting the cases." He walked over to an empty station and started to slide the equipment back into position. "Just push them back where they belong."

Those computer maintenance guys were Bobby Golden, a computer expert from the Gresham Police Department; Gilbert, my cameraman; and me. As part of a story about computer hacking for *Hard Copy,* on the Wednesday before Thanksgiving, we had gone into IDPLC. With the full knowledge and permission of Joseph Martin, the owner of the company, we had arranged to hack into them from an outside location. For good measure, we had also managed to find and lift some of IDPLC's check stock. No one in IDPLC had known we were phonies but Joseph, yet while we were there, no one questioned our fake work order or asked about what work we were doing.

Two days later, after visiting IDPLC—at about the same time Danny was making a mental note to tell Joseph Martin, his boss, what a mess those computer maintenance guys had left—I was sitting with my partners in crime in an office at Gresham P.D. headquarters. I watched in awe as Bobby Golden hacked into IDPLC's accounting system. Following my directions, he accessed the IDPLC check-writing program.

Laughing in amazement, we proceeded to write a check for $100,000 payable to *Hard Copy,* and then another one for

$10,000 to Joseph Martin. Using the check stock we'd stolen, we printed out the checks on Bobby's laser printer, then copied Joseph Martin's signature, which we had scanned from the company's annual report, onto the checks.

It was fast, clean, and easy. In seconds, we had shown just how easy it was to operate a cyber-con. And we had chosen to do it the hard way because we wanted to hack; a crook could have simply copied the check writing program onto diskettes, then gone home and printed checks on his own printer.

In the end, of course, we didn't pass any bad paper. We gave all the checks we'd printed back to Joseph Martin, then helped him show his management staff just how we had been able to hack into their system. When we showed him our checks, Joseph's expression was priceless. He went into his accounting office and compared ours with the legitimate checks that were being sent out that day. Neither he nor anyone else in the office could tell the difference.

"You could have cleaned out our bank account," Joseph said. He shook his head and sat down, realizing how dangerous hacking could be.

"And," Bobby commented, "If we'd used multiple wire transfers, by the time you had noticed that the money was gone, we, too, would have been gone, without a trace."

The computer hacking con I perpetrated for *Hard Copy* is, I am afraid, only a very simple forerunner of the sophisticated white-collar crimes that more of us can expect to experience in the future.

FUTURE SHOCK: HACKERS, "CRACKERS," AND CYBERSPACE CRIME

Let's work together to meet these goals: . . . every twelve-year-old must be able to log on to the Internet. . . ."[2]
—*President Bill Clinton*

As we leave the twentieth century, we are moving ever more completely into the information age. With every passing month, computer technology is changing, rapidly and dramatically. According to something called "Moore's Law," computing power roughly doubles every eighteen months. If that rate of change holds steady, it means that in fifteen years, standard-issue desktop computers will be 1,000 percent more powerful than they are today.[3] And while this, of course, translates to significantly greater power for individuals and businesses, it will also provide professional con artists with countless new and profitable criminal opportunities.

HACKING AND CRACKING

Today, it's already common for hackers to invade systems that were once thought to be impenetrable. A number of software programs are available that will enable the con artist to perpetrate cyber-cons. This software is available through news groups and Internet sites, where anyone can download it, free of charge. All one has to do is get on-line and type the keyword *hacking*, and instantly he will have accessed a list of hundreds of sites that give information—and sometimes, step-by-step instructions—on how to hack into other computers.

As each of us depends more and more on computers to store and regulate our financial lives, the risk that we'll encounter violations by high-tech thieves grows. Computer hackers have evolved into more dangerous crackers intent on perpetrating crimes in cyberspace. Sophisticated computer criminals have the ability to create thousands of financial casualties—all without leaving any kind of paper trail.

Today, the estimates for financial losses from computer crime go as high as $10 billion annually for corporate America, but not even the experts know for sure. The FBI reports that as many as 95 percent of all attacks are *undetected.*[4]

It seems inevitable that big-ticket computer cons will become more and more prevalent in coming years.

FRAUD ON THE INTERNET

Con artists have already found the Internet to be a rich new turf, and abuse of it will increase as it becomes more widely used. Even if you're not legitimate, it's easy to *appear* legitimate on the Internet. When the Federal Trade Commission conducted its Internet search on December 9, 1996, now known as Internet Pyramid Surf Day, it discovered more than 500 suspicious Web sites.[5]

On-line, business opportunity cons, pyramid and other investment scams, and work-at-home schemes are flourishing. In just the last five years experts have noticed a significant increase in fraud on the Internet. When the National Fraud Information Center first started monitoring on-line scams in 1992, it received twenty inquiries concerning possible Internet scams per day. More recently, it reported that it now receives 150 e-mails a week, and 350 phone calls a day.[6]

Another unsettling aspect of the rise of technology: as we become more tied to our computers and thus more physically isolated from one another, we might possibly become less skilled at reading people's characters. After all, most contact will be made via computer. Criminals already enjoy the anonymity of the Internet, where someone can be whoever he or she wants to be and easily take on a different identity.

DIGITAL CASH CONS

But the Internet will not be the only site of future cyber-cons. Today, most of us already use credit cards to make a variety of purchases, from food and clothing to vacation rentals and concert tickets. More and more of us are banking using direct deposits and withdrawals. All large cash transactions—paychecks, rent or mortgage payments, car payments—are already done automatically for some people.

Most banks have also begun to issue debit cards to their checking account holders, so that they can automatically deduct purchases from their cash reserves. More and more, we're moving into a brand-new financial world—the world of digital cash. In this new world, cyber-con artists are sure to find new scam opportunities.

SMART CARD SCAMS

Today, the smart computer con artist can already use your credit card to access your birth date and Social Security number. Meanwhile, more and more experts support the introduction of identity cards that would allow hackers access to even more information: your driver's license number, your employment information, and even your medical records. Not only could a con artist use such a smart card to drain your finances—he or she could also use the card to assume your identity.

By simply inputting a few numbers, a con artist can now access your driving record, your work history, your credit history, and your court records. The IRS, the FBI, the Social Security Administration, doctors, businesses: all of these already keep computer files on most of us. Although the proponents of smart cards believe that safeguards will prevent their fraudulent use, what the smart card will do is make a con artist's work easier than ever, by collecting all kinds of information about us in a single place.

THE CHANGING FACE OF WHITE-COLLAR CRIME

CON ARTISTS OF THE FUTURE

Technological advances won't be the only factor contributing to the types of cons prevalent in the future. Changing demographics will also play a role in the look of con artists of the future.

Georgette Bennett, in her fascinating book *Crimewarps: The Future of Crime in America,* discusses six social transformations that she predicts will substantially affect the way we live. Three of these trends directly address the white-collar crime wave:

1. There will be an increase in the number of older, better-educated criminals, including senior citizens. The number of crimes perpetrated by women will increase.

2. Crime will be freer of geography, thanks in large measure to the computer.

3. Less personal, more profitable white-collar crimes will become more pervasive.[7]

Due to the increased number of older, better-educated criminals, high-level fraud will increase; embezzlers and other swindlers are usually of an age and skill level that gives them access to positions of trust and power. They must be mature, experienced, and well educated, the kind of person one finds in managerial, administrative, and professional roles. In fact, banks presently lose eight times more money to employees and slick swindlers than they do to gun-toting bank robbers.[8]

The bulk of criminals currently arrested for fraud, embezzlement, counterfeiting, and forgery are between the ages of twenty-five and forty-four. During the next fifty years, the median age of the population will float within that range. What this means is that more people than ever will be of the right age to succeed at high-level fraud—or that more than likely, there will be more good con artists around than ever.[9]

Meanwhile, as growing numbers of women opt to pursue careers, criminal opportunities for women will also grow. According to sociologist Rita Simon, "If this trend continues, approximately equal numbers of men and women will be arrested for fraud and embezzlement by the 1990s and for forgery and counterfeiting, the proportion should be equal by the 2020s."[10]

WHO WILL CON ARTISTS
TARGET IN THE FUTURE?

According to Coates & Jarratt, a futurist consulting firm, approximately 40 percent of Americans will belong to a contingent workforce by the year 2020; instead of being on any one company's regular payroll, they will be on call for specific projects.[11] With greater job insecurity, more fraudulent job placement companies may surface.

With the future of Social Security bleak, and a growing portion of the workforce self-employed, individuals will have to rely more on themselves, and less on employers and the government, to provide for income and health care in their old age.[12] These individuals will be easy targets for investment scams.

As more and more members of both sexes remain single or marry later, there will likely be an increase in the number of personal ads and dating services, many of which will come into singles' homes via the Internet. This direct access will afford love cons an opportunity to find marks more easily than ever. And dating service cons, like one I investigated in which the proprietors matched prospective partners by throwing darts at pictures on the wall, will become more popular than ever.

According to the Census Bureau, more than a quarter of the population will be aged 60 years and older by the year 2025.[13] As a result, cons against seniors will flourish.

The older our population becomes, the more time we will spend in doctors' offices, hospitals, and long-term nursing care. Medical quackery and life insurance fraud will run rampant.

With a large aging population, there will be a tremendous demand for nursing home beds; as that demand increases, the likelihood of fraud against seniors with dementia and Alzheimer's will increase. Who will protect disabled seniors from charlatans who would take their last dollar, leaving them to die in misery and loneliness? Who will stop the forgers and counterfeiters looking to gain control of seniors' estates, who will be able to supply the official, signed paperwork for euthanasia?

Meanwhile, health maintenance organizations, which are focused more purely on minimizing costs and maximizing profits than traditional hospitals, may be tempted by dollars to make life-and-death decisions based solely on the ability to pay, and to forget about the Hippocratic oath. Consider the following: a name is moved to the top of the list for an organ transplant in exchange for an under-the-table payment. Possible? Absolutely, and probably already being done.

FIGHTING CRIME IN THE FUTURE

Law enforcement authorities will increasingly rely upon computer databases that contain extensive information about all kinds of cons and con artists. Computer programs will help law enforcement agents discern patterns in criminals' acts. We've seen how computers help construct ID sketches and help the FBI track serial killers; in the same way, computers will help the authorities track con artists.

But try as they might, the authorities will not be able to put an end to cons. The con artist will continue to rob us blind; he'll just be using different tools. To combat the ever growing number of swindlers, America's indifference to white-collar crime must change. More than ever, it will be imperative for us as individuals to remain vigilant in order to protect ourselves and our loved ones against cons and con artists. More of what we can do to fight back follows.

LESSON
....
While advances in technology mean greater opportunities for individuals and businesses, they also provide con artists with countless new

and profitable criminal opportunities. As our lives depend more and more on computers, the probability that our privacy will be invaded by high-tech con artists grows. Although it's likely that many traditional swindles will survive, high-tech con games of the future will depend heavily on getting past security safeguards. Individuals will have to become more vigilant in guarding their own personal security and fighting the white-collar electronic crime wave that rapidly approaches.

....

1. Vic Sussman, "Policing Cyberspace," *U.S. News and World Report* *118, no. 3 (January 23, 1995):54.*

2. William J. Clinton, "1997 State of the Union Address," *Vital Speeches of the Day* 63, no. 10 (March 1, 1997): 291.

3. Kristin Davis, "Fifty Years from Now," *Kiplinger's Personal Finance Magazine* (January 1997): 100.

4. Richard Behar, "Who's Reading Your E-Mail?" *Fortune* 135, no. 2 (February 3, 1997): 56-58.

5. Eric Sherman, "Why the Surge in Scams and Schemes?" *Home Office Computing* 15, no. 3 (March 1997): 19.

6. *Ibid.*

7. Georgette Bennett, *Crimewarps: The Future of Crime in America* (Garden City, N.J.: Anchor Press/Doubleday, 1987), pp. xiii-xiv.

8. *Ibid.*, p. 104.

9. *Ibid.*

10. Rita Simon, *Journal of Criminal Justice*. In Bennett, *Crimewarps*, p. 37.

11. Davis, "Fifty Years from Now," p. 102.

12. *Ibid.*

13. Bennett, *Crimewarps*, p. 57.

·17·

FIGHTING BACK AGAINST CON ARTISTS

You gotta understand, it's not what I want to do: I need to do it because I'm a gambling addict, and I need the extra dough to cover my losses. You understand, don't you?

—Mario LoPresso, swindler of business owners

STINGING THE CON

Renee Isengard was in a bind. Now that she was divorced, the mother of two no longer had the luxury of waiting for her highly specialized startup business to take off. Her long-term goals were being superseded by an immediate need for cash.

Renee looked out at her backyard; it resembled the stage set of an avant-garde play. Not long ago, she had begun a home-based business selling reproductions of antique outdoor furniture, gaslights, and other quaint furnishings. Until she could afford the rent on a shop somewhere in town, the backyard would have to serve as a makeshift showroom for her inventory. But now the question of whether she'd find a retail space had become moot. She had to sell her inventory—all of it—right away.

With that in mind, she placed an "Inventory Clearance Sale!" ad in the business opportunities section of her hometown paper's classifieds.

Much to Renee's delight and relief, a call came first thing the next day. A man wanted to look at her inventory, with an eye to buy. She gave him the address of her home in the suburbs, and he was there in less than an hour.

Mario LoPresso was a middle-aged man whose hair was combed carefully across his balding head. Dressed casually, he wore little half-glasses that he peered over when speaking to you. His manner was businesslike but friendly.

Renee's inventory was strewn all across her backyard: metal benches and chairs, light stanchions, all with a turn-of-the-century look. As he walked around, LoPresso made appreciative noises; occasionally, he stopped to ask a question about a particular piece. Renee trotted after him with increasing excitement, sensing that he was truly interested in the collection of faux antiques.

Stopping, LoPresso took out a little pad and began scribbling numbers. Several times, he walked over to an item, tapped it with his pencil, and wrote another figure. Renee's heart beat so quickly she thought she might be having an anxiety attack.

"Ms. Isengard, this stuff is just what I've been looking for, and I'll try not to insult you with this offer." LoPresso scratched a few more numbers on his pad. "How does $40,000 sound?"

Renee tried to hide her excitement. It wasn't as much as she'd hoped for, but it was a decent price. She decided to accept it.

LoPresso reached out his hand to shake on the deal. Renee eagerly took it.

Inside, over a cup of coffee, they finalized the details. *Great,* Renee thought when she saw LoPresso take out a purchase order pad and begin writing up the sale. *He's legitimate.* But then, when he showed the order to Renee, she was bewildered. It was from a dental office in another state.

"You're wondering about the dentist?" LoPresso asked, his glasses perched on the end of his nose.

"Yes, I guess so. What would a dentist want with this stuff?"

"Good question. The guy has more money than he knows what to do with. He's put braces on just about every kid in his town. So, he's kinda lookin' for a few places to put his money, and he's not particularly interested in making a quick buck. He wants to try a few ideas. I'm sort of his advisor. I've put him on the track of a few things, and when this came up I told him about it. So here I am."

Renee gave a quiet sigh of relief. "I'm glad you saw the ad. I didn't expect results so soon."

LoPresso shrugged. "It works this way sometimes."

When LoPresso left, Renee was overjoyed. Her problem was suddenly over, almost before it had begun. She didn't have the check in hand yet, but LoPresso had told her he would fax the purchase order to the dentist and she'd have her check in a matter of days.

The next day, a rental truck pulled up to Renee's house. In two hours, Mr. LoPresso and two burly young men got almost all of the heavy, more expensive pieces into it. Then, Mr. LoPresso shook hands with Renee again, wrote up an informal receipt for the inventory, and took off, promising to return that afternoon for the remainder.

But he never came back. And one month later, there was no sign of the check he'd promised. Finally, unable to wait any longer, Renee called the dental office number printed on the purchase order. When she reached the dentist, he told her the awful truth.

"Madam, I don't know how to tell you this, but I've never heard of Mario LoPresso. Somehow, he must have stolen one of my purchase order pads. I'm terribly sorry."

Feeling faint, Renee slumped into a kitchen chair. She'd been had—conned, scammed, grifted, swindled. By any name, it felt awful. She had lost most of her inventory—which made up most of her fortune. And there was nothing she could do about it.

Or was there? Suddenly, a voice went through Renee's head. *Why be a victim?* it said. *Why not fight back?*

Energized, Renee stood up and began pacing, deciding what steps she could take to fight back. First, she called the fraud division of her police department, and spoke to Mona Bellmore, who's seen and heard it all in the arena of fraud. Renee then filed a report about Mario LoPresso. Then, having seen my reports on scams on TV, she called me. After doing a little research, I told her what I'd learned about Mario LoPresso: He had committed similar crimes in the past, was in violation of his parole, and had a warrant outstanding for his arrest.

Reasoning that there might be others in her area who'd been victimized by LoPresso, she began calling others who had advertised in the business opportunities section of the newspaper. Sure enough, on the fifth call, she reached Crofton's Books, a bookstore across town.

"Have you ever been approached by a man named Mario LoPresso?" Renee asked the owner, Pam Crofton.

Pam gasped on the other end of the line. "Yes," Pam replied. "Why do you ask?"

"Well, a month ago, he ripped me off of almost my entire inventory," Renee said.

"Oh, my God! He just agreed to buy my entire stock today for $15,000. He said he had a purchase order from an out-of-town dentist, something about—"

"Wanting to diversify into new businesses, and using LoPresso as his agent? A Dr. Lawrence?"

"Oh, my God, yes! LoPresso's coming tomorrow to pick up the books."

"Good. The Fraud Division can meet him there."

The next day, Renee, the police, my cameraman, and I got to Crofton's Books early. A half hour later, when Mario arrived, he went directly to the owner, who was working behind the counter. Pam was very nervous, but she acted her part flawlessly.

"Hi, I'm Mario LoPresso."

"Well, I'm so glad you called. This is sure going to help me out. Cash flow has just really been poor. This time of year, not too many people are buying books, you know."

"Yeah, I know, business is really tough. I've been in business all my life; I've had similar problems myself in the past. Fortunately, I have a variety of buyers who work through wholesale networks throughout the United States, who are willing to take your books. Here's the purchase order we spoke about yesterday."

"Wow, I'm impressed." Pam gushed, taking the purchase order.

"Okay, well, let's get these books boxed up," Mario said, turning to signal through the door to his helpers that it was okay to come on in.

When the first box had been loaded on the truck, I emerged from behind the bookshelf where I'd been hiding with my cameraman. "Mr. LoPresso, I'd like to ask you a few questions about your business dealings," I said.

"Who are you?" LoPresso's eyes narrowed to slits.

"I'm Chuck Whitlock."

"I know you. You're that scam guy on TV. You son of a—"

Just then, the sheriff walked through the front door.

"Mr. LoPresso, we have a warrant for your arrest. Would you step into the back room please?"

THE CON ARTIST AND THE SHORT ARM OF THE LAW: IS JUSTICE SERVED?

> *Laws too gentle are seldom obeyed; too severe, seldom executed.* —*Benjamin Franklin*

The old adage that crime doesn't pay may apply to convicted rapists, drug dealers, armed robbers, and murderers. But most often, white-collar crime not only pays, it pays well—usually a con artist can do the crime without doing the time.

Again and again, we have seen the bad guys caught, and the good guys emerge victorious. *Dirty Harry, Cops*—according to TV shows and movies, when a crime is committed, justice is almost always served. Unfortunately, however, when it comes to con artists, real life seldom measures up to what we see on television or in the movies. Con artists usually manage to walk away from their crimes without any police cars in hot pursuit. They face no roadblocks, no all-points bulletins, no helicopter chases. In fact, no fanfare of any kind.

There are a variety of explanations for the fact that con artists and frauds almost never get caught, and the fact that when they do, they almost always go free or face a punishment that's not even close to just, given their crimes. For one thing, victims of white-collar crime often don't report the crimes because they are embarrassed and/or afraid of what might happen if the criminal finds out they've gone to the police. Other victims of cons do not even know they've been ripped off.

And if a swindler is caught and brought to trial, there's a good chance any witnesses against him will be senior citizens, since that age group more than any other attracts con artists. Which means that the witnesses will be more likely than most to have poor memories, bad eyesight or hearing, and other infirmities that may make their testimony less credible. And sweetheart scammers are especially hard to prosecute, because their victims usually give them access to their assets quite willingly.

Also contributing to the lack of justice served against con artists is the fact that all across the United States, police fraud departments are tremendously understaffed and overburdened. And then there's the fact that intent to defraud is hard to prove and time-consuming to prosecute, so prosecutors hesitate to file charges against con artists, or to extradite those who are caught outside their jurisdiction. And because they are usually not violent, judges tend to be lenient with white-collar criminals.

Finally—again because they're not violent—white-collar criminals are more likely than others to be released from prison early. The matrixing system is a perfect example of this philosophy. Under this system, when a county jail becomes overcrowded, by federal mandate it must release nonviolent criminals first.

In my years as an investigative journalist, I have seen far too many white-collar criminals go free or underpunished. Aside from those mentioned elsewhere in these pages, I could give you countless examples.

• There's Larry Nickelson, for example. After he conned the elderly Barbara Hammond out of her savings, a warrant was issued for his arrest—but he had already fled to another state, one considered too far away to make extradition proceedings worthwhile.

• And there's Julie Jones. After working for a couple of years as John Markham's secretary, this beautiful, tastefully dressed woman began embezzling the businessman's funds. Eventually, she was arrested, put on trial, and sentenced. But because of her "classy" appearance and sophisticated demeanor, the warden of her prison soon had her relocated to a halfway house; within months, she had left the halfway house, and a year later, she was arrested for embezzling once again.

• Or consider the case of Tony Shade. After siphoning some $170,000 out of the coffers of his local Masonic lodge where he was treasurer, he was arrested. But when the authorities tried to get the funds back, they found that on paper, at least, Tony was broke. By transferring everything he'd stolen to his wife, then divorcing her, he'd made the funds legally inaccessible.

• Finally, consider the case of Jane White. After marrying a meek elderly man, she managed to bilk him out of more than $200,000. But when she was arrested, she managed to remain free by offering restitution of $100,000. Because no one was injured by her crime, and because she returned half the money she'd stolen, the judge decided just to put her on probation— a sad but common story in southern California, according to my friend Detective Coffey, at least when it comes to fraud cases dealing with less than $1 million.

FIGHTING BACK AGAINST CON ARTISTS

All this doesn't mean there's nothing we can do to fight back against con artists or to protect ourselves from being conned in the first place. Like Renee Isengard, we can be proactive in the fight against white-collar crime.

Some of my favorite con stories are about con artists who, in a moment of weakness, allowed themselves to be conned. There's something I love about the way these con artists were hit where they live. And I like the way these stories show that, rather than being criminal geniuses, most con artists can succumb to human weaknesses, such as greed, just like you and me.

One of my favorite stories took place in New York City. There, the police targeted several types of criminals, including con artists, for a sting operation. First, the police set up a sham state bureau, the New York Division of Unclaimed Funds. Next, the "NYDUF" sent out letters to the last known addresses of 3,000 criminals, telling them that they were owed money due to bank error, inheritance, or government miscalculation. The money had to be claimed in person, the letter stated, so as to verify the identities of the recipients of the funds.[1]

Nearly 10 percent of the fugitives responded, showing up with their letters at the fake NYDUF office the police had set up, complete with undercover policemen playing the roles of receptionists and janitors. When they got there, the fugitives learned that they were being detained on outstanding warrants for their arrest.[2]

One con artist living in New Mexico had called the phone number listed on the letter three times trying to find out how much money he had coming to him. When this "lucky" man found out he was owed $6,000, he hopped on a bus and traveled the 3,000 miles to collect his money. Like the others who answered the letter, when he showed up, he was busted immediately. To add insult to injury, he received an additional narcotics charge for the bag of marijuana in his pocket.[3]

Another man tried in vain to outsmart the NYDUF by pretending to be the recipient of one of the letters. When he tried to claim his money, he was arrested for fraud.[4]

Another time, the New York Police Department worked a similar sting operation. They contacted fugitives from justice and told them that they'd been selected to meet star players from N.Y.'s beloved Yankees. The results that time were equally impressive.

RULES TO LIVE BY

Every time I go undercover to confront a con artist, I am basically operating a sting. In effect, I'm conning the cons—whether I'm posing as an ignorant motorist at a crooked auto repair shop or as a potential investor in a fraudulent real estate scheme. Every time I go undercover like this, I learn the same thing: just like you and me, the typical con man has his weaknesses; he, too, can be had.

While it may be difficult for you, the reader, to go so far as the police or I may go, there are still steps you can take to fight back against con artists, and to avoid being conned in the first place.

• *Trust your gut instincts.* Many of the people I've conned for the camera have told me they knew in their gut that something was wrong. They just didn't listen to their instincts. Make sure you listen to yours.

• *Do your homework.* Some con artists try to lend themselves credibility by hanging certificates from leading universities, or photos of famous people with personal inscriptions, on their walls. Clever con artists weave their stories with half truths; for example, Charles Keating's sales representatives at Lincoln Savings & Loan told depositors that deposits in the past had all been insured, that none of their depositors had ever lost a red cent, and that they would receive a much higher yield by switching from regular FDIC-insured deposits to bonds. All of which was absolutely true.

What the salespeople failed to mention was that the bonds were not guaranteed. By omitting some important information, Lincoln Savings & Loan was able to divert millions of dollars into noninsured investments. All of the depositors could have done their homework and learned that that was true—but many of them didn't.

To protect yourself, always go beyond the first level of information given to you in your investigation. Swindlers will often construct a first level of legitimacy, but they rarely go further than that. This is why it is so important to perform due diligence, whether investing in a company or preparing to hire someone. Ask for licenses, bonds, and references from contractors, to verify they are who they say they are.

Check to see that the contractor, businessperson, or financial advisor has been in business in your area for more than a short while; con artists have itchy feet, and someone who's been in business locally for only a short time is somewhat more likely than others to end up being crooked. Always investigate before you invest; make every effort to independently confirm what you've been told. Use independent experts to help you as needed.

• *Jealously guard your personal information.* Your Social Security number, bank account information, credit card information, driver's license number, phone number, and birth date should be protected and given out only after you've verified who the people are who are requesting it and why they need it.

• *Be wary of strangers or new friends who try to ingratiate themselves with you too quickly.* If a relative stranger begins to offer you dreams that seem too good to be true, be wary of him or her. If someone wants to get too close too soon, back off and give yourself some breathing space.

• *Be aware of your emotional vulnerability.* When somebody you love has just died, it's relatively easy for a funeral salesman to up-sell you—that is, to take advantage of your feelings and get you to spend more money than you want to. Stop and think about what kinds of pressures you're under. If you find yourself depressed or in a desperate situation and someone offers you an instant remedy, a red flag should immediately go up in your mind.

• *Don't jump into things.* To avoid being conned, it's important to stay focused and remain calm. Following natural disasters such as tornadoes, hurricanes and floods, gypsy home repair crews invariably appear out of the woodwork. Very often, unfortunately, these freelance repair crews do slipshod and even dangerous work. Rather than rushing to get your home fixed, you'd be better off to stick with established contractors. At the very least, make a quick check with your local Better Business Bureau and your state's consumer affairs agency before hiring someone. Better still, check with the state licensing board. It's been said before, but it bears repeating: Patience is a virtue in foiling swindlers.

• *Don't succumb to pressure tactics.* If someone insists you make a decision immediately, the odds are good that there is something fishy going on. Swindlers are very good at creating an atmosphere of urgency or panic to compel their victims to act quickly, so they won't seek second opinions.

One con artist I interviewed told me how he'd enter victims' homes by representing himself as being associated with a local air-conditioning and heating company. First, he would offer a free inspection of his mark's furnace and air conditioner. Then he'd go to the basement, where he would squirt the ceiling with water. Showing the homeowner that she had leaking pipes, he'd insist that time was of the essence—the longer the homeowner waited, he'd claim, the more extensive the damage would become. Fortunately, *he* could fix it right away—for a fee.

He would then bring some pipes in, along with some tools, and pretend to work in the basement. Of course, he never did any real repair work, because there was never a real problem. But he would charge his marks as much as $1,800. Had his marks simply not panicked but called a plumber for a second opinion, they would have protected themselves from being scammed.

• *Don't part with your money, assets, or other goods prematurely when concluding a business deal.* Wait until checks clear before considering a deal done. We've already seen from Renee Isengard what can happen when you give up possession of goods you're selling before payment has been made; she would have avoided trouble altogether if she'd insisted on a check from Mario LoPresso, then waited for it to clear—or if she'd insisted on a certified check—before letting him cart away all her faux antiques.

By the same token, if you're purchasing something, insist on taking possession of the merchandise at the same time you deliver payment—don't give con artists the chance to take your money and leave town before delivering goods as promised.

• *Get it in writing.* Avoid handshake deals. Good cons avoid written agreement or contracts, because they avoid creating evidence that can be used against them in court.

• *Don't participate in any illegal schemes.* No quick fix can take the place of hard work, good planning, and practical solutions. A con artist may promise you immediate relief for your problems, but so-called easy money isn't the solution.

• *Most important, remember: If it sounds too good to be true, it probably is.*

• *Contact the authorities.* If you've been conned, suspect you're being conned, or just know about a con, call the police. Even if you think you'll never see your money again, it's worth it to make the call. Your information may be just what fraud officers need to establish a con artist's pattern, and may result in an immediate arrest or in an arrest some time in the future. You may get some restitution, and you'll definitely be doing your civic duty, helping make society a safer, better place.

Scams have been with us since the beginning of time. And they'll be with us to the end of time. Until we all develop ESP, we will never be able to say with certainty just what the intentions are of the other people in our lives. In the end, vigilance is the main weapon we can have in the fight against con artists. Each of us must always be personally responsible for protecting ourselves and our loved ones from white-collar crime.

In closing, I hope these lessons, and others you learned in *Scam School,* will protect you for years to come.

---

1. Murray Weiss, "Sting Sticks Fugitives with Chance to 'Check' Out Jail," *New York Post* (February 4, 1997): 6.

2. *Ibid.*

3. *Ibid.*

4. *Ibid.*

FINAL EXAM
• • • • • • • • • • • • • •

1. A con artist usually
    a. has good verbal skills.
    b. is friendly.
    c. insists on a quick decision.
    d. offers a deal that is almost impossible to turn down.
    e. All of the above.

2. John was diagnosed with terminal cancer and told to get his affairs in order. He read in a homeopathic magazine about a nitric acid patch that killed tumors. The product was endorsed by a well-known celebrity. The ad also included scores of impressive testimonials from people who claimed that the patch saved their lives. What should John do?
    a. Send in his $299 and try the patch. What has he got to lose?
    b. Call his doctor for his professional opinion on the product.
    c. Check out the product with the FDA to see if the product is approved and if there are any complaints about the product.
    d. b and c

3. Why do people play three-card monte or the shell game?
    a. They see the shill make a lot of easy money
    b. Pure greed.
    c. People are drawn in by the excitement of the game.
    d. All of the above.

4. **Your roof was damaged in a wind storm. You select the name of a roofing contractor from several advertisements in your local paper. After inspecting your roof damage, he estimates it will cost about $2,200 to repair. He requires you to pay him $1,100 in advance for materials. You need the roof repaired immediately. What should you do?**

    a.   Pay the contractor the up-front fee and have him repair the roof.

    b.   Call two other contractors for bids.

    c.   Check all contractors' references, licenses, and bonds. Call the Better Business Bureau and your state's contractors board for any complaints against a contractor.

    d.   b and c

5. **What can you do to make it difficult for a con artist to assume your identity?**

    a.   Nothing.

    b.   Give your bank account information to a telemarketer if required.

    c.   Have a listed phone number.

    d.   Shred all personal documents before placing them in the garbage and do not put outgoing mail in your mailbox. Do not leave incoming mail in your mailbox overnight.

6. **An FBI agent calls you at home and asks that you help with an investigation. In confidence, the agent tells you that a bank manager at your bank is embezzling money. He wants you to withdraw $5,000 and meet him outside the bank in two hours. If the dishonest manager is caught, you could receive a $10,000 reward. What should you do?**

    a.   Go to the bank and withdraw $5,000 as instructed.

    b.   Refuse to cooperate and face the possibility of going to jail.

c. Comply with the request, but don't go to the bank alone.

d. Notify the police about the call immediately.

7. What is a "circle of friends" con?

a. A con artist cons his friends.

b. A con artist cons his mark's friends and relatives.

c. A con artist continues to con the same people over and over again.

d. A séance.

8. Mary wants to earn an income while she stays home with her new baby. According to an ad in her neighborhood paper, for just $49.95 she can earn $300 per week stuffing envelopes. The $49.95 covers supplies and pays for the preparation of her independent supplier contract. What should Mary do?

a. Send her check for $49.95 by certified mail so she can prove that they received it.

b. Find some other business that she can do at home. Mary shouldn't have to pay to get work, and chances are good this home business opportunity is a scam.

c. Pay the $49.95 in installment payments.

d. Since the couple can easily recover any up-front fees after the first week, Mary's husband should also pay $49.95 so that together they can make $600 per week.

9. What is the sweetheart con?

a. A con artist prostitutes herself, then kills the mark.

b. A con artist pretends to love his/her mark so he/she can steal from him/her.

c. A con artist stalks someone he/she loves.

d. a and c

10. You receive a post card informing you that you've won a travel sweepstakes. The post card shows a toll-free 800 number to call for details. When you call, you're told that in order to collect your prizes you first have to join a travel club which discounts fares, rental cars, and hotel stays. What should you do?

    a.   Ask what the prizes are and how much it costs to join the travel club.

    b.   Throw away the post card and forget about the prizes. You shouldn't have to join a club or pay a fee in order to win a legitimate sweepstakes.

    c.   So that you may collect your prizes sooner, allow the sweepstakes promoter to send a courier to your home to collect your check for the travel membership.

    d.   Provide the sweepstakes promoter with any personal financial information he requests to speed delivery of your prizes.

11. Exaggerating a loss fraudulently on an insurance claim is a crime.

    a.   True

    b.   False

12. You receive a chain letter in the mail from a man who tells you how you can earn large sums of money by mailing one dollar in cash to the five people listed on the letter. His instructions are simple: You are to remove the first name on the list and replace it with yours. Make 100 copies of the letter. Send $13 to the mailing list company named in the letter and you'll receive 100 labels in about a week. Don't put a return address on the outside of the envelope. Stamp and mail your letters. What should you do?

    a.   Put your name and return address on the envelopes before you mail them so you'll know how many aren't received.

b. Follow the instructions exactly. Even if nothing happens, you've only lost $18.

c. Make photocopies of the letter for all of your friends so that they can share in the wealth.

d. Toss the chain letter away. If you participate, your name will probably end up on a con artist's "suckers list" of people who've fallen for scams and are considered easy marks.

13. What are the features of pyramid schemes?

a. They make nearly all their profits from signing up new recruits.

b. There is always a minimal up-front investment.

c. Monetary rewards are based on sales of products.

d. Participants never profit from the payments of others who join later.

14. Which of the following statements is/are true?

a. To protect consumers, there is a three-day right to cancel any and all purchases.

b. Charitable organizations are not obligated by law to spend a certain percentage on the stated charitable purpose.

c. A store must honor a consumer's request for a refund, even if the return policy is not posted.

d. Swindlers often use the credibility of respected citizens or celebrities to sell an investment opportunity.

e. a and b

f. c and d

g. b and d

15. What is the best way to determine if you (or your child) has a future in modeling?

    a.   Pay for a photo shoot and buy an advertisement in a modeling magazine.

    b.   Apply for modeling jobs with advertising agencies.

    c.   Put an advertisement in the paper.

    d.   Visit a professional modeling agency and ask if you (or your child) meet the height, weight, and other requirements.

16. Danielle and James have been living together for almost a year. James has established a good credit record and has about $5,000 in his bank account, but Danielle hasn't been able to obtain her own credit cards because of a credit problem she experienced a few years ago. She's asked James if he'll help her out by adding her name to his credit card accounts. If he wants to protect his assets, which of the following *shouldn't* James do?

    a.   Suggest that Danielle apply for a secured credit card. Her charges would be guaranteed by an amount of money she deposited specifically for the account.

    b.   Suggest Danielle open a bank account and get a debit card to charge against the assets in the account.

    c.   Add Danielle's name to his credit card accounts and accept responsibility for her charges.

    d.   Ask Danielle to get a copy of her credit report from the major credit bureaus. There may be a legitimate way to help clean up her credit files.

17. In the "phantom employee" con,

    a.   the employee goes in and out of the building undetected.

    b.   the employee is fired, then rehired.

    c.   the employee does the job of two people.

    d.   employees that don't exist are created so the con artist can collect their paychecks.

18. A carpet cleaning service phones your home to announce an attractive home service bargain: They will clean all of the carpets in your home for what they would normally charge to clean the largest room. The offer sounds good to you and you schedule the work to be done. When the two workers arrive, they suggest you leave the house while they clean; they will finish the job faster if they don't have to work around you. You should:

    a.   Run some errands and let the workers clean your home while you're gone.

    b.   Send the workers away before they begin their work because it's highly likely they want to steal from you.

    c.   Call the Better Business Bureau to see if there are complaints against the company; if there aren't any complaints, leave your home as the carpet cleaners requested.

    d.   None of the above.

19. How do credit card con artists get hold of credit card numbers?

    a.   By going through the trash.

    b.   By paying corrupt waiters, waitresses, and clerks for the numbers.

    c.   By stealing your mail.

    d.   All of the above.

    e.   None of the above.

20. How can you prevent the automatic debit scam from happening to you?

    a.   Have all of your regular bill payments automatically debited from your bank account.

    b.   Allow someone who sold you something over the phone to debit your bank account.

    c.   Do not give your bank account number to anyone. Check your monthly bank statement carefully and only allow your mortgage holder or well-known, trusted creditor to automatically debit your account.

    d.   None of the above.

21. Why is it so easy for con artists to walk the fine line between legal and illegal activities?

    a.   It's often difficult to determine between a civil matter and a criminal violation.

    b.   It's hard to prove intent to defraud.

    c.   It's difficult to decide if someone is just a businessperson who's exercised poor judgment or if their representations were intentionally misleading.

    d.   All of the above.

22. What should you do before you make an investment?

    a.   Independently verify what you are told; if you don't know how to do this, contact a C.P.A. or attorney.

    b.   You don't need to do anything.

    c.   Pay any up-front fees quickly so you don't miss the opportunity.

    d.   None of the above.

23. Most victims of con artists get their money back since most judges insist on restitution.

    a.   True

    b.   False

24. Confident that you've found a trustworthy live-in caregiver for your elderly mother, you return to your home in California. When you speak to your mother a month later, you learn that the new caregiver has asked for power of attorney. The caregiver already has access to your mother's banking and checking accounts and is in the process of selling her home. How might you have prevented this disaster?

    a.   By personally staying in closer touch with your mother.

    b.   By routinely asking your mother direct questions about her ongoing financial dealings.

    c.   By recognizing the signs of financial abuse by caregivers and others.

    d.   By asking a trusted friend, attorney, church member, or other trusted party to routinely check on your mother's well-being.

    e.   All of the above.

    f.   None of the above.

25. Prosecutors have a difficult time indicting and successfully prosecuting con artists because

    a.   it is often difficult to prove intent to defraud.

    b.   law enforcement is often understaffed.

    c.   juries are usually sympathetic to con artists.

    d.   a and b

ANSWERS TO SCAM SCHOOL FINAL EXAM

1. e	14. g
2. d	15. d
3. d	16. c
4. d	17. d
5. d	18. b
6. d	19. d
7. b	20. c
8. b	21. d
9. b	22. a
10. b	23. b
11. a	24. e
12. d	25. d
13. a	

Give yourself one point for each question you answered correctly. If your score is:

24-25 Congratulations! You have the ability to spot scams and it's highly unlikely you'll be taken by a con artist. Give yourself an A+.

22-23 Excellent. You are very knowledgeable about most types of scams.

19-21 Good. You are aware of many types of scams but need to be more cautious.

16-18 Fair. You probably know a lot about some types of scams but are vulnerable to others.

10-15 Poor. You may be very vulnerable to con artists.

0-9 You are highly vulnerable to con artists. If you want to avoid becoming the victim of a swindler, reread this book and retake the test.

GLOSSARY
· · · · · · · · · · · · ·

addict   A victim who is taken in repeatedly by a con artist.

advance fee scam   Any form of con in which a swindler falsely promises goods or services in return for an up-front fee.

advertising solicitation scheme   A scam designed to convince businesses to place costly ads in nonexistent or misrepresented publications. These schemes often involve solicitations that look very much like invoices.

air bag scam   The recent failure of insurance companies to offer discounts on policies for vehicles equipped with safety and antitheft devices.

assumed identity scam   When a con artist, using an individual's birth date, Social Security number, bank accounts, credit card accounts, etc., assumes the identity of that individual.

autograph   A con game in which the victim is cajoled into signing a slip of paper that is later fraudulently changed into a negotiable check.

automatic debit scam   The making of unauthorized withdrawals from a victim's checking account.

bail bond con   In this scam, the con artist phones his victim in the middle of the night, posing as a neighbor's friend, and says that the neighbor has been unjustly tossed into jail and needs someone to post bail. The con artist goes to the victim's home and takes the bail money.

bait-and-switch   When a retail establishment attracts customers by offering for sale items that are not actually available, then tries to pressure customers into buying other, more expensive products instead.

bank examiner scheme   A classic con in which the con artist impersonates a bank examiner or law enforcement official, then gets victims to hand over withdrawals from their accounts by telling them that a bank teller is suspected of stealing money from the bank.

bankruptcy fraud   When a person or business uses federal bankruptcy laws to defraud creditors. For example, a con artist might establish a phony business with the intention of running up huge debts, then declaring bankruptcy.

big con   Any confidence game in which the victim is sent to retrieve funds, usually from his bank account. Big cons are generally more complex than "short cons," in which the victim is bilked out of the money he has on his person. Also known as a long con.

big store   A place of business created to fool a mark into thinking it's a legitimate business.

blind pool penny stock scam   An investment scam in which the victim is persuaded to invest in a near worthless stock. The company's promoter buys the stock at a fraction of what the public pays, constantly manipulates the stock price upward with boiler room sales tactics and hype, and then, when the stock reaches its peak, sells out; the price then collapses and the victim is left with worthless stock.

block hustle   A con in which a hustler is selling goods (which may have been stolen) on the street for a fraction of their retail value; the con artist convinces his victim not to open the box containing the goods until the victim gets home, revealing the fact that the box contains nothing but bricks or newspapers. Also known as rocks-in-the-box.

blow off   Get a mark to leave after he's been conned, without arousing his suspicion.

boiler room   A telemarketing enterprise that uses high-pressure—often false and misleading—sales tactics. Often operated out of low-rent headquarters.

bull and cow   *See* swoop and squat.

bunco (also bunk or bunko)   *See* confidence game.

c (or *"the c"*)   Abbreviation for confidence game.

call-sell operator   One who sells long-distance phone calls, frequently to poor immigrants, using stolen phone access codes or stolen credit calling card numbers.

canister con   A con in which canisters soliciting donations for bogus charitable causes are placed in businesses.

card activation system   A recently instituted credit card security procedure. The credit card cannot be used until the cardholder contacts the issuer and verifies his or her identity, usually with a Social Security number.

cash-back deposit con   Using bogus deposits to get cash back from a bank account.

cash drawer con   A con in which the criminal poses as an auditor in order to exchange his cash register drawer, containing only a small amount of cash, for a store clerk's register drawer full of cash, checks, and credit card receipts.

chain letter   See Ponzi scheme.

check bleaching   Erasing the pen ink on a check in order to create a blank check, which can be filled in by the con artist.

check kiting   An embezzlement scam that hustlers play on banks. The con artist opens a checking account at Bank A by giving the teller a check written on an empty account at Bank B. Then he deposits into his account at Bank B a check written on his account at Bank A. He continues to float, or kite, checks in this manner for several days, causing both accounts to swell at no cost to him. Then, suddenly, he withdraws the cash from both accounts and hits the road.

chump   *See* mark.

circle of friends con   A scam in which the con artist takes advantage of the friends, relatives, and other associates of a mark.

claimant fraud   A fraudulent insurance claim filed by a policyholder.

COD scam   A con in which a COD package is delivered unexpectedly to the victim. After paying the delivery fee, the victim finds out that the package is empty.

computer repair scheme   A con in which the criminal poses as a computer repair person in order to steal valuable computer equipment and/or gain access to a company's confidential and proprietary information.

computer virus   A computer program specifically created to alter or destroy data.

con mob   All of the hustlers involved in a particular confidence game; a ring of con artists.

confederate   *See* shill.

confidence game   A swindle or deceptive scheme in which fraud is perpetrated upon a victim after the perpetrator wins the victim's confidence. The victim is led to believe that he or she will profit—sometimes illegally— from the relationship. Also known as bunco and flimflam.

counterfeit product   An exact replica of a product, including the genuine article's brand name and logo.

coupon fraud   The fraudulent use of coupons originally intended to enable consumers to obtain a discount or free product or service. Coupon fraud may be committed by making and using counterfeit coupons, securing and selling coupons illegally, or redeeming coupons for merchandise never purchased.

cracking   Infiltrating another party's computer system for criminal purposes. Similar to hacking, which is a more general term used to describe the passion of often innocent, frequently antiauthoritarian computer aficionados.

credit repair scheme   Any scheme in which swindlers promise to clean up the credit records of individuals with poor credit for a fee. These schemes often involve creating a new identity for the victim.

damage claim artist   A con artist who pretends to be injured, threatens to sue, and then accepts an out-of-court settlement.

digital cash   Money in the form of digital bits, which may eventually eliminate the need for paper money and coins. Also known as DigiCash.

dirt-pile scams   A scam in which the mark is given the opportunity to invest in a gold mining operation by purchasing a quantity of unprocessed dirt from the mine. Although the dirt is guaranteed to contain enough gold to cover the cost of the investment, in reality, the investment is virtually worthless. Central to the scam: The mark is told that it will take one to three years to see a return on the investment. This gives the promoters time to get money from lots of investors before anyone gets suspicious.

diverter fraud   A fraud in which drugs are resold in order to bilk an insurance company: a healthy patient fills a prescription at a crooked pharmacy, then sells the prescription back to the pharmacy at a small fraction of the cost; the pharmacist then resells the prescription at its regular price.

dummy supply company   A phony vendor that invents purchase order records, using them to bill clients fraudulently.

Dumpster diver   An individual who delves into trash in the hope of recovering documents containing valuable information such as computer passwords, bank statements, credit card receipts, etc.

egg   *See* mark.

el toro y la vaca (bull and cow)   *See* swoop and squat.

embezzlement   The theft of company money or property by an employee or consultant.

file segregation   Creating a new identity for a person with poor credit so that he or she appears to have a clean credit history.

flimflam   *See* confidence game.

foreclosure forestallment scam   A con man posing as a financial counselor promises to postpone foreclosure on a victim's home for an up-front fee.

foreign bank investment scam   A con in which swindlers falsely promise victims huge profits from investments in overseas banks.

franchise fraud   Any scam in which a franchiser defrauds a franchisee by disappearing with investment money, going out of business with the intent to defraud, misrepresenting the amount of training or field support he will provide, etc.

friendship swindle   A scam that starts when a con artist befriends someone, usually a lonely old person, ostensibly for altruistic reasons. The con endears himself to the mark by spending time with him or her; then, after a while, he begins to borrow large sums of money from the victim.

front-end loading   An illegal method of forcing a new dis-tributor to buy a lot of products, which he may not be able to sell, up-front, before he's been able to make any money.

gold brick con   An old-time confidence game in which the swindler sells phony gold bricks.

green-goods racket   A scam in which a victim pays real money for what he believes is perfectly made counterfeit cash.

grifter   A skilled career con artist.

hacking   Illegally infiltrating others' computer systems. Unlike computer cracking, hacking is often done not with criminal intent, but for the sheer challenge of trying to break into a system.

home diversion game   A scam that starts when two con artists visit the home of their victim, usually an old per-son. While one con artfully distracts the victim, the other scours the house, searching for jewelry or cash.

hot seat   A con game in which the victim is convinced he's been hired to deliver a bundle of cash, then per-suaded to post a deposit with the con to demonstrate his goodwill. The bundle of cash turns out to be filled with shredded paper.

house of cards   *See* Ponzi scheme.

impostor   Someone who deceives others by assuming or creating a new identity.

inside man   A con artist who receives the mark brought in by an outside man.

Jamaican switch   A con game in which the victim is asked to hold a bundle of cash for a "visiting foreigner" while the foreigner, who is really a swindler, goes off to conduct some business. The victim is required to post a small deposit as earnest money, only realizing that he's been had when the bunco artist never returns, and he opens the "bankroll" to find that it's been switched for a wad of ripped-up newspaper.

knockoff product   An almost identical replica of a product. Unlike a counterfeit product, a knockoff intentionally changes the brand name or logo of the genuine article.

loan broker scam   See advance fee scam.

long con   See big con.

mail fraud   Any scheme to defraud that uses the mail as an important element.

mark   A term for the target or victim of a confidence game. Also referred to by con artists as the egg, the chump, or the sucker.

matrixing   A system mandated by the federal government which compels the release of prisoners whenever over-crowding exists in a jail.

medical mills   Medical and legal professionals who work together to defraud insurance companies, especially in workers' compensation cases. The doctors solicit patients to file fraudulent or exaggerated claims, then purposely overbill, or bill for services not rendered. The lawyers then negotiate settlements based on the fraudulent or exaggerated claims.

medical quackery   Health care fraud, often perpetrated by someone pretending to have medical training or medical knowledge.

mooch   A potential victim, especially of telephone swindlers.

need-help scams   A scam in which the criminal tells a stranger that his wife is sick, his car has broken down, or some other tale of woe. The swindler collects cash, a check or credit card, then disappears.

never received issue (NRI)   A credit card scam in which a card is intercepted and stolen before it ever gets to the legitimate cardholder.

obituary hoax   A scam in which the con artist pores over a newspaper's death notices, then visits the home of a bereaved person. There, he may demand payment on a debt owed by the dead person, or he may try to deliver a COD package addressed to the deceased that is worth far less than the cost of delivery.

office creeper   Someone who enters a place of business with the express purpose of stealing cash, credit cards, and other valuables.

outside man   Also known as a roper or a steerer. An outside man locates likely con victims, trying to bring them into the con game.

paper accident   A phony car accident created on paper by con artists hoping to bilk an insurance carrier. Hustlers, in manufacturing a paper accident, often forge wreck photos, police reports, and repair estimates. In some cases, they even create paper vehicles by providing vehicle identification numbers of cars that don't exist.

paper firm   A fictitious company—often an insurance company—created to defraud businesses.

paper pirates   Fraudulent telemarketers who call businesses, pitching office products that sound like good deals on quality goods, but are in reality shoddy and overpriced. Also known as toner phoners.

the payoff   An intricate, classic con game. A wealthy mark is made to believe he's betting on a fixed horse race in order to swindle a huge racing syndicate. At first the mark bets with money given to him by the con artists. His trust bolstered, he is then encouraged to raise all the betting money he can. The cons then pocket the cash and take off.

PBX fraud   *See* phone phreaking.

phantom employee   A nonexistent employee created by a con artist to bilk a company out of paychecks.

phone phreaking   Using computers to infiltrate and tamper with a phone system, usually to place costly calls that are charged to that system. Also called PBX fraud.

phony invoice scheme   A scam in which swindlers send legitimate-looking bills for undelivered goods or services to businesses.

pigeon drop   A classic street swindle that starts when at least one hustler meets a victim and then strolls along with him, only to "discover" a stray cache of money. The con artist convinces the victim that they should ask a lawyer what they should do with the money until the owner is found or the money can be legally distributed. The lawyer (who may be another con artist or may not even exist) recommends that the victim must put up earnest money while the cash is being held. The victim never sees his share of the funds that were discovered or the earnest money again.

plant   *See* shill.

playing the doctor   Street slang for executing a diverter fraud, a scam involving a pharmacist who resells drugs. *See* diverter fraud.

Ponzi scheme   An investment racket in which the scam operator collects investment money, then pays his clients interest (or commissions, fees, etc.) by skimming funds from the deposits made by later investors. Many investors actually make profits early in Ponzi scams, but later investors inevitably get bilked, because the operator ultimately runs off with their investments and/or the scheme collapses. Also known as a pyramid scheme, house of cards, chain letter, and snowball.

premium diversion fraud   The fraudulent diverting of insurance premiums paid by policyholders so that the money will not be available to pay claims later.

premium fraud   A scam in which dishonest employers steal from the workers' compensation system by misrepresenting their payrolls, employee job classifications, or loss histories in an effort to lower their premiums.

professional claimant   An individual who repeatedly submits fraudulent insurance claims.

pyramid scheme   *See* Ponzi scheme.

the rag   Like the payoff, this is a con game in which hustlers rip off a rich person by leading him to believe that he'll reap a huge profit at the expense of a big business. In this con, the grifters claim that they represent a legitimate stock brokerage aiming to financially break a phony brokerage. After helping their victim to profit on several initial investments, and then gaining his confidence, they fleece him.

reinsurance scam   Undercapitalized reinsurance companies—often outside the United States—which claim bogus or inflated assets. Insurance companies using these firms, having decreased their reserves accordingly, are often unable to meet legitimate demands for claims.

reload scam   A scam in which consumers who've already fallen for phony prize offers are called back by fraudulent telemarketers and given a chance to be suckered in yet again.

rocks-in-the-box   *See* block hustle.

roper   *See* outside man.

running the buckets   A scam pulled by crooked house painters. The cons use two or three buckets of paint in completing their work, then dip others in a vat of paint, so that it looks like twenty or so buckets have been used, all of which are charged to the victim.

salami slicing   The illegal electronic transfer of small amounts of money from a number of bank accounts into one's own account.

the send   The point in a con game at which the victim is sent home, or to the bank, to get money.

shill   A con artist who acts like a customer to help another con artist win the confidence of a potential victim. The victim sees the shill win or make a profit, and thus gains confidence in the con artist's proposal. Also called a plant or confederate.

short con   A con in which the victim is taken for only the money he is carrying at the time.

shoulder surfer   A criminal who steals victims' phone calling card numbers by loitering near phone booths and peering over callers' shoulders. Shoulder surfers usually haunt airports, hotels, and train stations, where banks of phones are prevalent. The card numbers are often sold.

slip and fall artists   Insurance claimants who orchestrate phony falls, then threaten litigation against the owner of the property where the "accident" occurred, and file claims with insurance companies for bogus injuries. One of the most widely practiced insurance scams.

snowballs   *See* Ponzi scheme.

social engineering   When a computer cracker talks someone into revealing a secret password. For instance, a social engineer might phone a company's secretary and, posing as an executive, say he's forgotten his password in order to gain access to the computer system.

soft tissue injury   An injury to flesh, tissues, or muscles. Typically, these are sprains or strains to the neck, head, spine, or joints. The injury of choice for many insurance fraud artists, because they don't show up on X rays or MRIs and so are easy to claim without physical proof.

staged auto accident   A vehicle accident orchestrated to defraud insurance companies.

steerer   *See* outside man.

straw man   Term used for someone who profits by posing as someone he's not, usually in a real estate transaction. For example, someone who's paid by a con to pose as a buyer or seller in a property deal, who has no real interest in the property.

suckers list   Used by telemarketers, this is a list of people who've been conned one or more times.

sweepstakes scam   A con in which the mark is advised that he's won a large prize, for which he must pay a fee or series of fees before taking delivery. After paying the fee(s), the mark never receives the prize, or receives only worthless trinkets.

sweetheart scam   A con in which the con artist romances his victim in order to obtain his or her money or other assets.

switch   The point at which a con artist guides a victim into a discussion of the mechanism of the scam so as to make the victim think it was his or her idea all along. Also, to substitute one item for another, such as a phony item for a legitimate one.

swoop and squat   A staged car accident orchestrated to collect insurance money. The squat vehicle, traveling in front of an unsuspecting motorist, is forced to stop suddenly when the swoop vehicle cuts in front of it; the unsuspecting victim runs into the squat car. Also called *el toro y la vaca* (bull and cow).

the tat   A gambling swindle used in nightclubs. The con asks his victim to play a dice game, such as craps, with him. The victim rolls a regular die, but the con uses a tat or crooked die, which always lands on the number the con wants it to.

teleblackmail   Blackmail of innocent employees who've been conned by fraudulent telemarketers, often toner phoners. The telemarketers blackmail employees who unknowingly purchase supplies at inflated prices by sending them gifts as well, then threatening to tell their bosses that they bought expensive office supplies and accepted extravagant gifts from a vendor.

telemarketing fraud   Any scheme that uses telecommunications to cheat victims out of their money.

three-card monte   A card game con in which victims try to find the queen in a trio of cards. The victim is able to "find the lady" easily at first, because the cons bend the corner of the queen card for him. But the victim's luck quickly goes sour when the cons bend the corners of the other cards, use trick cards, palm the cards, or secretly remove the queen from play.

toll fraud   Unauthorized use of long-distance phone services.

toner phoners   Swindlers who use the phone to peddle poor-quality copy machine ink or toner to businesses at inflated prices. Term used interchangeably with paper pirates.

touch   The money taken or scored from a victim.

trash and dash   A scam in which bunco artists dressed as janitors steal valuables from a business. Similar to office creeping.

travelers   Groups of Scottish-, Irish-, and English-Americans living as clans who perpetrate home repair fraud as they travel across the United States.

triple-A con   A con artist pretends to work for the American Automobile Association (AAA). Stopping his victim, the con artist informs the victim of a bogus car problem, then offers to fix it for a fee.

WATS line hustling   A term sometimes used by the police to describe the activities of high-pressure telemarketers.

work-at-home scam   A scam in which the perpetrator offers victims easy, quick money for work, such as envelope stuffing and product assembly, done in the home. These scams usually require the victim to pay a fee up front to learn the operation.

workers' compensation fraud   The filing of incorrect information to defraud the workers' compensation system by dishonest claimants, professionals, such as doctors, lawyers, and chiropractors, or employers.

yank down   A scam in which insurance fraudsters intentionally pull display items or other store merchandise on top of themselves or others in order to file injury claims.

RESOURCES
• • • • • • • • • • • • • •

Alliance Against Fraud in Telemarketing (AAFT)
1701 K Street NW, Suite 1200
Washington, DC 20006
202/835-3323

A program of the National Consumers League, its member-ship includes consumer groups, trade associations, unions, and governmental agencies that work to provide education to the public and prevent telemarketing fraud. Provides informa-tion on fraud practices, distributes educational materials, and develops public service announcements to alert consumers to telemarketing fraud.

American Association of Retired Persons (AARP)
601 E Street NW
Washington, DC 20049
202/434-2277 or 202/434-6030 for AARP consumer issues

Membership organization of persons fifty years of age or older, working or retired. AARP seeks to promote quality of life for older people, targeting the areas of health care, women's initiatives, worker equity, and minority affairs. Also sponsors community service programs on crime prevention, defensive driving, and tax aid. Publications include books on housing, health, exercise, retirement planning, money man-agement, and travel and leisure.

American Bankers Association (ABA)

1120 Connecticut Avenue NW
Washington, DC 20036
202/663-5000

Seeks to enhance the role of commercial banks as preeminent providers of financial services through communications, research, legal action, lobbying, and education and training programs.

American Insurance Association (AIA)

1130 Connecticut Avenue NW, Suite 1000
Washington, DC 20036
202/828-7100

Professional association of property and casualty insurance companies that serves as a clearinghouse for information on the insurance business for both consumers and insurance professionals.

American Medical Association (AMA)

515 N. State Street
Chicago, IL 60610
312/464-4818

National professional association of physicians. Works to promote high-quality medical practice through dissemination of information and the activities of its medical ethics committee.

American Society of Travel Agents (ASTA)

1101 King Street, 2d floor
Alexandria, VA 22314
703/739-2782

Professional association of travel agents and others in the travel industry. Among other activities, they seek to promote professional and ethical conduct in the travel agency industry and facilitate consumer protection and safety when traveling.

American Telemarketing Association (ATA)

4605 Lankershim Blvd., Suite 824

N. Hollywood, CA 91602-1891

818/766-5324

800/441-3335

Provides services and information to businesses that use telephone sales to market products. Seeks to dispel the public perception of telephone marketing as "junk calls."

Bankcard Holders of America (BHA)

524 Branch Drive

Salem, VA 24153

540/389-5445

A membership organization of bank and credit card holders that works to educate the public about the wise and careful use of credit. Conducts educational programs and surveys, monitors economic trends, and makes public service announcements promoting credit awareness.

Business Products Industry Association (BPIA)

301 N. Fairfax Street

Alexandria, VA 22314

703/549-9040

Industry association of manufacturers, manufacturers' representatives, wholesalers, and retailers dealing in office products, furniture, and machines. BPIA sponsors seminars, conducts research, and publishes an annual directory of its membership that includes a buyer's guide covering 554 product categories.

Business Technology Association (BTA)
12411 Wornall Road
Kansas City, MO 64145
816/941-3100

This association of retailers and suppliers of office machines offers seminars and conducts research. Provides information on returning unordered supplies and other related business fraud.

Consumer Federation of America (CFA)
1424 16th Street NW, Suite 604
Washington, DC 20036
202/387-6121

An organization of consumer groups and protection agencies that disseminates information on consumer issues and serves as an advocate for consumer rights.

Consumer Product Safety Commission (CPSC)
4330 Eastwest Highway
Bethesda, MD 20207
800/638-CPSC
800/638-8270 (TDD Line)

An independent federal regulatory agency that seeks to protect consumers from dangerous products. The agency has information on product-related injuries, recalls, and public safety, and conducts outreach programs for consumers, industry, and local governments. Consumers can also file product-related complaints.

Consumer Sourcebook
AnnaMarie Sheldon and Deborah J. Unterer, editors
Gale Research Inc.
800/877-GALE

A subject guide to approximately 7,000 federal, state, and local government agencies and offices; national, regional, and grassroots associations and organizations; and information centers, clearinghouses, and related consumer resources. Most larger libraries have this book in their reference collections.

Consumer's Resource Handbook

U.S. Office of Consumer Affairs
Consumer Information Center
Pueblo, CO 81009

A publication by the U.S. Office of Consumer Affairs that includes tips on getting the most for your money, how to prevent credit card fraud, and how to protect your privacy. It also lists offices one can contact for help with consumer problems. A single copy is available by writing to the above address.

Consumers Union of the United States, Inc. (CU)

101 Truman Avenue
Yonkers, NY 10703-1057
914/378-2000

CU is a nonprofit, independent organization that researches and tests consumer goods and services and disseminates the results in its monthly magazine, *Consumer Reports,* as well as other publications and media.

Council of Better Business Bureaus (CBBB)

4200 Wilson Boulevard, Suite 800
Arlington, VA 22203
703/276-0100

The CBBB is supported by local Better Business Bureaus and their membership of more than 240,000 businesses. It serves as a spokesperson for business in the consumer field, supports consumer education programs, and works to arbitrate consumer complaints. Local bureaus handle more than 11 million public contacts annually without charge. CBBB sponsors Auto Line, a national mediation and arbitration service between car owners with complaints and participating automobile companies. Look for your local Better Business Bureau office listed in the white pages of your telephone book.

Direct Selling Association (DSA)
1666 K Street NW, Suite 1010
Washington, DC 20006-2808
202/293-5760

A national trade association of the leading companies that manufacture and distribute goods and services sold directly to consumers. The DSA's mission is "to protect, serve, and promote the effectiveness of member companies and the independent business people they represent. To ensure that the marketing by member companies of products and/or the direct sales opportunity is conducted with the highest level of business ethics and service to consumers."

Federal Bureau of Investigation (FBI)
935 Pennsylvania Avenue NW
Washington, DC 20535
202/324-3000

The law enforcement arm of the Department of Justice, the FBI investigates all federal crimes except those assigned to other agencies. For the nearest office, check the white pages of your telephone book under "U.S. Government."

Food and Drug Administration (FDA)
Consumer Affairs and Information
5600 Fishers Lane
Rockville, MD 20857
301/827-5006
800/532-4440
Web site: www.fda.gov

The FDA provides information to the public through its thirty-two regional offices. Look for your local FDA office listed in the white pages of your telephone book under "U.S. Government."

Fraud & Theft Information Bureau (FTIB)

217 N. Seacrest Boulevard, Box 400

Boynton Beach, FL 33425

561/737-7500

Web site: www.checksbyphone.com

Part of the National Association of Credit Card Merchants, the FTIB publishes the *Bank Identification Number (BIN) Directory* for merchants, and *Credit Card and Check Fraud: A Stop Loss Manual,* along with other fraud-control publications.

Internal Revenue Service (IRS)

Commissioner

1111 Constitution Avenue NW, Room 3244

Washington, DC 20224

202/622-5000

800/829-1040

Consumers may file complaints against deceptive charitable organizations with the IRS. Written complaints should be directed to the Commissioner at the above address. For a local or regional office near you, check the white pages of your telephone book under the heading "U.S. Government."

International Anti-Counterfeiting Coalition, Inc. (IACC)

1620 L Street NW, Suite 1210

Washington, DC 20036

202/223-5728

IACC membership includes American, European, and Asian corporations and associations. It works to eliminate counterfeiting of a wide variety of merchandise, disseminates information to the public concerning the problems caused by purchasing counterfeit products, advocates strong law enforcement and conducts enforcement programs in the U.S., Thailand, and Italy.

International Franchise Association (IFA)

1350 New York Avenue NW, Suite 900
Washington, DC 20005
202/628-8000

Members include firms in fifty-eight countries involved in franchise businesses. Holds annual symposia, workshops, and trade shows on various aspects of the franchise business. Publishes *Franchise Opportunities Guide.*

National Association of Consumer Agency Administrators (NACAA)

1010 Vermont Avenue NW, Suite 514
Washington, DC 20005
202/347-7395

Organization of federal, state, county, and local governmental consumer protection agencies. The NACAA works to enhance consumer services, has an annual conference, conducts seminars and public policy forums to promote consumer interests, and publishes a newsletter ten times a year on scams and the latest enforcement activities.

National Association of Home Builders of the United States (NAHB)

1201 15th Street NW
Washington, DC 20005
202/822-0200

Professional association of single and multifamily home builders, commercial builders, and others associated with the building industry. Sponsors seminars and workshops on a variety of subjects related to the building industry.

National Association of Realtors (NAR)

430 N. Michigan Avenue
Chicago, IL 60611-4087
312/329-8200

The NAR is a federation of fifty state associations and 1,848 local real estate boards that promotes education and high professional standards in the real estate field.

National Association of Securities Dealers (NASD)

1735 K Street NW
Washington, DC 20006
202/728-8000

The self-regulatory agency for NASDAQ (National Association of Securities Dealers Automated Quotations) and over-the-counter markets.

National Charities Information Bureau (NCIB)

19 Union Square West
New York, NY 10003
212/929-6300

An organization founded in 1918 that provides a reporting and advisory service about national and international nonprofit organizations that solicit contributions from the public. The NCIB promotes high ethical standards in the field of philanthropy and provides donors with independent reports on the purposes, programs, and stability of nonprofit groups. Publications include: *Wise Giving Guide, The 1-2-3 of Evaluation, Charitable Giving: What Contributors Want to Know,* and *Standards in Philanthropy.*

National Consumers League (NCL)
1701 K Street NW, Suite 1200
Washington, DC 20006
202/835-3323

The NCL is a nonprofit membership organization working for consumer health and safety protection and fairness in the marketplace and workplace. Current principle issues include consumer fraud, food and drug safety, fair labor standards, child labor, health care, the environment, financial services, and telecommunications. The NCL develops and distributes consumer education materials and newsletters.

National Fraud Information Center (NFIC)
P.O. Box 65868
Washington, DC 20035
800/876-7060

A consumer service project of the National Consumers League, the NFIC offers free advice and information on current major frauds and counselors to assist those who have been defrauded with filing complaints.

National Futures Association (NFA)
200 W. Madison Street, Suite 1600
Chicago, IL 60606-3447
312/781-1410
800/621-3570

Industry association for brokers and others involved in the trading of futures on the commodity market. Works to provide more effective industry self-regulation and member qualification screening. Monitors and enforces customer protection rules and uniform business standards. The NFA also arbitrates customer disputes. They publish a free annual review, along with numerous informational pamphlets and guides.

National Health Care Anti-Fraud Association (NHCAA)

1255 23d Street NW, Suite 850

Washington, DC 20037

202/659-5955

Trade association of private insurance companies and public and private agencies that work against health insurance fraud and share information on claims.

National Insurance Consumer Helpline

800/942-4242

A toll-free consumer information telephone service sponsored by insurance industry trade associations that represent all segments of insurance. In addition to answering a wide range of questions about a variety of insurance concerns, helpline personnel refer complaints to appropriate sources and mail consumer brochures as requested.

National Insurance Crime Bureau (NICB)

10330 S. Roberts Road

Palos Hills, IL 60465

800/TEL-NICB (Consumer Hotline)

The NICB, a not-for-profit organization, is supported by approximately 1,000 property-casualty insurers and self-insured companies dedicated to combating insurance crime. The NICB provides insurance investigators, law enforcement officials, and NICB agents with access to 300 million vehicle and insurance claim-related records. Consumers can call their consumer hotline to report insurance claim fraud and auto theft.

North American Securities Administrators Association (NASAA)

1 Massachusetts Avenue NW, Suite 310

Washington, DC 20001

202/737-0900

Organization of state and local officials involved in enforcing securities sales laws.

Patent and Trademark Office
Office of Public Affairs
2121 Crystal Drive, Suite 0100
Crystal Park 2
Arlington, VA 22202
703/305-8341

The Patent and Trademark Office maintains and records patents and trademarks for products and product names. In addition, it provides information to individuals and businesses involved in litigation concerning infringement of patent and trademark rights.

Philanthropic Advisory Service
Council of Better Business Bureaus, Inc.
4200 Wilson Boulevard
Arlington, VA 22203
703/276-0100

Provides information about national fund-raising organizations. Complaints about national charities may be directed to the Philanthropic Advisory Service.

Securities and Exchange Commission (SEC)
Office of Consumer Affairs
450 5th Street NW (Mail Stop 11-2)
Washington, DC 20549
202/942-7040 (Investor information and complaint hotline)

Administers federal securities laws that seek to provide protection for investors to ensure that securities markets are fair and honest. Regulates public offers and sales of securities. Answers questions about securities dealings; verifies registration of securities dealers and firms. The Publications Unit offers materials to assist potential investors. Has nine regional and branch offices; check in the white pages under "U.S. Government" or call the Washington, DC, office for the branch in your area.

U.S. Copyright Office
Information Section
Room 401, James Madison Building
101 Independence Avenue SE
Washington, DC 20559
202/707-3000

The U.S. Copyright Office provides information about copyrights, copyright law, and registration procedures.

U.S. Department of Commerce (DOC)
14th Street between Constitution Avenue and E Street NW
Washington, DC 20230
202/482-2000

The DOC oversees all commerce within the United States, trade with foreign countries, and administers a wide variety of programs related to trade through its divisions.

U.S. Postal Service
475 L'Enfant Plaza SW
Washington, DC 20260-2166
800/654-8896 (Postal Crime Hotline)

Investigates reports of violations of federal postal laws, including bogus mail-order investment schemes, phony invoices, solicitations disguised as invoices, and any scheme that includes documents sent through the U.S. mail. Contact your local post office for help concerning mail fraud, or call the Postal Crime Hotline.

U.S. Social Security Administration (SSA)
Department of Health and Human Services
800/772-1213
800/269-0271 (Inspector General's Hotline)

The U.S. Social Security Administration conducts investigations into fraudulent activities involving Social Security funds or recipients. Contact your local Social Security office listed in the white pages under "U.S. Government." Call 800/HHS-TIPS to report fraud in any program administered by the DHHS or suspected crime committed by an employee or contractor of the DHHS.

Weiss Ratings Inc.
4176 Burns Road
P.O. Box 109665
Palm Beach Gardens, FL 33410
561/627-3300
800/289-9222

Publishes *Weiss Ratings' Guide to the Strongest Insurance Companies in America*; *Life, Health & Annuity Insurance Directory*; *Property & Casualty Insurance Directory*; *HMO & Insurance Directory*; *Brokerage Safety Directory*; and *Bank Safety Directory*, among others.

Specific addresses for the following may be found in the City, County, and State Government listings in the white pages of your telephone directory:

District Attorney's Office
State Attorney General's Office

Both the District Attorney's Office and the State Attorney General's Office investigate and prosecute fraud cases.

•

Social and Health Services
Social Services
Welfare Office

Report fraud and abuse of financial assistance programs, medical assistance programs, and food stamps to these local, county, and state agencies. They are known by a variety of names depending on the locality.

•

State Insurance Commissioner
State Insurance Department

Regulates the insurance industry in the state.

•

State Securities Commission
State Securities Department
Department of Corporations

All of the above regulate offers and sales of securities by companies in the state. You may need to contact your state capital's information bureau for more information.

BIBLIOGRAPHY
•••••••••••••••••••••

Adams, Susan. "The Strange Case of the Dangerous Intersection: Computers Are Helping Insurance Companies Track Down Phony Claims. Good News for the Average Motorist." *Forbes* 158, no. 13 (December 2, 1996): 122-24.

ATM Crime & Security Newsletter 7, issues 1-3 (January-March 1996): 10.

Behar, Richard. "Who's Reading Your E-Mail?" *Fortune* 135, no. 2 (February 3, 1997): 56-61ff.

Bennett, Georgette. *Crimewarps: The Future of Crime in America.* Garden City, N.J.: Anchor Press/Doubleday, 1987.

Blum, Richard H. *Deceivers and Deceived: Observations on Confidence Men and Their Victims, Informants and Their Quarry, Political and Industrial Spies and Ordinary Citizens.* Springfield, Ill.: Charles C. Thomas, 1972.

Clinton, William J. "1997 State of the Union Address." *Vital Speeches of the Day* 63, no. 10 (March 1, 1997): 290-96.

Council of Better Business Bureaus. *How to Protect Your Business from Fraud, Scams, & Crime.* Englewood Cliffs, N.J.: Prentice Hall, 1992.

Davis, Kristin. "Fifty Years from Now." *Kiplinger's Personal Finance Magazine* (January 1997): 98-106.

Davis, L. J. "Medscam." *Mother Jones* 20, no. 2 (March-April 1995): 26-29ff.

DeYoung, H. Garrett. "Thieves Among Us: If Knowledge Is Your Most Important Asset, Why Is It So Easily Stolen?" *Industry Week* 245, no. 12 (June 17, 1996): 12–14ff.

Diagnostic and Statistical Manual of Mental Disorders, 4th ed. Washington, D.C.: American Psychiatric Association, 1994.

Gordon, John Steele. "As Old As the Pyramid Scheme." *American Heritage* 45, no. 7 (Nov. 1994): 18ff.

Groves, Martha. "Allstate to Pay Record Fine in Handling of Fire Claims." *Los Angeles Times* (December 23, 1992).

Henderson, M. Allen. *How Con Games Work.* Secaucus, N.J.: Citadel Press, 1985.

Independent Sector. *Giving and Volunteering in the U.S.* Washington, D.C.: 1996.

Mannix, Margaret. "Fat Claims, Thin Results." *U.S. News and World Report* 122, no. 13 (April 7, 1997): 59.

Marvin, Mary Jo. "Swindles in the 1990s: Con Artists Are Thriving." *USA Today (Magazine)* 123, no. 2592, (September 1994): 80–82.

"Mistreating Workers Boosts Employee Theft." *USA Today (Magazine)* 124, no. 2611 (April 1996): 6.

National Association of Consumer Agency Administrators. "New Telemarketing Fraud Message." *NACAA News* 19, no. 10 (August 1996), 1.

National Charities Information Bureau. *Before You Give: A Contributor's Checklist.* New York, N.Y.: 1991.

Standards in Philanthropy. New York, N.Y.: June 1996.

National Insurance Crime Bureau. "Insurance Companies Crack Down on Con Artists Seeking to Exploit Soft Tissue Injury for Hard Cash." *Spotlight on Insurance Crime* 1 (1997): 6–7.

———,"Fraud in Homes and Businesses: Bodily Injury Insurance Fraud." *Report the Ripoff.*

———,"Fraud on the Job: The Schemers and the Schemes." *Report the Ripoff.*

———,"Fraud on the Job: Workers' Compensation Fraud." *Report the Ripoff.*

———,"Fraud on the Road: Putting a Dent in Staged Collisions." *Report the Ripoff.*

———,"Insurance Fraud: The $20 Billion Disaster." *Report the Ripoff.*

———,"Proactive Fraud Detection." *Report the Ripoff* (5/1/96).

———."Workers' Compensation Fraud." *Report the Ripoff.*

Scism, Leslie. "Prudential Restitution Could Top $1.6 Billion." *The Wall Street Journal* 136, no. 105 (May 30, 1997): A3–A4.

Sebastian, Pamela. "Charitable Giving Rises, Thanks to Gains in Personal Income and in Stocks." *The Wall Street Journal* 136, no. 104 (May 29, 1997): A1.

Shapiro, Esther. "Tragedy Brings Out Charity and Con Artists Too." Knight-Ridder/Tribune News Service (June 27, 1995): 0627K8390.

Sherman, Eric. "Why the Surge in Scams and Schemes?" *Home Office Computing* 15, no. 3 (March 1997): 19.

Stein, Gordon, and Marie J. MacNee. *Hoaxes! Dupes, Dodges & Other Dastardly Deceptions.* Detroit: Visible Ink Press, 1995.

Sussman, Vic. "Policing Cyberspace." *U.S. News & World Report* 118, no. 3 (January 23, 1995): 54–60.

U.S. Office of Consumer Affairs. *1996 Consumer Resource Handbook.* Washington, D.C.: October 1995.

Weiss, Murray. "Sting Sticks Fugitives with Chance to 'Check' Out Jail," *New York Post* (February 4, 1997): 6.

Western Insurance Information Service. "Insurance Fraud: Who Pays?" (4/95).

Whitlock, Charles R. *Easy Money.* New York: Kensington Books, 1994.

Zuber, Amy. "Businesses Pointing a Furious Finger at Bogus Yellow Pages." *Nation's Restaurant News* 31, no. 19 (May 12, 1997): 3–5.

INDEX
• • • • • • • •